SIR HENRY IRVING

A BIOGRAPHY

BY

PERCY FITZGERALD

AUTHOR OF "THE LIFE OF DAVID GARRICK," "FIFTY YEARS
OF CATHOLIC LIFE," "LADY JEAN," ETC.

"As in a theatre the eyes of men,
After a well-grac'd actor leaves the stage,
Are idly bent on him that enters next."

PHILADELPHIA
GEORGE W. JACOBS & CO.
PUBLISHERS

TO

GEORGE ALEXANDER

Preface

THUS early, after the death of the great actor, I venture to offer this new and revised account of his very romantic life and work. I have dwelt more especially on the former, as it is agreed that herein was found his chief power or attraction. It is, in fact, the story of his ever engaging character and fashions that I have attempted to bring home before the reader, showing him in his habit as he lived.

There have been many elaborate accounts of his acting and managerial career, set off plentifully with dates of performances, casts of characters, and criticisms. These things have beyond doubt their value; but they make heavy and uninteresting reading. You cannot see the wood for the trees. I prefer to let the agreeable and original actor promenade it about through these pages according to his humour. I had the advantage of knowing him for some thirty years; and from the first, as will be seen here, on the most intimate terms with him and his following—hence I can speak with full knowledge.

The present is practically the third issue of this life. It was written under Irving's hearty encouragement, and all the earlier sheets were revised and corrected by him. However, later on when I came to dealing critically with his performances it became a rather too delicate matter for an actor's supervision, and I felt that it was better to give over the submission of the sheets to him —I am afraid not exactly to his satisfaction.

It has been thoroughly revised—large additions have been made which cover a period of some ten years, and bring the work down to his lamented death.

It will be seen that I have written independently and freely. Unlike the general crowd of admirers, and perhaps flatterers, for whom everything in their hero was *"superbe!" "magnifique!" "dernier cri!"* &c., I have pointed out all that might seem faulty or exaggerated to trained and impartial judges. I have dwelt on what were his real gifts and merits, as well as on their limits. Praising indiscriminately is no praise at all.

I may add that particular attention has been given to the illustrations in this volume. No one has been so copiously "limned" as this actor. I myself have filled some twenty huge folios with such pictures. I may call attention to the fine portrait which forms the frontispiece, as a truly artistic and successful rendering of Irving's thoughtful and expressive features, adapted as it were to the part he was playing. With this the reader may contrast the one given at the close of the volume, which shows him with his everyday countenance and costume, the former worn and sharpened—aged also—by the wear and tear of performances.

Contents

————◆◇◆————

CONTENTS

CONTENTS

List of Illustrations

xv

xvi LIST OF ILLUSTRATIONS

IRVING'S BIRTHPLACE AT KEINTON MANDEVILLE.
(The house on the right is where the great actor was born.)
Photo by E. S. Russell.

To face p. 1.

CHAPTER I

SCHOOL-DAYS—EARLY TASTE FOR THE STAGE— FIRST APPEARANCE

HENRY IRVING was born at Keinton, near Glastonbury, in Somersetshire, on February 6, 1838. His real name was John Henry Brodribb. "The last place God made" has been the description given of this little town—Keinton-Mandeville. The house in which the future actor was born is still pointed out—a small two-storied dwelling—lately "bought in" for £600.

Henry Irving's mother was Sarah Behenna, a woman of strong, marked character, who early took the child into Cornwall to her sister Penberthy. Thus was he brought up among miners and mining captains in a district "stern and wild," where lessons of dogged toil and perseverance were to be learned. The earliest books he read were his Bible, some old English ballads, and "Don Quixote," a character which he had long had a fancy for performing. In an intimate *causerie* with his and my friend Joseph Hatton, he strayed back to these early days of childhood, when he called up some striking scenes of those old mining associations. This aunt Penberthy was a resolute, striking woman, firm and even grim of purpose, and the scenes in which she figured have a strong flavour, as Mr. Hatton suggests, of Currer Bell's stories.

Shortly after his birth the father removed to London, but the wife—a woman of purpose—resolved to bring up the child in the country. He was accordingly left to the care of his aunt Penberthy, married to a strange being, captain of a Cornish mine near St. Ives. As Irving told Mr. Hatton, one day the giant uncle was angry. "He walked," said Sir Henry, "into the kitchen where we youngsters were, and began to smash everything he could lay his hands on. He took up the chairs and broke them across his knee, and they were pretty strong, too—nothing, however, to him; he snapped them as if they had been the merest sticks. Drawers, tables, he smashed everything; then walked out and went back to the mine. We were all terrified while this was going on. As for me, I got behind the door or anywhere else out of his way."

But the tactful aunt healed the sore. She did not scold. But when the captain returned in the evening, "he paused at the open doorway of the kitchen, flung back his chest, and gave forth a great burst of laughter. You never heard such a laugh; it was tremendous. My aunt laughed, too. What do you think he laughed at? The wreck of the furniture had been got together and displayed by my aunt, as if the whole business was a huge joke. Broken chairs, table-legs, a cupboard door, pieces of an old seat, all manner of things were hung upon the walls, as if they were pictures, articles of virtu, bric-a-brac. And this was all that occurred. There was no scene ; only the laughter. During the next day or two the place was put to rights, and never for a moment did the affair disturb the happiness of the household ; she knew how to live with her husband, and he loved her in his big, devil-may-care kind of way." [1]

He was early sent to a school then directed by Dr. Pinches, in George Yard, Lombard Street, close by the "George and Vulture," which still happily stands, and where Mr. Pickwick always put up when he was in town. There were about a hundred boys, one of whom was called Dickens. At this academy, on some exhibition day, he proposed to recite a rather gruesome piece called 'The Uncle,' to which his preceptor strongly objected, when he substituted the more orthodox 'Defence of Hamilton Rowan,' by Curran.

More than thirty years later, when the boy had become famous, and was giving a benefit at his own theatre to a veteran player—Mr. Creswick— the latter, coming before the curtain, related to the audience this little anecdote. "I was once," he said, "invited to hear some schoolboys recite speeches previous to their breaking up for the

[1] *Daily News*, Oct. 16, 1905. Before his death, the actor was dictating to Mr. Austin Brereton a long and minute account of these early, childish days—which has recently been issued.

holidays. The schoolmaster was an old friend of mine, whom I very much respected. The room was filled from wall to wall with the parents and friends of the pupils. I was not much entertained with the first part; I must confess that I was a little bored; but suddenly there came out a lad who at once struck me as being rather uncommon, and he riveted my attention. The performance, I think, was a scene from ' Ion,' in which he played Adrastus. I well saw that he left his schoolfellows a long way behind. That schoolboy was Master Henry Irving. Seeing that he had dramatic aptitude, I gave him a word of encouragement, perhaps the first he had ever received, and certainly the first he had received from one in the dramatic profession, to which he is now a distinguished honour." Sir Edward Clarke, who was sent to the school after Irving left it, long after made humorous complaint at a Theatrical Fund dinner that, on exhibiting his own powers at the same school, he used to be regularly told, "Very good—very fair; but you should have heard Irving do it."

On leaving the school, it was determined that the future actor should adopt a commercial career, and he was placed in the offices of Messrs. Thacker, "Indian Merchants in Newgate Street." He was then about fourteen, and remained in the house four years.[1] Mr. Edward Russell, of the old Haymarket, was with him at Thacker's, and describes his elation

[1] 87 was the number; and Messrs. Lyons and Co., who now occupy the premises, are having a tablet placed on the wall to commemorate the actor.

at the purchase of some stage properties, also the
affection of the worthy old Thacker for his clerk.
His eyes were even now straying from his desk
to the stage. He was constantly reading plays
and poetry, and seeking opportunity for practice
in the art in which he felt he was destined so to
excel, and even reciting in the street.

At this time, about 1853, the late Mr. Phelps'
intelligent efforts, and the admirable style in which
he presented classical dramas, were exciting interest
and even enthusiasm among young men. I now
look back with pleasure to the pilgrimages to
the far-off Sadler's Wells Theatre, where so intellectual an entertainment was provided and sustained
with admirable taste for many seasons. What was
called " The Elocution Class" was one of the
results. It was directed by a Mr. Henry Thomas
with much intelligence ; his system was to encourage
his pupils to recite pieces of their own selection, on
which the criticisms of the listeners were freely
given and invited. " On one evening," says one
of Irving's old class-fellows, "a youth presented
himself as a new member. He was rather tall for
his age, dressed in a black suit, with what is called
a round jacket, and a deep white linen collar turned
over it. His face was very handsome, with a mass
of black hair, and eyes bright and flashing with
intelligence. He was called on for his first recitation, and fairly electrified the audience with an
unusual display of elocutionary and dramatic intensity." This was Henry Irving. By and by
the elocution class was moved to the Sussex

Hall, in Leadenhall Street, when something more
ambitious was attempted in the shape of regular
dramatic performances. The pieces were chiefly
farces, such as ' Boots at the Swan,' or ' Little
Toddlekins,' though more serious plays were performed. It was remarked that the young performer
was invariably perfect in his "words." In spite
of his youth he gave great effect to such characters
as Wilford in ' The Iron Chest,' and others of a
melodramatic cast. A still more ambitious effort
was Tobin's ' Honeymoon,' given at the little
Soho Theatre, with full accompaniments of scenery,
dresses, and decoration ; and here the young
aspirant won great applause.

It was to be expected that this success and these
associations should more and more encourage him
in his desire of adopting a profession to which he
felt irresistibly drawn. He was, of course, a visitor
to the theatres, and always recalled the extraordinary impression left upon him by Phelps' performances. In every one's experience is found one of
these " epoch-making " incidents, which have an
influence we are often scarcely conscious of ; and
every thinking person knows the value of such
" turning-points " in music or literature. The young
man's taste was no caprice, or stage-struck fancy ;
he would try his powers deliberately; and before
going to see a play would exercise himself in
regular study of its parts, attempting to lay out
the action, business, &c., according to his ideas.
Many years later, in America, he said that when
he was a youth he never went to a theatre

except to see a Shakespearian play—in fact, for instruction.

At Sadler's Wells there was a painstaking actor called Hoskins, who was attracted by the young fellow's conscientious spirit, and who agreed to give him a few lessons in his art. These were fixed for eight o'clock in the morning, so as not to interfere with commercial business. Hoskins introduced him to Phelps, who listened to his efforts with some of that gnarled impassibility which was characteristic of him ; then in his blunt, good-natured way, gave him this advice : " Young man, have nothing to do with the stage ; *it is a bad profession !* "

Such, indeed, is the kindest counsel that could be given to nine-tenths of the postulants of our time. Their wish is to " go on the stage "—a different thing from becoming an actor. The manager had nothing before him to show that there were here present the necessary gifts of perseverance, study, and intelligence. Struck, however, by his earnestness, he proposed to give him an engagement of a very trifling kind, which the young man, after deliberation, declined, on the ground that it would not afford him opportunities of thoroughly learning his profession. The good-natured Hoskins, who was himself leaving the theatre to go to Australia, gave him a letter to a manager, with these words : " You will go on the stage ; when you want an engagement present that letter, and you will obtain one." He, indeed, tried to induce him to join him on his tours, but the offer was declined.

His mother, however, could not reconcile herself

to his taking so serious a step as "going on the stage." "I used frequently," writes his companion at the elocution class, "to visit at her house to rehearse the scenes in which John and I were to act together. I remember her as being rather tall, somewhat stately, and very gentle. On one occasion she begged me very earnestly to dissuade him from thinking of the stage as a profession ; and having read much of the vicissitudes of actors' lives, their hardships, and the precariousness of their work, I did my best to impress this view upon him." But it is ever idle thus striving to hinder a youth's purpose when it has been deliberately adopted.

Having come to this resolution, he applied earnestly to the task of preparing himself seriously for his profession. He learned a vast number of characters ; studied, and practised ; even took lessons in fencing, attending twice a week at a school-of-arms in Chancery Lane. This accomplishment, often thought trifling, was once an important branch of an actor's education ; it supplies an elegance of movement and bearing.

"The die being now cast," according to the accepted expression, John Brodribb, now become Henry Irving, bade adieu to his desk, and bethinking him of the Hoskins letter, applied to Mr. Davis, a country manager, who had just completed the building of a new theatre at Sunderland. With a slender stock of money he set off for that town. By an odd coincidence the name of the new house was the Lyceum. The play appointed was

'Richelieu,' and the opening night was fixed for September 29, 1856. The young actor was cast for the part of the Duke of Orleans, and had to speak the opening words of the piece.

Mr. Alfred Davis, a well-known provincial actor, and son of a northern manager, used often to recall the circumstances attending Irving's "first appearance on any stage." "The new theatre," he says, "was opened in September, 1856, and on the 29th of that month we started. For months previously a small army of scenic artists had been at work. Among the names of the *corps dramatique* were those of our old friend, Sam Johnson (now of the Lyceum); Miss Ely Loveday (sister of H. J. Loveday, the much respected stage-manager of the Lyceum); and a youthful novice, just eighteen, called Henry Irving. Making his first appearance, he spoke the first word in the first piece (played for the first time in the town, I believe), on the first or opening night of the new theatre.[1] The words of the speech itself, '*Here's to our enterprise!*' had in them almost a prophetic tone of aspiration and

[1] Monday Evening, Sept. 29, 1856.
The Season will commence, with Sir E. L. Bulwer Lytton's beautiful play,

R I C H E L I E U.

| Louis the Thirteenth ... ... | Mr. Courtenay. |
| Gaston (Duke of Orleans) ... ... | Mr. Irving. &c. |

After 'Richelieu' came:
The highly successful New Piece of Oriental Sentimentality or Sentimental Orientality, extracted from Dreams of the Arabian Nights, by the indefatigable Visionary Hoo-Zure-Attar, and which to be appreciated must be seen, as the

success. So busy was I in front and behind the scenes, that I was barely able to reach my place on the stage in time for the rising of the curtain. I kept my back to the audience till my cue to speak was given, all the while buttoning up, tying, and finishing my dressing generally, so that scant attention would be given to others. But even under these circumstances I was compelled to notice, and with perfect appreciation, the great and most minute care which had been bestowed by our aspirant on the completion of his costume. In those days managers provided the mere dress. Accessories, or 'properties' as they were called, were found by every actor. Henry Irving was, from his splendid white hat and feathers to the tips of his shoes, a perfect picture ; and, no doubt, had borrowed his authority from some historical picture of the Louis XIII. period."

" The impersonation," as the neophyte related it long afterwards, " was not a success. I was nervous, and suffered from stage fright. My second appearance as Cleomenes in ' A Winter's Tale,' was even more disheartening, as in Act V. I entirely forgot my lines, and abruptly quitted the scene, putting out all the other actors. My manager, however, put down my failure to right causes, and instead of

most extravagantly laudatory ecomiums (*sic*) must fall immeasurably short of the gigantic merit of

THE ENCHANTED LAKE !

Or the Fisherman and the Genie.

Near the end of the cast occurs the following line :

Cooks ... Messrs. Brunt, Irving, Waite, Broderick, Owen., &c.

dispensing with my services, gave me some strong and practical advice."

All which is dramatic enough, and gives us a glimpse of the good old provincial stage life. That touch of encouragement instead of dismissal, is significant of the fair, honest system, which then obtained in this useful training school.

Of this stage fright he did not quite shake himself clear for a long time. Once acting in 'A Winter's Tale,' he entered boldly enough, but all the words passed from his memory. In desperation he called out, "Come to the market-place and I well tell you further," and so exit.

CHAPTER II

1857–1859

EDINBURGH AND THE SCOTTISH THÉATRES

AT the Sunderland Theatre he remained only four months, and though the manager pressed him to stay with him, the young actor felt that here he had not the opportunities he desired. He accordingly accepted an engagement at the Edinburgh Theatre, which began on February 9, 1857.

Among the faces that used to be familiar at any "first night" at the Lyceum were those of Robert Wyndham and his wife. There is something romantic in the thought that these guests of the London manager and actor in the height of his success and prosperity should have been the early patrons of the unfriended struggling player. Wyndham was one of the successors of that sagacious Murray to whom the Edinburgh stage owes so much that is respectable. Here our actor remained for two years and a half, enjoying the benefits of that admirable, useful discipline, by which alone a knowledge of acting is to be acquired—viz., a varied practice in a vast round of characters.   This experience, though acquired in a hurried and perfunctory fashion, is of enormous value in the way of training. The player is thus introduced to every shade and form of character, and can practise himself in all the methods of expression.   Now that "stock companies" are abolished, and have given place to the "travelling ones," the actor has few opportunities of learning his business, and the result is a "thinness" or meagreness of interpretation.   In this Edinburgh school our actor performed "a round," as it is called, of no fewer than three hundred and fifty characters! This seems amazing.   It is, in truth, an extraordinary list, ranging over every sort of minor character.

He here also enjoyed opportunities of performing with famous "stars" who came round the provinces, Miss Helen Faucit, Mrs. Stirling, Vandenhoff, Charles Dillon, Madame Celeste, "Ben" Webster, Robson, the facetious Wright, the buoyant Charles Mathews, his life-long friend Toole, of "incompressible humour," and the American, Miss Cushman.[1] This, it is clear, was a period of useful drudgery, but in it he found his account.   The company

[1] Long after, in his prosperity, he recalled to American listeners an excellent piece of advice given him by this actress.   He was speaking of the invaluable practice of revealing thoughts in the face before giving them utterance, where, he said, it "will be found that the most natural, the most seemingly accidental, effects are obtained when the working of the mind is seen before the tongue gives its words.   This lesson was enjoined on me when I was a very young man by that remarkable actress, Charlotte Cushman."

visited various Scotch towns, which the actor has described pleasantly enough in what might seem an extract from one of the old theatrical memoirs. He had always a vein of quiet humour, the more agreeable because it was unpretending and without effort.

It would be difficult to give an idea of the prodigious labour which this earnest, resolute young man underwent while struggling to "learn his profession." The iron discipline of the theatre favoured his efforts, and its calls on the exertions of the actor seem, nowadays, truly extraordinary, though in another laborious profession, the office of "deviling" for a counsel in full practice, which entails painful gratuitous drudgery, is welcomed as a privilege by any young man who wishes to rise. A few of these Edinburgh bills are now before me, and present nights of singularly hard work for so young a man. We may wonder, too, at the audience which could have stomach for so lengthy a programme. Thus, one night, January 7, 1858, when the pantomime was running, the performances began with the pantomime of 'Little Bo-Peep,' in which we find our hero as Scruncher, "the Captain of the Wolves." After the pantomime came 'The Middy Ashore,' in which he was Tonnish, "an exquisite," concluding with 'The Wandering Boys,' in which we again meet him as Gregoire, "confidential servant to the Countess Croissey." We find him nearly always in three pieces of a night, and he seems, in pieces of a light sort, to have been "cast" for the gentlemanly captain of the "walking" sort; in more

NEW ROYAL LYCEUM THEATRE

Licensed Pursuant to Act of Parliament.

Proprietor & Manager, — **MR. E. D. DAVIS**

The Erection being completed, the NEW ROYAL LYCEUM THEATRE

WILL BE OPENED

FOR THE RECEPTION OF THE PUBLIC

ON MONDAY EVENING NEXT, SEPT. 29th. 1856

Mr. DAVIS wishes that his kind Friends and Patrons should themselves judge of the efforts ma for their accommodation rather than be guided by any comments from him, he will therefo only express his hopes that it will be apparent to all how anxiously he has laboured to rede the promise made as to the time of opening.

Architect - - - - **MR. THOS. MOORE.**
Assistant Architect and Superintendent of Works, - - **MR. JOS. POTTS**
The Decorative Department from the Pencil of **MR. JAS. LINDSAY.**
Executed under his direction by Messrs. SAUNDERS & JOHNSON
The Masonry by **MESSRS. THOMPSON AND TERRY**
The Joiner Work by **MR. J. TAYLOR.**
The Gas and other Fittings by Mr. DANNATT and Mr. CLASPER.
The Upholstery by Messrs. ALCOCK, BRYDON, HERRING. &c.
The Painting Work by Mr. ARNISON.

MONDAY EVENING, Sept. 29, 1856

The Season will commence with Sir E. L. BULWER LYTTON'S beautiful Play

RICHELIEU

Louis the Thirteenth........Mr. COURTENAY   Gaston (Duke of Orleans).......Mr. IRVIN
The Sieur de Beringhen (a Courtier)...................Mr. ALFRED DAVIS
Baradas (Favourite of the King)..Mr. ORVELL   The Chevalier de Mauprat..Mr. J. C. COWPE
Richelieu, (First Time in Sunderland)...................Mr. DAVIS
Father Joseph Mr. FOOTE Huguet a Spy)Mr. BRUNT Francois(a Page Miss AGNES MARKHA
Pages to Richelieu......................Misses POULSON and MONTAGUE
Pages to the King...........................Misses MILNER, LEIGH, CARTER
Count de Clermont...........Mr. GIBSON   Captain of Guard...........Mr. WAITE
Gaoler.............Mr. BRODERICK   Governor...........Mr. S. JOHNSON
First Secretary Mr. MASTERS Second Do. Mr. EDOUIN Third Do. Mr. MORELI
Julia de Mortemar (Richelieu's Ward)...................Mrs. ALFRED DAVIS
Marion de Lorme...........................Miss DE CLIFFORD

To Conclude with the highly successful New Piece of Oriental Sentimentality, or Sentimental Orientality, extracted fro Dreams of the Arabian Nights, by the indefatigable Visionary, HOO-ZURE-ATAR, and which to be appreciated must be seen, as the most extravagantly laudatory ecomiums must fall immeasurably short of the gigantic merit of

THE ENCHANTED LAKE!

OR THE FISHERMAN AND THE GENIE.

Achmet (Autocrat of Bagdad, of imperial splendour and imperious disposition) Mr. S. JOHNSON
Mooney Pacha (his much-abused Vizier) Mr. FOOTE Abdallah (the Black Enchanter) Mr. MASTER
Hassan (a Fisherman, who finds out that honesty is the best policy) Mr. ALFRED DAVIS
Monkey (who though at first, "a beast," ultimately proves himself 'a gentleman") Mr. EDOUIN
Genius of theBottle.................(who has no connection with the Bottle Imp).................Mr. COURTENAY
Selim.....................Cook of the Palace).................Mr. GIBSON
Azor and Azim.............(Two Young Princes).............Mrs. COURTENAY and Miss CARTER
Cooks...........Messrs. BRUNT, IRVING, WAITE, BRODERICK, OWEN
Fatima and Zelica (interesting young Ladies, Daughters of Achmet) Misses OWEN and DE CLIFFORD
Queen of the Peri.........................Miss MILNER
Peris Misses LEIGH, POULSONS, C. BROCK, B. BROCK and F. BROCK, &c.

[To face page

serious ones, for the melodramatic and dignified characters. In 'Nicholas Nickleby' he was the hero; and Jack Wind, the boatswain, the chief mutineer, in 'Robinson Crusoe.' In the course of this season Toole and Miss Louisa Keeley came to the theatre, when Irving opened the night as the Marquis de Cevennes in 'Plot and Passion,' next appearing in the "laughable farce" (and it *is* one, albeit old-fashioned), 'The Loan of a Lover,' in which he was Amersfort, and finally playing Leeford, "Brownlow's nephew," in 'Oliver Twist.' As Mr. Wyndham informed me : "During the short period he was under our management, both Mrs. Wyndham and myself took a most lively interest in his promotion, for he was always perfect, and any character, however small, he might have been called upon to represent, was in itself a study ; and I believe he would have sacrificed a week's salary—a small affair, by the way—to exactly look like the character he was about to portray."

The young man, full of hope and resolution, went cheerfully through these labours, though "my name," as he himself tells us, "continued to occupy a useful but obscure position in the playbill. Nothing occurred to suggest to the manager the propriety of doubling my salary, though he took care to assure me I was 'made to rise.'" This salary was the modest one of thirty shillings a week, then the usual one for what was termed "juvenile lead." The old classification, "walking lady," "singing chambermaid," "heavy father," &c., will have soon altogether disappeared, simply

because the round of characters that engendered
it has disappeared. Now the manager selects, at
his goodwill and pleasure, anybody, in or out of
his company, who he thinks will best suit the
character.

Of these old Edinburgh days Irving thought
fondly. At the Scottish capital he was later welcomed with an affectionate sympathy ; and the
various intellectual societies of the city—Philosophical and others—were always glad to receive
instruction and entertainment from his lips. In
November, 1891, when he was visiting the
Students' Union Dramatic Society, he told them
that some thirty years before " he was member of
a University there—the old Theatre Royal. There
he had studied for two years and a half his beautiful art, and there he learnt the lesson that they
would all learn, that—

> " ' Deep the oak must sink its roots in earth obscure,
> That hopes to lift its branches to the sky.' "

In some of his later speeches " of occasion " he
has scattered little autobiographical touches that are
not without interest. On one occasion he recalled
how he was once summoned over to Dublin to
supply the place of another actor at the Queen's
Theatre, then under the direction of two " manager-
twins," the Brothers Webb. The Queen's was but
a small house, conducted on old-fashioned principles,
and had a rather turbulent audience. When the
actor made his appearance he was, to his astonishment, greeted with yells, general anger, and dis-

approbation. This was to be his reception through nearly the whole engagement, which was luckily not a long one. He, however, stuck gallantly to his post, and sustained his part with courage. He described the manager as perpetually making "alarums and excursions" in front of the curtain to expostulate with the audience. These "Brothers Webb, who had found their twinship profitable in playing the 'Dromios,' were worthy actors enough, and much respected in their profession; they had that marked individuality of character now so rarely found on the boards. He discovered, at last, what his offence was, viz., the taking the place of a dismissed actor—an unconscious exercise of a form of 'land-grabbing'—but his placid good-humour gradually made its way, and before the close of the engagement he had, according to the correct theatrical phrase, 'won golden opinions.'"

At the close of the season—in May, 1859—the Edinburgh company set out on its travels, visiting various Scotch provincial towns. During this peregrination, when at Dundee, the idea occurred to him and a brother-player of venturing "a reading" in the neighbouring town of Linlithgow. This adventure he has himself related in print. Our actor had an agreeable vein of narrative, marked by a quiet, rather placid humour, also found in his occasional speeches. The charm and secret of this is the absence of affectation or pretence; a talisman ever certain to win listeners and readers.

" I had been about two years upon the stage, and was fulfilling my first engagement at Edinburgh. Like all young men, I was full of hope. It happened to be vacation time—'preaching week,' as it is called in Scotland—and it struck me that I might turn my leisure to account by giving a reading. I imparted this project to another member of the company, who entered into it with enthusiasm. He, too, was young and ambitious. I promised him half the profits.

" Eight o'clock drew near, and we sallied out to survey the scene of operations. The crowd had not yet begun to collect in front of the town-hall, and the man who had undertaken to be there with the key was not visible. As it was getting late, we went in search of the doorkeeper. He was quietly reposing in the bosom of his family, and to our remonstrance replied, ' Ou, ay, the reading ! I forgot all aboot it.' This was not inspiriting.

" The time wore on. The town clock struck eight, and still there was no sign of 'the rush.' Half-past eight, and not a soul to be seen—not even a small boy ! I could not read the ' Lady of Lyons ' to an audience consisting of the manager, with a face as long as two tragedies, so there was nothing for it but to beat a retreat. No one came out even to witness our discomfiture.

" This incident was vividly revived last year, as I passed through Linlithgow on my way from Edinburgh to Glasgow, in which cities I gave, in conjunction with my friend Toole, two readings on behalf of the sufferers by the bank failure, which

produced a large sum of money.   My companion in
the Linlithgow expedition was Mr. Edward Saker
—now one of the most popular managers in the
provinces."

In March, 1859, we find our actor at the old
Surrey Theatre, playing under Mr. Shepherd and
Mr. Creswick, for a "grand week," so it was announced, "of Shakespeare, and first-class pieces;
supported by Miss Elsworthy and Mr. Creswick,
whose immense success during the past week has
been *rapturously endorsed* by crowded and enthusiastic audiences."   "Rapturously endorsed" is good.
In 'Macbeth' we find Irving fitted with the modest
part of Siward, and this only for the first three
nights in the week.   There was an after-piece, in
which he had no part, and 'Money' was given on
the other nights.

But he had now determined to quit Edinburgh,
lured by the prospect of "a London engagement,"
an *ignis fatuus* for many an actor, who is too soon
to find out that a London engagement does not
mean exactly a London success.   In 1859 he made
his farewell appearance in 'Claude Melnotte,' and
was received in very cordial fashion.   As he told
the people of Glasgow many years later, he ever
thought gratefully of the Scotch, as they were the
first who gave him encouragement.

Now a London engagement was offered to him
by Mr. A. Harris, then managing the Princess's
Theatre.   It was for three years.   But when he
arrived he found that the only opening given him
was a part of a few lines in a play called 'Ivy Hall.'

As this meagre employment promised neither improvement nor fame, he begged his release. This
he obtained, and courageously quitted London,
determined not to return until he could claim a
respectable and conspicuous position. Thus we
find him, with perhaps a heavy heart, once more
returning to the provinces, just as Mrs. Siddons
had to return to the old drudgery after her failure
at Drury Lane. Before leaving London, that
wholesome taste for appealing to the appreciation
of the judicious and intellectual portion of the community, which had always been "a note" of his
character, prompted him to give two readings at
the old palace of Crosby Hall. In this he was
encouraged by City friends and old companions,
who had faith in his powers. It was something to
make this exhibition under the roof-tree of that
interesting old pile, not yet "restored"; and the
locale, we may imagine, was in harmony with his
own refined tastes. He read the ' Lady of Lyons '
on December 19, 1859, and the somewhat artificial
' Virginius ' on February 1, 1860. These performances were received with favour, and were pronounced by the public critics to show scholarly
feeling and correct taste.

I have before me a curious little criticism of this
performance taken from an old and long defunct
journal that bore the name of *The Players*, which
will now be read with a curious interest :

"We all know the ' Dramatic Reading.' We
have all—at least, all who have served their
apprenticeship to theatrical amusements—suffered

the terrible infliction of the Dramatic Reader; but
then with equal certainty we have all answered to
the next gentleman's call of a 'Night with Shakespeare, with Readings, &c.,' and have again under-
gone the insufferable bore of hearing our dear old
poet murdered by the aspiring genius.   Thinking
somewhat as we have above written the other evening, we wended our editorial way towards Crosby
Hall, where our informant 'circular' assured us Mr.
Henry Irving was about to read Bulwer's 'Lady of
Lyons.'   We asked ourselves, Who is Mr. Henry
Irving? and memory, rushing to some hidden cave
in our mental structure, answered—Henry Irving,
oh! yes, to be sure; how stupid!   We at once
recollected that Mr. Irving was a gentleman of
considerable talent, and a great favourite in the
provinces.   We have often seen his name honourably figuring in the columns of our provincial con-
temporaries.   Now, we were most agreeably disappointed on this present occasion; for instead of
finding the usual conventional respectable-looking
'mediocrity,' we were gratified by hearing the
poetical 'Lady of Lyons' poetically read by a most
accomplished elocutionist, who gave us not only
words, but that finer indefinite something which
proves incontestably and instantaneously that the
fire of genius is present in the artist.   It would be
out of place now to speak of the merits of the piece
selected by this gentleman, but the merits appeared
as striking and the demerits as little so as on any
occasion of the kind in our recollection.   Claude's
picture of his imaginary home was given with such

poetic feeling as to elicit a loud burst of approval
from his hearers, as also many other passages
occurring in the play. Mr. Irving was frequently
interrupted by the applause of his numerous and
delighted audience, and at the conclusion was unanimously called to receive their marks of approval."
It was at this interesting performance that Mr.
Toole, as he tells us, first met his friend.

A very monotonous feature in too many of the
dramatic memoirs is found in the record of dates,
engagements, and performances, which in many
instances are the essence of the whole. They are
uninteresting to any one save perhaps to the hero
himself. So in this record we shall summarise such
details as much as possible. Our actor went straight
to Glasgow, to Glover's Theatre, whence he passed
to the Theatre Royal, Manchester, where he remained for some four years, till June, 1865. Here
he met fresh histrionic friends, who "came round"
the circuit in succession—such as Edwin Booth,
Sothern, Charles Mathews, G. V. Brooke, Miss
Heath, and that versatile actor and dramatist and
manager, Dion Boucicault. Here he gradually
gained a position of respect—respect for his unfail-
ing assiduity and scrupulous conscientiousness,
qualities which the public is never slow to note.
In many points he offers a suggestion of Dickens,
as in his purpose of doing whatever he attempted
in the very best way he could. There are other
points, too, in which the actor strongly recalled the
novelist ; the sympathetic interest in all about him,
the absence of affectation combined with great

SIR HENRY IRVING.
From a photograph taken in the early sixties by Chancellor & Son, Dublin.

To face p. 23.

talents, the aptitude for practical business, the knowledge of character, the precious art of making friends, and the being unspoiled by good fortune. Years later he recalled with grateful pleasure the encouragement he had received here. And his language is touching and betokens a sympathetic heart :—

"I lived here for five years, and wherever I look —to the right or to the left, to the north or the south—I always find some remembrance, some memento of those five years. But there is one association connected with my life here that probably is unknown to but a few in this room. That is an association with a friend, which had much to do, I believe, with the future course of our two lives. When I tell you that for months and years we fought together and worked together to the best of our power, and with the means we had then, to give effect to the art we were practising ; when I tell you we dreamt of what might be done, but was not then done, and patted each other on the back and said, 'Well, old fellow, perhaps the day will come when you may have a little more than six-pence in your pocket;' when I tell you that that man was well known to you, and that his name was Calvert, you will understand the nature of my associations with Manchester. I have no doubt that you will be able to trace in my own career, and the success I have had, the benefit of the communion I had with him. When I was in Manchester I had very many friends. I needed good advice at that time, for I found it a very difficult thing as an actor to pursue my profession and to do justice to certain things that I always had a deep, and perhaps rather an extravagant, idea of, on the sum of £75 a year. I have been making a calculation within the last few minutes of the amount of money that I did earn in those days, and I found that it was about £75 a year. Perhaps one would be acting out of the fifty-two weeks of the year some thirty-five. The other part of the year one would probably be receiving nothing. Then an actor would be tempted perhaps to take a benefit, by which he generally lost £20 or £30. I have a very fond recollection, I have an affection for your city, for very many reasons. The training I received here was a severe training; I must say at first it was very severe. I found it a difficult thing to make my way at all with the audience; and I believe the audience to a certain extent was right; I think there was no reason that I *should* make my way with them. I don't think I had learnt enough; I think I was too raw, too unacceptable. But I am very proud to say that it was not long before, with the firmness of the Manchester friendship which I have always found, they got to like me."

The man that could trace these faithful records of provincial stage life, and speak in this natural heartfelt fashion of memories which many would not perhaps wish to revive, must have had a courageous and sympathetic nature.

Many years later, in his prosperity, he came to Bolton to lay the first stone of a new theatre, on which occasion other old memories recurred to him.

" I once played here," he said, "for a week, I am
afraid to say how many years ago, and a very good
time we had with a little sharing company from
Manchester, headed by an actor, Charles Calvert.
The piece we acted was called ' Playing with Fire ' ;
and though we did not play with too much money,
we enjoyed ourselves thoroughly.   I always look
back to that week with very great pleasure.   The
theatre then had not certainly every modern appli-
ance, but what the theatre lacked the audience made
up for, and a more spontaneous, good-natured public
I never played to."

On another occasion he again indulged in a retro-
spect ; indeed, his eyes seem always to have fondly
turned back to Manchester and these early days of
struggle : " I came all the way from Greenock with
a few shillings in my pocket, and found myself in
the splendid theatre now presided over by our
friend Captain Bainbridge.   The autumn dramatic
season of 1860 commenced with a little farce, and a
little two-act piece from the French, called ' The
Spy,' the whole concluding with ' God Save the
Queen,' in which, and in the little two-act piece
from the French, I took prominent parts ; so you
see, gentlemen, that as a vocalist I even then had
some proficiency, although I had not achieved the
distinction subsequently attained by my efforts in
Mephistopheles.   Besides ' Faust and Marguerite,'
there was a burlesque of Byron's, ' The Maid and
the Magpie,' in which I also played, the part being
that of an exceedingly heavy father ; and you will
forgive me, I am sure, for saying that the very

heavy father was considered by some to be anything but a dull performance. But though the
houses were poor, we were a merry family. Our
wants were few : we were not extravagant. We
had a good deal of exercise, and what we did not
earn we worked hard to borrow as frequently as
possible from one another."

In his Manchester recollections, as we see, there
are hints of very serious struggles and privations.
Such are, as says Boswell, "bark and steel for the
mind." A man is the better for them, though the
process is painful ; they assuredly teach resource
and patience. Years after, the actor, now grown
celebrated and prosperous, used to relate, and
relate dramatically, this very touching little story
of his struggles. That he should record it is
evidence of his frank and unaffected nature. It
is as pathetic as it is characteristic :—

" Perhaps the most remarkable Christmas dinner
at which I have ever been present was the one at
which we dined upon underclothing. Do you
remember Joe Robins—a nice genial fellow who
played small parts in the provinces ? Ah, no ; that
was before your time. Joe Robins was once in the
gentleman's furnishing business in London city. I
think he had a wholesale trade, and was doing well.
However, he belonged to one of the semi-Bohemian
clubs, associated a great deal with actors and journalists, and when an amateur performance was organised for some charitable object, he was cast for the
clown in a burlesque called 'Guy Fawkes.' He
determined to go upon the stage professionally and

become a great actor. Fortunately, Joe was able to dispose of his stock and goodwill for a few hundreds, which he invested so as to give him an income sufficient to prevent the wolf from getting inside his door in case he did not eclipse Garrick, Kean, and Kemble. He also packed up for himself a liberal supply of his wares, and started in his profession with enough shirts, collars, handkerchiefs, stockings, and underclothing to equip him for several years.

" The amateur success of poor Joe was never repeated on the regular stage. He did not make an absolute failure ; no manager would entrust him with parts big enough for him to fail in. But he drifted down to general utility, and then out of London, and when I met him he was engaged in a very small way, on a very small salary, at a Manchester theatre.

"Christmas came in very bitter weather. Joe had a part in the Christmas pantomime. He dressed with other poor actors, and he saw how thinly some of them were clad when they stripped before him to put on their stage costumes. For one poor fellow in especial his heart ached. In the depth of a very cold winter he was shivering in a suit of very light summer underclothing, and whenever Joe looked at him the warm flannel undergarments snugly packed away in an extra trunk weighed heavily on his mind. Joe thought the matter over, and determined to give the actors who dressed with him a Christmas dinner. It was literally a dinner upon underclothing, for most of the shirts and drawers which Joe had cherished so long went to the pawnbroker's or the slop-shop to provide the money for the meal. The guests assembled promptly, for nobody else is ever so hungry as a hungry actor. The dinner was to be served at Joe's lodgings, and before it was placed on the table Joe beckoned his friend with the gauze underclothing into a bedroom, and pointing to a chair, silently withdrew. On that chair hung a suit of underwear which had been Joe's pride. It was of a comfortable scarlet colour ; it was thick, warm, and heavy ; it fitted the poor actor as if it had been manufactured especially to his measure. He put it on, and as the flaming flannels encased his limbs he felt his heart glowing within him with gratitude to dear Joe Robins.

"That actor never knew—or, if he knew, could never remember—what he had for dinner on that Christmas afternoon. He revelled in the luxury of warm garments. The roast beef was nothing to him in comparison with the comfort of his under-vest; he appreciated the drawers more than the plum pudding. Proud, happy, warm, and comfortable, he felt little inclination to eat ; but sat quietly, and thanked Providence and Joe Robins with all his heart. 'You seem to enter into that poor actor's feelings very sympathetically.' 'I have good reason to do so,' replied Irving, with his sunshiny smile, '*for I was that poor actor !*'"

This really simple, most affecting, incident, he himself used to relate when on his first visit to America.

Most actors have a partiality for what may be called fantastic freaks or "practical jokes"; to be accounted for perhaps by a sort of reaction from their own rather monotonous calling. Sothern delighted in such pastimes, and Mr. Toole was not exactly indifferent to them. The excitement caused by that ingenious pair of mountebanks, the Davenport Brothers, will still be recalled: their appearance at Manchester early in 1865 prompted our actor to a lively method of exposure, which he carried out with much originality. With the aid of another actor, Mr. Philip Day, and a prestidigitator, Mr. Frederic Maccabe, he arranged his scheme, and invited a large number of friends and notables of the city to a performance in the Athenæum. Assuming the dress characteristics of a patron of the Brothers, one Dr. Ferguson, Irving came forward and delivered a grotesque address, and then, in the usual familiar style, proceeded to "tie up" his coadjutors in the cabinet, with the accompaniments of ringing bells, beating tambourines, &c. The whole was, as a matter of course, successful. It was not, however, strictly within the programme of an actor who was "toiling at his oar," though the vivacity of youth was likely enough to have prompted it.

On the eve of his departure from Manchester he determined on an exceedingly ambitious attempt, and played 'Hamlet' for his own benefit. The company good-naturedly favoured his project, though they fancied it was beyond his strength. It was, as he used to tell, an extraordinary success, and the performance was called for on several nights—a high compliment, as it was considered, in the city, where the custom was to require a "new bill" every night.   He himself did not put much faith in the prophecies of future eminence that were uttered on this occasion ; he felt that, after all, there was little likelihood of his emerging from the depressing monotonous round of provincial histrionics. But rescue was nearer at hand than he fancied. The stage is stored with surprises, and there, at least, it is the unexpected that always, or usually, happens.

Leaving Manchester, he passed to Edinburgh, Bury, Oxford, and even to Douglas, Isle of Man, where the assembly-room used to do duty as a "fit-up" theatre.   For six months, from January to July, 1866, he was at Liverpool with Mr. Alexander Henderson.

Thus had he seen many men and many theatres and many audiences, and must have learned many a rude lesson, besides learning his profession.   At this moment, as he described it long after, he found himself one day standing on the steps of the theatre looking hopelessly down the street, and in a sort of despair, without an engagement, and no very likely prospect of engagement, not knowing, indeed, which way to turn, unless some "stroke of luck" came.   But the "actor's luck," as he said, "is really *work;*" and the lucky actor is, above all, a worker.   At this hopeless moment arrived unexpectedly a proposal from Dion Boucicault that he should join him at Manchester and take a leading

character in his new piece. He accepted; but with
some shrewdness stipulated that should he succeed
to the author's satisfaction, he was to obtain an
engagement in London. This was acceded to, and
with a light heart he set off.

Mr. Boucicault, indeed, long after in America
boasted that it was his good fortune to "discover
Irving" in 1866, when he was playing in "the
country." The first performance took place on
July 30, 1866. "He was cast for a part in
'Hunted Down,' and played it so admirably that I
invited my friend Mr. Charles Reade to go and see
him. He confirmed my opinion so strongly, that
when 'Hunted Down' was played in London a few
months afterwards, I gave it conditionally on Mr.
Irving's engagement. That was his *début* in
London as a leading actor." He added some
judicious criticism, distinguishing Irving as "an
eccentric serious actor" from Jefferson, who was
"an eccentric comic actor." "His mannerisms are
so very marked that an audience requires a long
familiarity with his style before it can appreciate
many merits that are undeniable. It is unquestion-
able that he is the greatest actor as a tragedian that
London has seen during the last fifty years." [1]

---

[1] It is not surprising that many more should have been found
to claim the credit of "discovering" Henry Irving. Mr. W.
Reeve writes: "A long talk again with Miss Herbert. As I
have two theatres on my hands and a company, decided not to
go. She seemed very disappointed; asked me what she should
do. Thought of Henry Irving, who followed me in Manchester;
advised her to write to Mr. Chambers; promised to do so, as
well, if engaged, for Mr. Knowles to release him. Wrote to

In this piece, ' Mary Leigh and her Three Lives '
(which later became ' Hunted Down '), the heroine
was performed by Miss Kate Terry, at that time
the only member of a gifted family who had made
a reputation.   Irving's character was Rawdon
Scudamore, a polished villain, to which he imparted
such force and *finesse*, that it impressed all who
witnessed it with the belief that here was an actor
of striking power.   It at once gave him " a position,"
and an impression of his gifts was of a sudden left
upon the profession, upon those even who had not
seen him.   No fewer than three offers of engagement were made to him.   The author of the piece,
as we have seen, was particularly struck with his
powers ; his London engagement was now secure,
and he was to receive a tempting offer, through
Mr. Tom Taylor, from the management of the
St. James's Theatre, about to open with the new
season.

Chambers about Irving." All which, as I know from the best
authority, is somewhat imaginative. The engagement was
entirely owing to Boucicault.

IRVING AND ANOTHER.
From an early photograph.

To face p 53.

CHAPTER III

1866

THE ST. JAMES'S THEATRE—'HUNTED DOWN'—THE
NEW VAUDEVILLE THEATRE—'THE TWO ROSES'

THE directress of the new venture at the St.
James's Theatre was Miss Herbert, a graceful, sympathetic person of much beauty, with
exquisite golden hair and almost devotional features,
which supplied many of the Pre-Raphaelite brethren
with angelic faces for their canvases. On the stage
her efforts were directed by great sympathy and
spirit, and she was now about to essay the difficulties and perplexities of management. Like so
many others, she had before her a very high ideal
of her office: the good, vivacious old comedies,
with refined, correct acting, were to entice the way-
ward public; with pieces by Reade, Tom Taylor,
and Boucicault. This pleasing actress was destined
to have a chequered course of struggle and adventure, a mingled yarn of success and disappointment,
and has long since retired from the stage.

At the St. James's Theatre the company was
formed of the manageress herself; of Walter Lacy,

4

an actor of fine polish and grace ; of Addison, one
of the old school ; with that excellent mirth-making
pair, the Frank Mathews'.   The stage-manager was
Irving.   Here, then, he found himself, to his inexpressible satisfaction, in a respected and respectable
position, one very different from that of the actor-
of-all-work in the provinces.   Not the least com-
forting reflection was that he had won his way to
this station by remarkable talent and conscientious
labour.   The theatre opened on October 6, 1866.
'Hunted Down' was the piece originally fixed
upon, but it could not be got ready in time, so a
change was made to the lively old comedy of the
'Belle's Stratagem,' the name which it had been
originally proposed to give to Oliver Goldsmith's
'She Stoops to Conquer.'

The actor tells us of this interesting occasion :
"I was cast for Doricourt, a part which I had never
played before, and which I thought did not suit
me ; I felt that this was the opinion of the audience
soon after the play began.   The house appeared to
be indifferent, and I believed that failure was con-
clusively stamped upon my work, when suddenly,
upon my exit after the mad scene, I was startled by
a burst of applause, and so great was the enthusiasm
of the audience, that I was compelled to reappear
upon the scene, a somewhat unusual thing except
upon the operatic stage."[1]   This compliment was

---

[1] Related in one of his conversations with Mr. Joseph Hatton.
I have heard Walter Lacy describe the modest, grateful fashion
in which our actor received some hints given him at rehearsal by
this old and experienced performer as to the playing of his part.

nearly always paid to our actor when he performed
this part.

In the criticisms of the piece the efforts of the
interesting manageress-actress, of course, received
the chief attention. Dramatic criticism, however,
at this time was of a somewhat slender kind, and
the elaborate study of an individual performer's
merits was not then in fashion. The play itself
was then "the thing," and accordingly we find the
new actor's exertions dealt with in a curt but encouraging style : " Mr. H. Irving was the fine
gentleman in Doricourt : but he was more, for his
mad scenes were truthfully conceived and most
subtly executed." Thus the *Athenæum*. And Mr.
Oxenford, with his usual reserve, after pronouncing
that the comedy was "a compound of English
dulness and Italian pantomime," added that Doricourt " was heavy company till he feigns madness,
and the mock insanity represented by Mr. H. Irving
is the cause of considerable mirth." This slight
and meagre tribute contrasts oddly with the elaborate
fulness of stage criticism in our day.

It was at one of the Irving suppers, and most amusing was it to
find the veteran struggling to claim his share in the success.   " I
noticed the poor young fellow—he was all astray—'Pardon me,
Mr. Irving,' I said, ' if you will allow me to show you. Here,
bring down a sofa to the front.' "   But none of the old school
could sincerely have approved of Irving's methods.   I even once
heard the good old Howe, who was ever loud in praise of his
generosity—" He was a Prince"—give him this unconscious
stroke.   I was speaking of the excessive decoration in the
Shakespeare plays, " My dear sir, if you take all that away,
what have we left? "

The piece continued in the actor's *répertoire*, after being compressed into a few scenes. The rich, old-fashioned dress and powder suited the performer and set off his intelligent features, which wore a smiling expression, as though consciously enjoying the comedy flavour of the piece.

A little later, on November 5th, 'Hunted Down' was brought forward, in which the actor, as Rawdon Scudamore, made a deep impression. It was declared that the part "completely served the purpose of displaying the talent of Mr. Henry Irving, whose ability in depicting the most vindictive feelings, *merely by dint of facial expression*, is very remarkable." Facial expression is, unhappily, but little used on our English stage, and yet it is one of the most potent agencies—more so than speech or gesture.[1] It was admitted, too, that he displayed another precious gift—reserve—conveying even more than he expressed : a store of secret villainy as yet unrevealed. Among the spectators were George Henry Lewes and George Eliot, when the former is said to have exclaimed, " In twenty years he will be at the head of the English stage!" on which his companion, "He is there already." I myself heard Dickens speak with enthusiasm of the same performance, saying it was most remarkable. I heard, too, that he was much delighted with the actor's Mr. Chenevix in 'Uncle Dick's Darling,'

[1] I may be allowed to refer those who would learn the importance of this agent of " facial expression " to a little treatise of my own, "The Art of Acting "—a lecture at the Royal Institution, where it is fully discussed.

which was a suggestion of his own Mr. Dombey.
It was not noted at the time that Digby Grant in
the 'Two Roses' with some of the plot was boldly
transferred from the same story. Mr. Disraeli was
said to have once humorously remarked, "I think
he might be mistaken for *me!*" Many were
the compliments paid him on this creation; and
friends of Charles Dickens know how much struck
he was with the new actor's impersonation. The
novelist was always eager to recognise new talent
of this kind. Some years later, "Charles Dickens
the younger," as he was then called, related at a
banquet how his celebrated father had once gone
to see the 'Lancashire Lass,' and on his return
home had said: "But there was a young fellow in
the play who sits at the table and is bullied by Sam
Emery; his name is Henry Irving, and if that
young man does not one day come out as a great
actor, I know nothing of art." A worthy descendant
of the Kembles, Mrs. Sartoris, also heartily appreciated his powers.[1] During the season a round of

---

[1] Of this night, my friend Mr. Arthur A'Beckett has recently
recalled some memories: "All the dramatic critics were
assembled. John Oxenford—kindest of men and ripest of
scholars—for the *Times*, E. L. Blanchard for the *Daily Telegraph*,
John Hollingshead (still amongst us), the predecessor of my good
friend Moy Thomas of the *Daily News*, Leicester Buckingham
for the *Morning Star*, Desmond Ryan (I think) for the *Standard*,
Heraud for the *Illustrated London News*, Tomlins or Richard
Lee for the *Advertiser*, and Joseph Knight (again one of our
veterans) for the *Sunday Times*. We were assembled to see a
new piece by Dion Boucicault, then one of the most prolific of
dramatists. Well, we were waiting for the curtain to draw up on
the first act of the new play. It was called 'Hunted Down,' and

pieces were brought forward, such as 'The Road to Ruin,' 'The School for Scandal' (in which he played young Dornton and Joseph Surface), 'Robert Macaire,' and a new Robertson drama, 'A Rapid Thaw,' in which he took the part of a conventional Irishman, O'Hoolagan! It must have been a quaint surprise to see our actor in a Hibernian character. After the season closed, the company went "on tour" to Liverpool, Dublin, and other towns.[1]

Miss Herbert's venture, like so many other ventures planned on intellectual basis, did not flourish exceedingly; and in the course of the years that followed we find our actor appearing rather fitfully at various London theatres, which

it was buzzed in the stalls that Dion had picked up a very clever young actor in the provinces, who, after a short career in town, had made his mark in Manchester. He was called Henry Irving."

[1] At this time I happened to be living in Dublin, and recall with pleasure the comedian's striking face and figure, and the entertainment that he imparted. Once buying a newspaper in a shop that was close by the fine old Theatre Royal, since destroyed by fire, a "characteristical" pair entered, whom I recognised from having seen them on the stage. I was particularly struck with the pale, well-marked features, the black flowing hair, the dress of correct black, the whole very much suggesting Nicholas Nickleby, or some other of Dickens' "walking gentlemen." There was something strangely attractive about him, with a courteous, kindly tone to the owner of the shop as he made his purchase. When the pair had departed the lady's tongue "grew wanton in his praise." "Oh, but Mr. Irving," she said enthusiastically, "he is the *one;* a perfect gentleman! Every morning he comes in to buy his newspaper, and he do speak so *nicely*. I *do* think he is a charming young man," &c.

at this time, before the great revival of the stage, were in rather an unsettled state. He went with Sothern to play in Paris, appearing at the Théâtre des Italiens, and in December, 1867, found an engagement at the Queen's Theatre in Long Acre, a sort of "converted" concert-room, where nothing seemed to thrive.

Mr. Labouchere, who has really supplied one of the best accounts of Irving, describes the Queen's Theatre in his own pleasant, satirical way. "In the sixties I was the owner of a London theatre; sometimes I let it, and sometimes I produced plays there. Irving was my stage manager, and all the time he was with me, an exceptionally good one." Here for the first time he played with Miss Ellen Terry, in 'Catherine and Petruchio' (a piece it might be well worth while to revive occasionally); and in that very effective drama, 'Dearer than Life,' with Brough and Toole; in 'The School for Scandal'; also making a striking effect in 'Bill Sikes.' I fancy this character, though somewhat discounted by his Dubosc, would have added to his reputation. We find him performing the lugubrious Falkland in 'The Rivals.' He also played Redburn in the highly popular 'Lancashire Lass,' which "ran" for many months. At the Queen's Theatre he remained for over a year, not making any marked advance in his profession, owing to the lack of favourable opportunities. He had a part in Watts Phillips' drama of 'Not Guilty.'

It was in 1869, when he was playing at the Queen's Theatre in Long Acre, that he was married to Florence, the daughter of an Army surgeon, Surgeon-General Daniel James O'Callaghan of the Indian Army. This importantly-sounding officer is not likely to have approved the alliance with a "play-actor," neither could the actor's friends have thought it a prudent step in his struggling condition. Indeed, it does not seem to have been a very successful alliance, as a separation, on the ground, I believe, of unsuitability of disposition, took place a little later. They only met again, I believe, in Westminster Abbey, when Lady Irving walked behind the bier. Two clever sons were born; the eldest, with much of the father's originality and fervent style, is more than likely to take a high place in his profession; the other, Laurence, full of an impetuous energy and ardour—witness his violent denunciatory speech in Robespierre's impeachment. The eldest is married to the fair 'Trilby'—Dorothea Baird; the other to a clever actress, Miss Mabel Hackney, who had been his father's "leading lady" in his latter days.

In 1869 he came to the Haymarket, and had an engagement at Drury Lane in Boucicault's 'Formosa,' a piece that gave rise to much excited discussion on the ground of the "moralities." His part was, however, colourless, being little more than a cardboard figure : anything fuller or rounder would have been lost on so huge a stage. It was performed, or "ran," for over a hundred nights. With his sensitive, impressionable nature the performance of so barren a character must have been positive pain : his dramatic soul lay blank and

fallow during the whole of that unhappy time.
Not very much ground had been gained beyond
the reputation of a sound and useful performer.
Relying on my own personal impressions—for I
followed him from the beginning of his course—
I should say that the first distinct effort that left
prominent and distinct impression was his performance at the Gaiety Theatre, in December,
1869, of the cold, pompous Mr. Chenevix, in
Byron's 'Uncle Dick's Darling.' It was felt at
once, as I then felt, that here was a rich original
creation, a figure that lingered in the memory, and
which you followed, as it moved, with interest and
pleasure. There was a surprising finish and reserve.
It was agreed that we had now an actor of *genre*,
who had the power of creating a character. The
impression made was really remarkable, and this
specimen of good, pure comedy was set off by
the pathetic acting of "friend Toole," who played
Uncle Dick. This was a turning-point in his
career, and no doubt led to an important advance.
But these days of uncertainty were now to close.
I can recall my own experience of the curious
pleasure and satisfaction left by the performance
of this unfamiliar actor, who suggested so much
more than the rather meagre character itself conveyed. I found myself drawn to see it several
times, and still the feeling was always that of
some secret undeveloped power in the clever,
yet unpretending, performer.[1]

[1] Irving could tell a story in the pleasantest "high comedy"
manner, and without laying emphasis on points. In being enter-

About this time an attractive actor, who had been much followed on account of his good looks, one Harry Montague, had joined in management with two diverting drolls—as they were then— James\ and Thorne, the pillars of burlesque at the Strand Theatre. All three felt a sort of inspiration that they were capable of something higher and more "legitimate"—an impression which the event has more than justified. The two last, by assiduous study and better opportunities, became admirable comedians. A sort of club that had not prospered was lying unused in the Strand, and a little alteration converted it into a theatre. The three managers were anxiously looking for a piece of modern manners which would exhibit to advantage their several gifts. A young fellow named Albery, who had left his desk for playwriting, had brought them

tained by the "Savages," he related this adventure of his early Bohemian days, in illustration of the truth that "it is always well to have a personal acquaintance with a presiding magistrate." "I had driven one night from the Albion to some rooms I occupied in Old Quebec Street, and after bidding the cabman farewell, I was preparing to seek repose, when there came a knock at the door. Upon opening it I found the cabman, who said that I had given him a bad half-crown. Restraining myself, I told him 'to be—to begone.' I shut the door, but in a few moments there came another knock, and with the cabman appeared a policeman, who said, with the grave formality of his office, 'You are charged with passing a bad half-crown, and must come with me to the police-station.' I explained that I was a respectable, if unknown, citizen, pursuing a noble, though precarious, calling, and that I could be found in the morning at the address I had given. The policeman was not at all impressed by that, so I jumped into the cab and went to the station, where the charge was entered upon the night-sheet, and I was briefly

a sort of comedy which was in a very crude state, but which, it seemed likely, could be made what they wanted; and by the aid of their experience and suggestions, it was fashioned into shape. Indeed, it proved that never was a piece more admirably suited to the company that played it. The characters fitted them all, as it is called, "like gloves." They were bright, interesting, natural, and humorous; the story was pleasing and interesting, and the dialogue agreeable and smart. Such was 'The Two Roses,' which still holds the stage, though it now seems a little old-fashioned. Irving was one of the performers, and was perhaps the best suited of the group. The perfect success of the piece proved how advantageous is the old system of having a piece "written in the theatre," when the intelligence of the performers and that of the managers are brought in aid of

requested to make myself at home. 'Do you intend me to spend the night here?' I said to the inspector. 'Certainly,' he said; 'that is the idea.' So I asked him to oblige me with a pencil and a piece of paper, which he reluctantly gave me. I addressed a few words to Sir Thomas Henry, who was then presiding magistrate at Bow Street, and with whom I had an intimacy, in an unofficial capacity. The inspector looked at me. 'Do you know Sir Thomas Henry?' he said. 'Yes,' I said, 'I have that honour.' The officer suddenly turned round to the policeman and said, 'What do you mean by bringing such a charge against this gentleman?' Then he turned fiercely on the cabman, and nearly kicked him out of the office. I returned home triumphantly in the cab. I cannot give a young 'Savage' first starting on his career a sounder piece of advice than this— 'Always know your own mind, and also a magistrate.'" Practised *littérateurs* might well envy the pleasant facility and point with which this was told.

each other. The little house opened on April 16,
1870, with a piece of Mr. Halliday's; and it was
not until a few weeks later that the comedy was
brought forward—on June 4th. The success was
instantaneous.

The unctuous Honey, in his own line an excellent
original actor, raised in the good old school of the
"low comedian," which has now disappeared, was
the good-natured Bagman—a part taken later by
James, who was also excellent. Thorne was efficient,
and sufficiently reserved, in the rather unmeaning
blind Caleb Decie; while Montague was the gallant
and interesting hero, Jack Wyatt. The two girls
were represented in pleasing fashion by Miss Amy
Fawcitt and Miss Newton. The piece, as I have
said, owed much to the actors, though these again
owed much to the piece. It is difficult to adjust
the balance of obligation in such cases; but good
actors can make nothing of a bad play, whereas
a good play may make good actors. Irving, as
Digby Grant, was the chief attraction, and his
extraordinarily finished and varied playing of that
insincere and selfish being excited general admiration.

It has not been noticed, in these days of appro-
priation, that the piece was practically an ingenious
variation, or adaptation, of Dickens' 'Little Dorrit.'
For here we find old Dorrit, his two daughters,
and one of their admirers; also the constant loans,
the sudden good fortune, and the equally sudden
reverse. It was easy to see that the piece had
been formed by the evolution of this one character,

the legitimate method, it has always seemed to me, of making a play; whereas the average dramatist adopts a reverse practice of finding a story, and then finding characters for it. Character itself *is* a story. The character of Digby Grant was the first that gave him firm hold of public favour. It belongs to pure comedy—a fidgety, selfish being, self-deluded by the practice of social hypocrisies, querulous, scheming, wheedling. It is curious that a very good actor, who later filled the part, took the villainy *au sérieux*, giving the complaint, " *You annoy me very much !* " repeated so often, as a genuine reproach, and with anger. Irving's was the true view—a simulated vexation, " *You annoy me very much !* " The audience sees that he is *not* " annoyed very much."

After our actor's visit to America, his performance was noticed to be more elaborate and laboured—overdone in fact—it had lost some of its spontaneousness—a result which, it has been noted, is too often the result of playing to American audiences, who are pleased with broad effects. This piece continued to be played for about a year—then thought to be a prodigious run, though it is now found common enough—during which time Irving's reputation steadily increased.[1]

[1] The good-looking Montague, following the invariable development, seceded from the management and set up a theatre for himself. This not proving successful, he went to America, where he died early.

CHAPTER IV

1871

'THE BELLS'—WILLS'S 'CHARLES I.'

AMONG those who had taken note of Irving's efforts was a "long-headed" American manager, whose loudly-expressed criticism was that "he ought to play Richelieu!" This was a far-seeing view. Many years before, this manager had been carrying round the country his two "prodigy" daughters, who had attracted astonishment by their precocious playing in a pretty piece of juvenile courtship, called 'The Young Couple.' The elder later won favour by her powerful and intense acting in 'Leah'; and he was now about taking a theatre with a view of bringing forward his second daughter, Isabel. It seems curious now to think that the handsome, elegantly-designed Lyceum Theatre, built by an accomplished architect on the most approved principles, was then lying derelict, as it were, and at the service of any stray *entrepreneur*. It could be had on very cheap terms, for at this time the revival of theatrical interest had not yet

IRVING AS "MATTHIAS" IN "THE BELLS."
Photo by the London Stereoscopic Co.

To face p 46.

come; the theatre, not yet in high fashion, was conducted on rather rude and coarse lines. The attractions of the old correct comedy, as seen at the Haymarket, were waning, and the old companies were beginning to break up. Buckstone and Webster were in their decay, yet still lagged ingloriously on the stage. The pit and galleries were catered for. Theatres were constantly opening, and as constantly closing. Burlesques of the Gaiety pattern were coming into favour. In this state of things the shrewd American saw an opportunity. He had an excellent coadjutor in his wife, a clever, hard-working lady, with characteristics that often suggested the good-natured Mrs. Crummles, but without any of her eccentricities. Her husband took the Lyceum, and proceeded to form a company; and one of his first steps was to offer an engagement to Irving.

"At a public function my father," said Miss Bateman, "heard him recite 'The Dream of Eugene Aram,' and returned home in a perfect frenzy of admiration. 'I have found the greatest English actor of this age,' he cried, and he backed his opinion by taking the Lyceum Theatre. My father had an unconquerable habit of relying on his own judgment. As you know, Irving in those days had plenty of detractors, and it was quite amusing to see the effect these had on Mr. Bateman. He looked as though he would annihilate any one who dared to whisper a doubt of Irving's genius. I remember seeing a man pinned by him against a wall while he blazed out, 'You look as if you didn't admire him,' in a tone that was sufficient to make an unfortunate critic tremble in his shoes."

It is difficult to conceive what a dilapidated sort of place the Lyceum was in the poor old "Colonel's" day.   No one had the awe or respect for it that it later was to gain; it was in a ruined state, associated with all kinds of "scratch" exhibitions and performances.   It was not, however, until Irving had taken over the lease and made arrangements with Mr. Arnold, the landlord, that anything was done to put it in good order.   It was to cost him enormous sums in the way of enlarging and patching up.   He eventually contrived to make it one of the most stately theatres in London. The arrangements were elegant, and he retained the vast green curtain—a true dramatic element.

The new venture started on September 11, 1871, with an unimportant piece, 'Fanchette,' founded on George Sand's 'Petite Fadette,' in which our actor had a character quite unsuited to his gifts, a sort of peasant lover.[1] The object was to introduce the manager's daughter in a fantastical part, but the piece was found "too French," and rather farfetched. It failed very disastrously. The young actor, of course, had to bear his share in the failure; but he could not have dreamt at that moment that here he was to find his regular home, and that for twenty long years he was destined never to be

---

[1] It has been stated, I know not with what truth, that he was engaged at a salary of £15 a week, which was raised on the success of 'The Bells' to £35.

IRVING AS "JINGLE."
Photo by the London Stereoscopic Co.

To face p. 49.

away from the shadow of the great portico of the Lyceum.

The prospect for the American manager was not encouraging. He had made a serious mistake at starting. In a few weeks he had replaced it by a version of " Pickwick," with a view of utilising his chief comedian's talent as Jingle. The play was but a rude piece of carpentry, without any of the flavour of the novel, hastily put together and acted indifferently ; the actors were dressed after the pictures in the story, but did not catch the spirit of their characters. Irving in face and figure and dress was thoroughly Pickwickian, and reproduced Seymour and Hablot Browne's sketch, very happily catching the recklessness and rattle of the original. Still, it was difficult to avoid the suggestion of ' Jeremy Diddler,' or of the hero of ' A Race for a Dinner.' The reason, perhaps, was that the adaptation was conceived in too farcical a spirit. It has always seemed to me that " the Immortal Pickwick " should be treated as comedy rather than farce, and would be more effective on the stage were the Jingle scenes set forth with due seriousness and sincerity. The incidents at the Rochester Ball, for instance, belong to pure comedy, and would be highly effective. Some years later Irving put the work into the not very skilful hands of Albery, who reduced it to the proportions of a farce with some pathetic elements. It was called ' Jingle.'

At this time there was " hanging loose on " the theatres, as Dr. Johnson once phrased it, one

Leopold Lewis, who had been seduced from an
office by the enchantments of the stage. He had
made a translation of a very striking French play,
' Le Juif Polonais,' which was shown to the new
actor.   This, as is well known, was by the gifted
pair   Erckmann-Chatrian,   whose   realistic   but
picturesque stories, that call up before us the old
" Elsass " life, show extraordinary dramatic power.
This ' Juif Polonais ' is more a succession of tableaux
than a formal play, but, like ' L'Ami Fritz ' of the
same writers, it has a charm that is irresistible.   It
is forgotten that a version of this piece had already
been brought before the public at one of the minor
theatres, which was the work of Mr. F. C. Burnand,
at that time a busy caterer for the theatres, chiefly
of melodramas, such as the ' Turn of the Tide ' and
' Deadman's Point.'

   " Much against the wish of my friends," says our
actor, " I took an engagement at the Lyceum, then
under the management of Mr. Bateman. I had
successfully acted in many plays besides ' The Two
Roses,' which ran three hundred nights. It was
thought by everybody interested in such matters
that I ought to identify myself with what they called
' character parts ' ; though what that phrase means,
by the way, I never could exactly understand, for I
have a prejudice in the belief that every part should
be a character. I always wanted to play in the
higher drama. Even in my boyhood my desire
had been in that direction. When at the Vaudeville
Theatre, I recited the poem of ' Eugene Aram,'
simply to get an idea as to whether I could impress

an audience with a tragic theme. I hoped I could, and at once made up my mind to prepare myself to play characters of another type. When Mr. Bateman engaged me he told me he would give me an opportunity, if he could, to play various parts, as it was to his interest as much as to mine to discover what he thought would be successful—though, of course, never dreaming of 'Hamlet' or of 'Richard III.' Well, the Lyceum opened, but did not succeed. Mr. Bateman had lost a lot of money, and he intended giving it up. He proposed to me to go to America with him." [1]

Our actor, always earnest and persuasive, pressed his point, and at last extorted consent—and the play, which required scarcely any mounting, was performed on November 25, 1871. At that time I was living in the south of France, in a remote and solitary place, and I recollect the surprise and curiosity with which I heard and read of the powerful piece that had been produced, and of the more extraordinary triumph of the new actor. Every

---

[1] "He knew 'The Bells,'" said the manager's daughter, "and when Irving showed him Leopold Lewis's translation he put it in rehearsal at once. This, of all the pieces, was the financial success ; but the rest were mostly artistic successes, of which my people were very proud. They always had a romantic love of art for its own sake. How we all lived through those days I don't know. Every night Irving supped with us, and then on far into the night went excitedly planning and arranging and mapping out all the details of the play in prospect. In everything he was encouraged by my people, and his mind, worn with long work in the provinces, grew brisk and alert, and all his ambitions revived. His Hamlet was a revelation."

one, according to the well-worn phrase, seemed to be "electrified." The story was novel, and likely to excite the profoundest interest.

An extraordinary alteration, due, I believe, to the manager, was the introduction of the vision of the Jew in his sledge, a device unmeaning and illogical. In the original the morbid remorse of the guilty man is roused by the visit of a travelling Jew, which very naturally excites his perturbed spirit. But this vision discounts, as it were, and enfeebles the *second* vision. The piece would have been presented under far more favourable conditions had it been prepared by or adapted by some one of more skill and delicacy.

The success was really owing to the contrasts to the existing methods of performance, and to the impassioned hysterical, almost frantic style in which Irving played it. It was truly a grand *tour de force*, but taken as a display of dramatic character, it was forced and unreal and did not represent the situations. Years later it was played by Coquelin— according to the truer and more correct methods of interpretation. He represented a sober, crafty bourgeois, who did not "give himself away" so easily, and with great gain to the dramatic interest of the piece. Of course staunch Irvingites laughed him to scorn and could only admit the home article. But the French actor's reading was convincing, however one might admire Irving's wonderful display.

For over twenty years and more this remarkable impersonation kept its hold upon audiences, and whenever revived for an occasional performance or for a longer "run," it never failed to draw full houses. It was his introduction to the American audiences.

The new actor was now becoming a "personality." Every one of note discovered that he was interesting in many ways, and was eager to know such a man. The accomplished Sir E. Bulwer Lytton wrote that his performance was "too admirable not to be appreciated by every competent judge of art," and added, "that any author would be fortunate who obtained his assistance in some character that was worthy of his powers." A little later the actor took this hint, and was glad to do full justice to several pieces of this brilliant and gifted writer.

At this time there was a clever young man "on town" who had furnished Mr. Vezin with a fine and effective play, 'The Man o' Airlie,' from a German original. He was a poet of much grace, his lines were musical, and suited for theatrical delivery ; he had been successful as a novelist, and was, moreover, a portrait-painter in the elegant art of pastel, then but little practised. In this latter direction it was predicted that he was likely to win a high position, but the attractions of the stage were too strong for him. Becoming acquainted with the popular actor, a subject for a new creation was suggested by his very physique and dreamy style. This was the story of the unhappy Charles I. Both the manager and the player welcomed the suggestion, and the dramatist set to work. Though possessed of true feeling and a certain inspiration, the author was carried away by his ardour into a neglect of the canons of the stage, writing masses of poetry of inordinate length, which he brought to his friends at the theatre, until they at last began to despair. Many changes had to be made before the poem could be brought into satisfactory shape ; and, by aid of the tact and experience of the manager and his actor, the final act was at last completed to the satisfaction of all.[1]

'Charles I.' was brought out on September 28, 1872. Having been present on this night, I can recall the tranquil pleasure and satisfaction and absorbing interest which this very legitimate and picturesque performance imparted, while the melodious and poetical lines fell acceptably on the ear. This tranquil tone contrasted effectively with the recent tumult and agitation of 'The Bells.' It was a perfect success, and the author shared in the glories.

Many years ago now we followed the once popular Wills to his grave in the Brompton Cemetery. His somewhat erratic and, I fear,

---

[1] Originally the piece opened with the second act. The manager was said to have exclaimed : " Oh, bother politics ! *give us some domestic business.*" This led to the introduction of the tranquil, pastoral scene at Hampton Court. The closing scene, as devised by the author, represented the capture of the king on the field of battle. " Won't do," said the " Colonel " bluntly ; " must wind up with *another* domestic act." Sorely perplexed by this requirement, which they yet felt was correct, both author and actor tried many expedients without success, until one evening, towards the small hours, the manager, who appeared to be dozing in his chair, suddenly called out : " Look at the last act of ' Black-eyed Susan,' with the prayer-book, chain, and all." All which may be legendary, and I give it for what it is worth.

troubled course closed in the month of December, 1891. There was a curious suggestion, or reminiscence, of his countryman Goldsmith in his character and ways. Like that great poet, he had a number of "hangers-on" and admirers who were always welcome to his "bit and sup," and helped to kill the hours. If there was no bed, there was a sofa. There were stories, too, of a "piece purse" on the chimney to which people might apply. He had the same sanguine temperament as Goldsmith, and the slightest opening would present him with a magnificent prospect, on which his ready imagination would lavish all sorts of roseate hues. He was always going to make his fortune, or to make a "great hit." He had the same heedless way of talking, making warm and even ardent protestations and engagements which he could not help forgetting within an hour. But these were amiable weaknesses. He was careless about his interests; and there was a story current that on being bidden to the Palace to paint one of the Princesses, he sent an excuse that he had an engagement. I remember my "tempestuous" friend, John Forster, loudly expressing his approbation. But he had a thoroughly good heart, was as sensitive as a woman, or as *some* women, affectionate and generous. His life, I fear, was to the close one of troubles and anxiety. He certainly did much for the Lyceum, and was our actor's favourite author. 'Charles I.,' 'Eugene Aram,' 'Olivia,' 'Iolanthe,' 'Faust,' 'The Vicar of Wakefield,' 'Vanderdecken' (in part), 'Don Quixote'—these were his contributions.

'Charles I.' was written after the correct and classical French model. The opening scene, as a bit of pictorial effect—the placid garden of Hampton Court, with a startling reproduction of Vandyke's figure—has always been admired, and furnishes "the note" of the play. All through the actor presented a spectacle of calm and dignified suffering, that disdained to resent or protest ; some of his pathetic passages, such as the gentle rebuke to the faithless Huntley and the parting with his children, have always made the handkerchiefs busy.

The leading actor was well supported by Miss Isabel Bateman in the character of the Queen, to which she imparted a good deal of pathetic feeling and much grace. For many years she was destined to figure in all the pieces in which he played. This, it need not be said, was of advantage for the development of her powers. Even a mediocre performer cannot withstand the inspiration that comes of such companionship ; while constant playing with a really good actor has often made a good actress. But the manager, who had some odd, native notions of his own, as to delicacy and the refinements generally, must have rather inconvenienced or disturbed—to say the least of it—our actor, by giving him as a coadjutor, in the part of Cromwell, an effective low-comedy actor of *genre*, in the person of Mr. George Belmore, who did his work with a conscientious earnestness. By and by he supplied another performer who was yet more unsuited—viz., the late Mr. John Clayton —who used to open the night's proceedings in a

IRVING AS "CHARLES I"
Photo by the London Stereoscopic Co.

face p. 56

light, rattling touch-and-go farce, such as 'A Regular Fix.' Both these actors, excellent in their line, lacked the weight and dignified associations necessary for the high school of tragedy.[1]

One of those vehement and amusing discussions which occasionally arise out of a play, and furnish prodigious excitement for the public, was aroused by the conception taken of Cromwell, which was, in truth, opposed to tradition; for the Protector was exhibited as willing to condone the King's offences, and to desert his party, for the " consideration " of a marriage between himself and one of the King's daughters! This ludicrous view, based on some loose gossip, was, reasonably enough, thought to degrade Cromwell's character, and the point was debated with much fierceness. But somehow it answered dramatically.[2]

During the "run" of 'Charles I.' the successful dramatist was busy preparing a new poetical piece on the subject of Eugene Aram. It is not generally known that the author himself dramatised his story. This was produced on April 19, 1873, but the tone seemed to be too lugubrious, the actor

[1] I recall the manager's complacent anticipation of the success of his *coup*. "Clayton," he said, "was a clever, spirited fellow, and would assuredly make a hit in the part." He certainly played respectably, and made up by earnestness what he lacked in other points. He was particularly proud of his own " make-up." But his inharmonious voice was against him, and it was impossible to "take him " seriously.

[2] "The Colonel," however, artfully encouraged the two factions, and was said to have sent persons into the gallery to shout for Cromwell and Charles.

passing from one mournful soliloquy to another.
There was but little action.   The ordinary versions
are more effective.   But the actor himself produced
a deep, poetical impression.

The manager, now in the height of success,
adopted a style of " bold advertisement," that
suggested Elliston's amusing exaggerations.[1]   The
piece ran for over one hundred and fifty nights, to
May 17, 1873, and during a portion of the time the
versatile player would finish the night with ' Jeremy
Diddler.'

The new season of 1873 began on September 27,
with Lord Lytton's ' Richelieu.'   It is a tribute to
the prowess of that gifted man that his three
pieces—the ever-fresh and fair ' Lady of Lyons,'
' Money,' and ' Richelieu '—should be really the
only genuine stock-pieces of the modern stage.
They never seem out of fashion, and are always
welcomed.   It used to be said, indeed, that there
was hardly a night on which the ' Lady of Lyons '

[1] " *Lyceum—Charles I., Mr. Henry Irving.*   The profound
admiration that has been manifested by all classes (for the
past four months) in this noble poetic play, and the unqualified
approval bestowed by the most illustrious auditors upon Mr.
Henry Irving's great creation of the martyr-king, have marked
a new era in public taste.   The manager is proud to be able
to announce that the immense audiences nightly assembled
render any change in the performances impossible.—*Miss Isabel
Bateman*, in her tender and exquisitely pathetic portraiture
of Queen Henrietta Maria.—*Mr. George Belmore*, in his vigorous
and masterly assumption of Oliver Cromwell."   Thus the modern
Elliston.   It was said that the whole outlay on this modest
revival did not exceed £100 : a startling contrast to the eight or
ten thousand pounds later to be expended.

was not *somewhere* acted.   In 'Richelieu' the actor presented a truly picturesque figure—he was aged, tottering, nervous, but rallying to full vigour when the occasion called.   The well-known scene, where he invokes "the curse of Rome," produced extraordinary enthusiasm, cheers, waving of handkerchiefs, and a general uproar from the pit.   It was in this piece that those "mannerisms" which have been so often "girded at," with too much pitilessness, began to attract attention.   In this part, as in the first attempt in 'Macbeth,' there was noted a lack of restraint, something hysterical at times, when control seemed to be set aside.   The truth is, most of his attempts at this period were naturally *experiments*, and very different from those deliberate, long-prepared, and well-matured representations he offered under the responsibility of serious management.

This piece was succeeded by an original play, 'Philip,' by an agreeable writer who had made a name as a novelist, Mr. Hamilton Aïdé—a dramatic story of the average pattern, and founded on jealousy.   It was produced on February 7, and enjoyed a fair share of success.

CHAPTER V

1874

'HAMLET'—'OTHELLO'—'MACBETH'—DEATH OF
"THE COLONEL"—'QUEEN MARY'

B UT now was to be made a serious experiment,
on which much was to depend. Hitherto
Irving had not travelled out of the regions of
conventional drama, or of what might be called
romantic melodrama ; but he was now to lay hands
on the ark, and attempt the most difficult and
arduous of Shakesperian characters, Hamlet. Every
actor has a dream of performing the character, and
fills up his disengaged moments with speculations
as to the interpretation. The vitality of this
wonderful play is such that it nearly always is a
novelty for the audience, because the character is
fitfully changeful, and offers innumerable modes of
interpretation.

The momentous trial was made on October 31,
1874. It had long and studiously been prepared
for : and the actor, in his solitary walks during the
days of his provincial servitude, had worked out a
formal conception of the character. There was

much curiosity and expectation; and it was noted that so early as three o'clock in the afternoon a dense crowd had assembled in the long tunnel that leads from the Strand to the pit door. I was present in the audience, and can testify to the excitement. Nothing I have ever seen on the stage, except perhaps the burst that greeted Sarah Bernhardt's speech in 'Phèdre' on the first night of the French Comedy in London, has approached the tumult of the moment when the actor, after the play scene, flung himself into the King's chair.

This whirlwind, though much praised at the time, might make the judicious grieve. There was no warrant for it in the text—no reason for taking possession of the chair or throne. The King, moreover, had betrayed himself to his court, so there was no need of such wild jubilation—which was opposed to Hamlet's patient and deliberate methods of vengeance. His utmost display should be sardonic triumph. It further " broke up " the whole scene.

Our actor judiciously took account of all criticisms, and with later performances subdued or toned down what was extravagant. The whole gained in thoughtfulness and in general meditative tone, and it is admitted that the meaning of the intricate soliloquies could not be more distinctly or more intelligibly conveyed to an audience. He played a good deal with his face, as it is called : with smilings of intelligence, as if interested or amused. But, as a whole, his conception of the character may be said to have remained the same as it was on that night.

The play was mounted with the favourite economy of the manager, and contrasted with the unsparing lavishness of decoration which characterised its later revival. But the actors were good. The sound, "full-bodied" old Chippendale was Polonius; Swinburne, also of the old school, was the King; and the worthy Mead, long ago a star himself, and one of Mr. Phelps' corps, "discharged" the Ghost with admirable impression and elocution.[1] He has now passed away, after long service, to "that bourne," &c. Miss Bateman was interesting, and Mrs. Pauncefort, who remained long at the Lyceum, was an excellent Queen. Actor and manager expected much success for 'Hamlet,' and counted on a run of eighty nights, but it was performed for two hundred! To the present hour it has always continued—though sparingly revived—the most interesting of the actor's performances, looked for with an intellectual curiosity.

In March the hundredth night of 'Hamlet' was celebrated by a banquet, given in the saloon of the Lyceum Theatre, at which all the critics and literary persons connected with the stage were

---

[1] I have seen in an old criticism a notice of a leading performer who in similar fashion "condescended"—so it was phrased—to the part of the Ghost, and whose impersonation was declared to be "more than usually *gentlemanlike and reputable.*" It were well, however, that the old system of slow charnel-house tones was now given up. There is no reason why this sort of *chaunt* should be adopted.

SIR HENRY IRVING AS "HAMLET."
From the Statue in the Guildhall, by E. Onslow Ford, R.A.

e p. 62.

present. This method of festivity became familiar enough, owing to the never-flagging hospitality of the later manager of the Lyceum, and offered a striking contrast to the older days, when it was intimated that "*chicken and champagne*" was a ready method of propitiating a critic. Mr. Pigott, who had recently been appointed the Licenser of Plays, a man of many friends, from his amiability, proposed the health of the lessee, which was followed by the health of the actor and of the author of the establishment, the latter, as it was rather sarcastically said, "giving the hundred and odd literary men present the oft-repeated illustration of how far apart are authorship and oratory." The good old Chippendale told how he had played Polonius to the Hamlet of Kemble, Kean, Young, and other famous tragedians; but protested that "the most natural and, to his mind, the most truthful representation he had seen was that of his friend here." Something must be allowed for post-prandial exuberance, and no one could more shrewdly appreciate their value than the actor himself. We may be certain that in his "heart of heart" he did not agree that he had excelled Kemble, Kean, Young, and the others. It was interesting, however, to meet such histrionic links with the past, which are now broken. Mr. Howe was perhaps the only other then surviving who could have supplied reminiscences of the kind. Since then what a number of Hamlets have we not seen! Forbes Robertson, Martin Harvey, our actor's son—H. B. Irving—and the divine Sarah herself.

A second Shakespearian piece was now determined on, and on February 14, 1875, 'Othello' was brought out. This, it was admitted, was not a very effective performance. It was hysterical, and in his agitation the actor exhibited movements almost panther-like, with many strange and novel notes. At some bursts there was even indecorous and disrespectful laughter. The ascetic face, too, was not in harmony with the dusky lineaments of "the Moor." Here, again, his notion of the character was immature.

But in the full tide of all this prosperity, theatre-goers were startled to learn that the shrewd and capable manager, the energetic "old Colonel," was dead. This event occurred, with great suddenness, on Monday, March 22, 1875. On the Sunday he had been at a banquet at a Pall Mall restaurant in company with his leading actor and other friends, but on the next day, complaining of a headache, he lay down. His daughter went as usual to the theatre, to which word was soon brought that he had passed away peacefully. It was thought advisable to let the performance be completed, and the strange coincidence was noted that while his child was bewailing the loss of her theatrical sire, the old Polonius, she was unconscious of the blow which had deprived her of her real parent.

There was much speculation as to what arrangement would follow, and some surprise when it was announced that the widow was ready to step intrepidly into his place, and carry on matters exactly as before. The mainstay of the house

was ready to support her, and though bound
by his engagement, he would, had he been so
inclined, have found it easy to dissolve it, or make
it impracticable. He resolved to lend his best
efforts to support the undertaking, in which his
views would, of course, prevail. It was hardly
a prudent arrangement, as the result proved, for
the three years that followed were scarcely advantageous to his progress. The management was to
be of a thrifty kind, without boldness, and lacking
the shrewd, safe instincts of the late manager;
while the actor had the burden, without the
freedom, of responsibility. It struck some that
the excellent Mrs. Bateman was "insisting" somewhat too much upon the family element. The
good-hearted, busy, and managing lady was in
truth unsuited to bear the burden of a great
London theatre, and what woman could be? her
views were hardly "large" enough, and too old-
fashioned. The public was not slow to find all this
out, and the fortunes of the theatre began almost
at once to change. Our actor, ambitious, and
encouraged by plaudits, was eager to essay new
parts; and the manageress, entirely dependent
on his talent, was naturally anxious to gratify
him. But Irving was, in truth, in a false position.
Here it was that the deliberation of the "old
Colonel" became valuable. He would debate a
question, examine it from all points, feel the public
pulse, and this rational conduct influenced his
coadjutor.

'Macbeth' was speedily got ready, and produced

6

on September 18, 1875. Miss Bateman, of Leah
fame, was the Lady Macbeth, but the performance
scarcely added to her reputation. The actor, as
may be conceived, was scarcely then suited, by
temperament or physique, to the part, and by a
natural instinct made it conform to his own particular qualifications. His conception was that of
a dreamy, shrinking being, overwhelmed with
terrors and remorse, speaking in whispers, and
enfeebled by his own dismal ruminations. There
was general clamour and fierce controversy over
this reading, for by this time the sympathetic
powers of the player had begun to exercise their
attraction. He had a large and passionately enthusiastic following; but there were Guelphs and
Ghibellines, Irvingites and anti-Irvingites — the
latter a scornful and even derisive faction. I
could fancy some of the old school, honest " Jack "
Ryder, for instance, as they patrolled the Strand
at midday, expatiating on the folly of the public :
" Call *him* an actor ! " Some of them had played
with Macready, " and *they* should think they knew
pretty well what acting was ! " This resentful tone
has been evoked again and again with every new
actor.[1]

Objection was taken to the uncertainty in the

---

[1] Old Cibber thus grumbled at Garrick's rise, and other
quidnuncs at Kemble's; and when Edmund Kean came, there
was the old prompter, who, when asked his opinion if he were
not equal to Kemble, said: " Very clever young man indeed,
very clever; but Lord bless you, sir, Mr. Kemble *was a different
thing altogether.*"

touches; the figure did not "stand out" so much as it ought. Much of this, however, was owing to the lack of effect in the Lady Macbeth, who, assuming hoarse and "charnel-house" tones, seemed to suggest something of Meg Merrilies. On the later revival, however, his interpretation became bold, firm, and consistent. The play had, however, a good deal of attraction, and was played for some eighty nights.

The King in Tennyson's play-poem, 'Queen Mary,' I have always thought one of the best, most picturesque, of Irving's impersonations, from the perfect realisation it offered of the characters, impressions, feelings of the historic figure he represented: it was complete in every point of view. As regards its length, it might be considered trifling; but it became important because of the *largeness* of the place it fitted. Profound was the impression made by the actor's Philip—not by what he had to say, which was little, or by what he had to do, which was less, or by the dress or "make-up," which was remarkable. He seemed to speak by the expression of his figure and glances; and apart from the meaning of his spoken words, there was another meaning beyond—viz., the character, the almost diseased solitude, the heartless indifference, and other odious historical characteristics of the Prince, with which it was plain the actor had filled himself. Mr. Whistler's grim, antique portrait conveys this perfectly.

His extraordinary success was now to rouse the jealousy, and even malignity, which followed his course in his earlier days, and was not unaccompanied with coarse ridicule and caricature, directed against the actor's legs even. "Do you know," said a personage of Whistlerian principles—"do you know, it seems to me there is a great deal of *pathos* in Irving's legs, particularly in the *left* leg!"

A letter had appeared, in January, 1876, in *Fun*, the *Punch* of the middle and lower class, addressed to "The Fashionable Tragedian." It affected alarm at the report that, "so soon as the present failure can with dignity be withdrawn," he intended to startle the public and Shakespearian scholars with a new tragedy. In the name of that humanity "to which, in spite of your transcendent abilities, you cannot help belonging," he was entreated to forbear, if only for the sake of order and morality. "With the hireling fashion of the press at your command, you have induced the vulgar and unthinking to consider you a model of histrionic ability." In the course of the investigation the article was traced to a writer who has since become popular as a dramatist, and who, as might be expected, has furnished a fair proportion of murders and other villainies to the stage. What was behind the attack it would be difficult to say; but there are people to whom sudden unexpected success is a subject of irritation. Just as hypocrisy is the homage paid to vice, so it may be that the attacks of this kind are some of the penalties that have to be paid for success. But the satire led to police-court proceedings before Sir R. Carden, the modern Sir Peter Laurie, who sagely remarked, "No one ever shed a tear who saw Toole"; on which Irving tranquilly, "I am sorry to hear you say that." The paper was withdrawn with due apologies.

When the theatre closed in 1876, the indefatigable manageress organised a tour of the company in the provinces, with the view of introducing the new tragedian to country audiences. There are, as may be conceived, a prodigious curiosity to see him, and the tour was very successful. She brought to the task her usual energy and spirit of organisation; though with so certain an attraction the tour, like a good piece, might be said to "play itself," on the principle of *ma femme et cinq poupées*. I can recall the image of the busy lady on one of these nights at Liverpool or Birmingham, seated in her office, surrounded by papers, the play going on close by, the music of a house crowded to overflowing being borne to her ears. There was here the old Nickleby flavour, and a primitive, homely spirit that contrasts oddly with the present brilliant system of "touring," which must be "up to date," as it is called, with special train, and a company perhaps a hundred strong, and supported by almost as much lavishness and magnificence as is expected in the Metropolis. After the piece came the pleasant little supper at the comfortable lodgings.

On this occasion he was to receive the first of those intellectual compliments which have since been paid him by most of the leading Universities. At Dublin he excited much enthusiasm among the professors and students of Trinity College. He

was invited to receive an address from both Fellows
and students, which was presented by Lord Ash-
bourne, later Lord Chancellor of Ireland, then a
Queen's Counsel.   This was conceived in the most
flattering and complimentary terms.   The University
was never slack in honouring him, and later gave
him the degree of Doctor of Letters.

About this time there arrived in England the
Italian actor Salvini, of great reputation in his own
country.   He presented himself at Drury Lane, then
a great, dilapidated " Dom-Daniel," stored with
ancient scenery, wardrobes, and nearly always associated with disaster.   In its chilling area, and under
these depressing conditions, he exhibited a very
original and powerful conception of the Moor,
chiefly marked by Southern fire and passion.   The
earlier performances were sad to witness, owing to
the meagre attendance, but soon enthusiasm was
kindled.   It was likely that meaner natures, who
had long resented the favour enjoyed by the
English actor, should here see an opportunity of
setting up a rival, and of diminishing, if possible,
his well-earned popularity.   Comparisons of a rather
offensive kind were now freely made, and the next
manœuvre was to industriously spread reports that
he was stung by so unworthy a jealousy, that the
very presence of the Italian was torture to him, and
that he would not even go to see his performance.
These reports were conveyed to the Italian, who
was naturally hurt, and stood coldly aloof.   The
matter being thus inflamed, Irving, himself deeply
resenting the unjust imputation made on him, felt it

would be undignified to seek to justify himself for offences that he had not committed. Every one knows that during a long course of years no foreign actor had visited the Lyceum without experiencing, not merely the lavish hospitality of its manager, but a series of thoughtful kindnesses and services.

Indeed, as the actor day by day rose in public estimation, the flood of caricatures, skits, &c., never relaxed. He could afford to smile contemptuously at these efforts, and after a time they ceased to appear. The tide was too strong to be resisted, and the lampooners even were constrained to join in the general eulogy.[1] At one of them he must himself have been amused—a pamphlet which dealt with his mannerisms and little peculiarities in a very unsparing way. It was illustrated with some malicious but clever sketches, dealing chiefly with the favourite topic of the "legs." Mr. William Archer, who has since become a critic of high position, about this time also wrote a pamphlet in which he examined the actor's claims with some severity. Yet so judicial was the spirit of this inquiry, that the subject of it could not have been offended by it, owing to some just compliments which seemed to be, as it were, extorted by the actor's merit.

The new Lyceum season opened with yet one more play of Shakespeare's—'Richard III.' As might have been expected, he put aside the old,

---

[1] I have a vast collection of these things, filling some twenty great folio volumes—an extraordinary tribute to the actor's success.

well-established Cibberian version, a most effective
piece of its kind, and restored the pure, undiluted
text of the Bard, to the gratification, it need not be
said, of all true critics and cultivated persons.   It
was refreshing to assist at this intellectual feast, and
to follow the original arrangement, which had all
the air of novelty.[1]

A happily-selected piece was to follow, the old
melodrama of 'The Courier of Lyons,' which was
brought out on May 19, 1877, under a new title, 'The
Lyons Mail'—the title was furnished by my friend
Walter Pollock, who always contended that the old
one was a mistranslation, "courier" really signifying
a mail-bag.   The success of 'The Bells' had shown
that for a certain class of romantic melodramas the
actor had exceptional gifts; and it may be added
that he had a *penchant* for portraying characters of
common life under exciting and trying circumstances.   This play is an admirable specimen of
French workmanship.   The characters are marked,
distinct, amusing; every passage seems to add

[1] At the close of the performance, Mr. Chippendale presented
to him the sword used by Kean when playing Richard.   Later a
friend gave him "the George," which the great actor also wore in
the part.   Lady Burdett-Coutts, always one of his great admirers,
added Garrick's ring, "in recognition of the gratification derived
from his Shakespeare representations, uniting to many characteristics of his great predecessors in histrionic art (whom he is too
young to remember) the charm of original thought."   I may add
that I was the medium of conveying to him Macready's dress as
Virginius, at the request of Mrs. John Forster, to whose husband
it had been given by the great tragedian, with the accompanying
"tinfoil dagger" with which he used to immolate Virginia.

IRVING AS "DUBOSC."
From a bust by the Author.

To face p. 73.

strength to the interest, and with every scene the
interest seems to grow.

In pieces of this kind, where one actor plays
two characters, a nice question of dramatic propriety arises, viz., to how far the point of likeness
should be carried.   In real life no two persons could
be so alike as a single person, thus playing the two
characters, would be to himself.   The solution I
believe to be this, that likenesses of this kind, which
are recognised even under disguise, are rather
mental and intellectual, and depend on peculiar
expression—a glance from the eye, smiles, &c.
Irving, it must be said, contrived just so much
likeness in the two characters as suited the situations and the audience also.   Superficially there
was a resemblance, but he suggested the distinct
individualities in the proper way.   The worthy
Lesurques was destined to be one of his best
characters, from the way in which he conveyed the
idea of the tranquil, innocent merchant, so affectionate to his family, and so blameless in life.
Many will recall the pleasant, smiling, wondering
fashion in which he would listen to the charges
made against him.

A yet bolder experiment was now to be made,
—another piece in which Charles Kean made a
reputation, ' Louis XI.,' was brought out on
March 9, 1878.   It may be said without hesitation
that this is one of the most powerful, finished, and
elaborate of all Irving's efforts, and the one to
which we would bring, say, a foreign actor who
desired to see a specimen of the actor's talents.

This marvellous performance ripened and improved year by year, gaining in suggestion, fulness of detail, and perfect ease. In no other part was he so completely the character. There was a pleasant good-humour—a chuckling cunning—an air of indifference, as though it were not worth while to be angry or excited about things. His figure was a picture, and his face, wonderfully transformed; yet it seemed to owe scarcely anything to the "making-up." Nowhere else did he speak so much with his expressive features. You could see the cunning thought rising to the surface before the words. There was the hypocritical air of candour or frankness suddenly assumed, to conceal some villainous device. There was the genuine enjoyment of hypocrisy, and the curious shambling walk. How admirably graduated, too, the progress of decay and mortal sickness, with the resistance to their encroachments. This, with the portrait of his Richard—not the old-established, roaring, stamping Richard of the stage, but the weightier, more composed and refined—dwells long in the memory, especially such touches as his wary watchings, the looking from one to the other while they talk, as if cunningly striving to probe their thoughts; and the curious scraping of his cheek with the finger, the strange senile tones, the sudden sharp ferocity betokening the ingrained wickedness, and the special leer, as though the old fox were in high good humour.[1]

[1] Irving always recalled with pleasure any spontaneous and unaffected tributes which his acting has called forth. A most

IRVING AS "VANDERDECKEN."
From a bust by the Author.

To face p. 75.

A few years before this time Wagner's weird opera, 'The Flying Dutchman,' had been performed in London, and the idea had occurred to many, and not unnaturally, that here was a character exactly suited to Irving's methods. He was, it was often repeated, the "ideal" Vanderdecken. He himself much favoured the suggestion, and after a time the "Colonel" entrusted me and my friend Wills with the task of preparing a piece on the subject. For various reasons the plan was laid aside, and the death of the manager and the adoption of other projects interfered. It was, however, never lost sight of, and after an interval I got ready the first

flattering one is associated with 'Louis XI.'—a critical work which one of his admirers had specially printed, and which enforced the actor's view of Louis's character. "You will wonder," the authors said, "why we wrote and compiled this book. A critic had said that, as nothing was really known of the character, manners, &c., of Louis XI., an actor might take what liberties he pleased with the subject. We prepared this little volume to put on record a refutation of the statement, a protest against it, and a tribute to your impersonation of the character." Another admirer printed his various thoughts on Charles I. This was set off with beautifully-executed etchings, tailpieces, &c., and the whole richly bound and enshrined in a casket. The names of these enthusiasts are not given.

One night, during the performance of 'Hamlet,' something was thrown from the gallery on to the stage. It fell into the orchestra, and for a time could not be found. A sad-looking working-woman called at the stage-door to ask about it, and was glad to learn it was found. It was only a cheap, common thing. "I often go to the gallery," she said, "and I wanted Mr. Irving to have this. I wanted him alone in the world to possess it." "This," he added, telling the story, "is the little trinket which I wear on my watch-chain."

act, which so satisfied Irving that the scheme
was once more taken up. After many attempts and
shapings and re-shapings, the piece was at last
ready—Wills having undertaken the bulk of the
work, I myself contributing, as before, the first act.
The actor himself furnished some effective situations, notably the strange and original suggestion of
the Dutchman's being cast up on the shore and
restored to life by the waves.

I recall all the pleasant incidents of this venture,
the journeys to Liverpool and Birmingham to consult on the plot and read the piece; above all, the
company of the always agreeable Irving himself,
and his placid, unaffected gaiety. Indeed, to him,
as to "Boz," apply forcibly the melodious lines—

> "A merrier man,
> Within the limits of becoming mirth,
> I never spent an hour withal,
> His eye begets occasion for his wit,
> Which his fair tongue, conceit's expositor,
> Turns to a mirth-moving jest."

'Vanderdecken,' as it was called, was produced
on July 8, 1878, but was found of too sombre a cast
to attract. It was all, as Johnson once said, "inspissated gloom," but there was abundant praise for
the picturesque figure of the actor. Nothing could
be more effective than his first appearance, when he
was revealed standing in a shadowy way beside the
sailors, who had been unconscious of his presence.
This was his own subtle suggestion. A fatal
blemish was the unveiling of the picture, on the

due impressiveness of which much depended, and which proved to be a sort of grotesque daub, greeted with much tittering—a fatal piece of economy on the part of the worthy manageress. An unusually sultry spell of summer that set in caused "the booking to go all to pieces"—the box-keeper's consolatory expression. Our actor, how-ever, never lost faith in the subject, and a year or two later he encouraged me to make another attempt ; while Miss Terry has been always eager to attempt the heroine, in which she was confident of producing a deep impression.

At this time our actor's position was a singular one. It had occurred to many that there was something strange and abnormal in the spectacle of the most conspicuous performer of his time, the one who "drew" most money of all his con-temporaries, being under the direction of a simple, excellent lady, somewhat old-fashioned in her ideas, and in association with a mediocre company and economical appointments. There was here power clearly going to waste. It soon became evident that his talents were too heavily fettered, and that he had now attained a position which, to say the least, was inconsistent with such surroundings. His own delicacy of feeling, and a sense of old obligation, which, however, was really slender enough, had long restrained him ; but now, on the advice of friends, and for the sake of his own interests, he felt that matters could go on thus no longer, and that the time had arrived for making some serious change. The balancing of obligations is always

set herself to do battle with fortune in a new and lower sphere.   She secured the old theatre Sadler's Wells, which she partially rebuilt and beautified, and on the opening night was encouraged by a gathering of her old friends, who cheered her when she appeared, supported by her two faithful daughters.   Even this struggle she could not carry on long.   She took with her some of her old company, Bentley, the Brothers Lyons, and others, and she furnished melodramas, brought out in a somewhat rude but effective style, suited to the lieges of the district.   Later, Mr. Charles Warner, greatly daring, gave a whole course of Shakespearian characters, taking us through the great characters *seriatim*.   It was, indeed, a very astonishing programme.   But the truth was, she had fallen behind the times ; the old-fashioned country methods would no longer "go down."   In a few years she gave up the weary struggle, and, quite worn out, passed away to join the "old Colonel."

higher artistic distinction and complete prosperity. In conclusion, Mrs. Bateman ventures to express her gratitude for the kindness and generosity extended to her by the public—kindness that has overlooked many shortcomings, and generosity that has enabled her to faithfully carry out all her obligations to the close of her tenancy.—Lyceum, August 31, 1878."

CHAPTER VI

1878

THE NEW MANAGER OF THE LYCEUM—MISS TERRY—
HIS SYSTEM AND ASSISTANTS

THE Lyceum was designed by a true architect at a time when a great theatre was considered to be a building or monument, like a public gallery or museum. In these days little is thought of but the *salle* or interior, designed to hold vast audiences in galleries or shelves, after the pattern of a dissenting chapel. The Lyceum was really a fine structure, with entrances in four different streets, an imposing portico, abundance of saloons, halls, chambers, and other *dependances*, which are necessary in all good theatres. There was a special grace in its lobby and saloon, and in the flowing lines of the interior, though it suffered somewhat from unavoidable alterations.[1] The stage was a truly noble one, and offered the attraction of supplying a dignity and theatrical illusion to the figures or scenes that were

---

[1] It was built in 1830, so it was then over sixty-five years of age. The lease, held from Lord Exeter, had not many years to run—some twenty or so, I believe. It is now a music-hall.

7

exhibited upon it ; thus contrasting with the rather
mean and prosaic air which the low and contracted
stages of most modern houses offer.   This dignified
effect is secured at a heavy cost to the manager, for
every extra foot multiplies the area of scenery to a
costly degree, and it requires many figures to fill the
void.   Beazely, a pleasant humorist and writer of
some effective dramas, was the architect of this
fine temple, as also of the well-designed Dublin
Theatre[1]—of which Irving was ever boundless in
praise—since destroyed by fire.

It may be imagined that the financial portion
of the transaction could have offered little diffi
culty.   A man of such reputation inspires confi
dence ; and there are always plenty ready to come
forward and support him in his venture, his abilities
being the security.   A story was long industriously
circulated that he was indebted to the generosity of
a noble lady well known for her wealth and liberality
who had actually "presented him with the lease of the
theatre."   Shortly after Irving's death this statement
was recklessly repeated, and drew from Mr. Burdett
Coutts a spirited and categorical statement that
Irving had never received a shilling from this great
lady.   The truth was that Irving entirely relied on
his own talent and resources.   According to a state

---

[1] He was described by a friend as "always just arrived by the
mail in time to see the fish removed, or as going off by the early
coach after the last dance at four in the morning."   He wrote his
own epitaph—

"Here lies Samuel Beazely,
Who lived hard and died easily."

ment which he found it necessary to have circulated, he borrowed a sum of money on business terms, which he was enabled to pay off gradually, partly out of profits and partly out of a substantial legacy. His first repayment was made out of the gains of his provincial tour.

The new manager's first effort was to gather round him an efficient and attractive company. He was to make a brilliant *coup*, which settled and assured the future of the enterprise. It became presently known that Miss Ellen Terry was to be his partner and supporter on the stage, and it was instantly, and almost electrically, felt that triumph had been already secured. People could see in advance, in their mind's eye, the gifted pair performing together in a series of romantic plays; they could hear the voices blending, and feel the glow of dramatic enjoyment. This important step was heartily and even uproariously acclaimed. No manager ever started on his course cheered by such tokens of goodwill and encouragement, though much of this was owing to a natural and selfish anticipation of coming enjoyment.

The new actress, a member of a gifted family, was endowed with one of those magnetically sympathetic natures, the rarest and most precious quality a performer can have. It may be said to be "twice blessed," blessing both him that gives and him that takes—actor and audience. She had a winning face, strangely expressive, even to her tip-tilted nose, "the Terry nose," and piquant, irregular chin; with a nervous, sinuous figure, and a voice charged with melodious, heart-searching accents. She indeed merely transferred to the stage that curious air of fitful *enjouement* which distinguished her among her friends, which often thus supplied to her performances much that was unfamiliar to the rest of the audience. She had, in short, a most marked *personality.*[1]

---

[1] I possess a rare and possibly unique bill of one of Miss Ellen Terry's earliest child-performances, which it may be interesting to insert here :

LECTURE HALL, CROYDON.

FOR ONE NIGHT ONLY !

Tuesday Evening, March 13th, 1860.

MISS KATE TERRY

AND

MISS ELLEN TERRY,

The original representatives of Ariel, Cordelia, Arthur, Puck, &c (which characters were acted by them upwards of one hundred consecutive nights, and also before her Most Gracious Majesty the Queen), at the Royal Princess's Theatre, when under the management of Mr. Charles Kean, will present their new and successful

ILLUSTRATIVE AND MUSICAL

DRAWING-ROOM ENTERTAINMENT,

In Two Parts, entitled,

'DISTANT RELATIONS,' AND 'HOME FOR THE HOLIDAYS,'

In which they will sustain several

CHARACTERS IN FULL COSTUME.

N.B.—This entertainment was produced at the Royal Colosseum, and represented by the Misses Kate and Ellen Terry thirty consecutive nights to upwards of 30,000 persons—

and so on.

ELLEN TERRY.
From an early photograph by Elliott & Fry.

To face p. 85.

In her rather fitful course, Ellen Terry [1] had gone
on the stage, left it, and had gone on it again.   Her
performance at the Prince of Wales's Theatre, the
little home of comedy, in the piece of 'Masks and
Faces,' had left a deep impression, and I well recall
the sort of passionate intensity she put into the part.
It must be said that there was some uncertainty as
to how she was likely to acquit herself in the very
important round of characters now destined for her ;

[1] The actress is of a genuinely theatrical family.   Readers of
Scott's Life will recall the clever, industrious Terry, who was long
connected with the Edinburgh stage, and had himself adapted so
many of the Scott novels.   Miss Terry's father was also long connected with the Edinburgh stage ; her three sisters, her brother,
her two children, have all found their way to the "boards."   Even
the precocious child performer, Minnie Terry, is different from
other prodigy children, and imparts a distinction to what is usually
a disagreeable sort of exhibition.   I take from the pages of *The
Theatre* the following minute account of Miss Terry's career :—
"Miss Ellen Terry was born at Coventry on February 27, 1848.
Her first appearance on the stage was made at the Princess's
Theatre, under the management of Mr. Charles Kean, on April
28, 1856.   On October 15 of the same year she appeared as
Puck in the revival of 'A Midsummer Night's Dream.'   In Mr.
Kean's production of 'King John,' on October 18, 1858, she
acted the part of Arthur.   She next appeared at the Royalty and
Haymarket Theatres, and at the latter house she played in 'Much
Ado About Nothing.'   In March, 1863, she acted Gertrude in
'The Little Treasure,' at the Haymarket.   She then acted at the
Queen's Theatre in Long Acre, where, on October 24, 1867, she
sustained the character of Rose de Beaurepaire in 'The Double
Marriage,' also in 'Still Waters Run Deep'; and, on December
26 of the same year, she acted for the first time with Mr. Henry
Irving, playing Katherine to his Petruchio in 'The Taming of
the Shrew.'   Miss Terry then retired from the stage for some
years, reappearing on February 28, 1874, at the Queen's Theatre,
as Philippa Chester in 'The Wandering Heir.'   On April 18 of

despotic where need required it, and eke genial and forbearing too. The wonderful and ambitious development at the Lyceum has drawn on all his resources, equipping him with an experience which few stage-managers have opportunities of acquiring. When, as during the performance of 'Henry VIII.,' a crowd of over five hundred persons passed through the stage-door of the Lyceum, a stage-manager must needs have gifts of control of a high order to maintain discipline and direct his forces. And who has not known the sagacious and ever-obliging Hurst, who controlled the box-office for many a year! This proper selection of officials is all-important in an enterprise of this kind. Where they are well chosen, they help to bind the public to the house. It is well known that the manager was well skilled in reading the book of human character, and rarely made a mistake in choosing his followers. On their side, they have always shown much devotion to the interests of their chief. The two first—Bram Stoker and Loveday—were with him in service for nigh thirty years, and both were close at hand on the fateful night of his death.

Not the least important of these assistants was an accomplished artist, Mr. Hawes Craven, the painter of the scenery, the deviser of the many elaborate settings and tableaux which have for so long helped to enrich the Lyceum plays. The modern methods of scenery now require an almost architectural knowledge and skill, from the "built-up" structures which are found necessary, the gigantic portals and porticoes of cathedrals, houses, squares, and statues. Monumental constructions of all kinds are contrived, the details, carvings, &c., being modelled or wrought in *papier-mâché* material. It may be doubted whether this system really helps stage illusion as it affects to do, or whether more sincere dramatic effects would not be gained by simpler and less laboured methods. To Mr. Craven, too, we owe the development of what is the "medium" principle—the introduction of atmosphere, of phantasmagoric lights of different tones, which are more satisfactory than the same tones when produced by ordinary colours. The variety of the effects thus produced has been extraordinary. As might be expected, the artistic instincts of the manager have here come in aid of the painter, who with much readiness and versatility has been ready to seize on the idea and give it practical shape by his craft.[1] I remember being

---

[1] Amiable and forbearing as Irving always showed himself to his subordinates, he could be resolute in seeing that what he wished or wanted was carried out. Schemes of scenery found available on trial were again and again condemned because they failed to bring about the effect desired. This, however, was the secret of the unity and homogeneousness of his productions. It is admitted that even in the matter of the elaborate orchestral music, which we might fancy he would have left to the professors, he had much to say and alter. It might strike him as not being suited to the situation. Fresh experiments would have to be made, to be also set aside, to the despair of the composer. Then the *difficile* manager would be heard to attempt, vocally, some rude outline of what he desired, and this suggestion the ready musician would grasp and put into shape, and it would be agreed *nem. con.* that somehow this last attempt suited the situation exactly. This sense of perfect propriety *in omnibus* was a "note" of the manager's character.

with him when he was reviewing a little model scene and being struck by the gracious and amiable fashion in which he made his objections, which, however, involved a complete reconstruction.

Mr. Craven, years ago, practised his art on the boards of the old Dublin Theatre Royal, under Mr. Harris, where his scenery attracted attention for its brilliancy and originality. It had the breadth and effect of rich water-colour drawings of the Prout school. Scenic effect is now seriously interfered with by the abundant effulgence of light in which the stage is bathed, and in which the delicate middle tints are quite submerged. The contrast, too, with moulded work is damaging, and causes the painted details to have a "poorish," flat air. Another point to which much prominence had been given from the first at the Lyceum was the music. A fine and full orchestra—on an operatic scale almost—with excellent conductors, who were often composers of reputation, was provided. This rich and melodious entertainment sets off a play and adds to its dignity, and may be contrasted with the meagre music ordinarily provided in theatres.

Once, travelling in the North, the manager met at a hotel a young musician, who, like himself, "was on tour," with some concert party it might be, and fell into conversation with him on their respective professions. This young man chatted freely, and imparted his ideas on music in general, and on theatre music in particular. The manager was pleased with the freshness and practical character of these views, and both went their way. Long

after, when thinking of a successor to Stöpel—
the old-established Lyceum conductor—he recalled
this agreeable companion, who was Mr. Hamilton
Clarke, and engaged him, at the handsome salary
of some six hundred a year, to direct the music.
He was, moreover, a composer of great distinction. His fine, picturesque overtures and incidental
music to 'The Merchant of Venice,' and other
Lyceum pieces, still linger in the memory. In
due time this connection was severed. The
manager later applied for aid to such composers
as Sir Arthur Sullivan, Sir A. Mackenzie, Sir
Julius Benedict, Sir Charles Stanford, Jacobi, and
Mr. German.

Anticipating a little, I may say here that the
Lyceum company, though not affecting to contain
any brilliant "stars," from the beginning exhibited
a true homogeneousness in sound, conscientious
actors who have always "discharged" their characters in an effective way, suited to the requirements
of the piece. With a certain logical consistency,
the manager has ever considered the requirements
of his audience and the theatre. The introduction
of Mrs. Stirling, an actress of the first rank, in such
a part as the Nurse, however welcome as a performance, almost disturbed the dramatic harmony,
and made an inferior part too prominent. This
may seem hypercritical, but there can be no doubt
as to its truth, and it shows what tact is necessary
to secure an even performance. Those members
of the *corps* who had been with him almost from
the beginning, the manager had thoroughly leavened

with his own methods and his own spirit, thus securing a general harmony. Such useful auxiliaries
include Johnson (a low comedian of the older
school), Tyars, Archer (another low comedian),
Haviland (a most useful performer, who improved
with every year), and Andrews. Another service-
able player was Wenman, who seemed in physique
and method to be exactly suited to Burchell in
'Olivia.' During past seasons, however, this
worthy man has been removed from the company
by death. On a stranger these players might produce little effect; but the *habitués* of the theatre
have grown familiar with their ways and faces and
figures, and would miss them much were they
absent from a new play.

In addition to this permanent body, the manager
was accustomed occasionally to call to his aid performers of mark, such as Terriss and Forbes
Robertson, the former an admirable actor in special
characters suited to his robustness, though his
powers would have gained by some refining.
Forbes Robertson is a picturesque performer
of many resources, who can supply colour and
passion at need. Arthur Stirling and Macklin
—excellent, well-trained actors both—have been
found at the Lyceum, as also Mr. Bishop.
Of the ladies there are Miss Genevieve Ward,
the excellent Mrs. Pauncefort (of the school of
Mrs. Chippendale), Miss Coleridge, occasionally the
vivacious Miss Kate Phillips, and Miss Emery,
now Mrs. Cyril Maude, who took Miss Terry's
place in case of indisposition or fatigue.

The new manager made some decorative alterations in the theatre which, considering the little
time at his disposal, did credit to his taste and
promptitude. The auditorium was treated in
sage green and turquoise blue ; the old, familiar
"cameos" of Madame Vestris's day, ivory tint,
were still retained, while the hangings were of blue
silk, trimmed with amber and gold, with white lace
curtains. The ceiling was of pale blue and gold.
The stalls were upholstered in blue, "a special
blue" it was called ; escaloped shells were used
to shield the glare of the footlights. The dressing-
rooms of the performers, the Royal box, and Lady
Burdett-Coutts' box were all handsomely decorated
and rearranged, the whole being directed by Mr.
A. Darbyshire, a Manchester architect. This,
however, was but the beginning of a long series of
structural alterations, additions, and costly decorations, pursued over a term of a dozen years.

On Monday, December 30, 1878, the theatre was
opened with the revived ' Hamlet.' This was the
first of those glittering nights—or *premières*—which
were to become a feature of the London season.
From the brilliancy of the audience—which usually
included all that was notable in the arts and professions—as well as from the rich dresses, jewels, and
flowers, which suggested the old opera nights, the
spectacle became one of extraordinary interest, and
invitations were eagerly sought. Here were seen
the regular *habitués*, who from the first were
always invited ; for the constancy of the manager to
his old friends was well known.

The play was given with new scenery, dresses, music, &c. The aim was to cast over the whole a poetical and dreamy glamour, which was exhibited conspicuously in the treatment of the opening scenes when the Ghost appeared. There were the mysterious battlements seen at a distance, shadowy walls, and the cold blue of breaking day. There were fine halls, with arches and thick pillars of Norman pattern. Irving's version of the part was in the main the same as before, but it was noted that he had moderated it, as it were ; it became more thoughtful.

Of course, much interest and speculation was excited by the new actress, who exhibited all her charming grace and winsomeness, with a tender piteousness, when the occasion called. "Why," she told an interviewer, " I am so high strung on a first night, that if I realised there was an audience in front staring at me, I should fly off and be *down at Winchelsea in two twos !*" On this momentous night of trial she thought she had completely failed, and without waiting for the fifth act she flung herself into the arms of a friend, repeating, " I have failed, I have failed !" She drove up and down the Embankment half a dozen times before she found courage to go home.

This successful inauguration of his venture was to bear fruit in a long series of important pieces, each produced with all the advantages that unsparing labour, good taste, study, and expense could supply. Who could have dreamed—or did *he* dream on that night ?—that no fewer than nine of Shakespeare's

IRVING AS "HAMLET."
From the painting by Edwin Long, A.R.A.
(By kind permission of Mr. Burdett-Coutts.)

ace p. 94.

greatest plays, a liberal education for audiences, were destined to be his contribution to the "public stock of harmless pleasure"? Every one of taste is under a serious obligation to him, having consciously or unconsciously learnt much from this accomplished man.

On this occasion, adopting a custom since always adhered to, the manager had his arrangement of the play printed, with an introduction by a good Shakespearian student, who was destined to be a well-known figure in the *entourage* of the Lyceum. This was "Frank Marshall," with his excited, bustling ways, and eccentric exterior. He was always *bon enfant*. He had written one very pleasing comedy, 'False Shame,' and was also rated as a high authority on all Shakespearian matters. He published an elaborate "Study of Hamlet," and later induced Irving to join him in an ambitious edition of Shakespeare, which took some years to complete. He was also a passionate bibliomaniac, though not a very judicious one, lacking the necessary restraint and judgment. He had somewhat of a troubled course, like so many a London *littérateur*.

At this time the average theatrical criticism, from lack of suitable stimulant to excite it, was not nearly so discriminating as it is now, when there is a body of well-trained, capable men, who sign their names and carry out their duty with much independence. It is extraordinary what a change has taken place in this respect. At the opening of Irving's management there was certainly a tendency to wholesale and lavish panegyric. Not unnaturally, too, for all were grateful to one who was making such exertion to restore the stage to elegance. Some of the ordinary newspapers, however, overwhelmed him with their rather tedious, indiscriminate praises ; it seemed as though too much could not be said. There is no praise where *everything* is praised ; nor is such very acceptable to its object. A really candid discussion on the interpretation of a character, with reasonable objections duly made, and argued out with respect, and suggestions put forward—this becomes of real profit to the performer. Thus in one single short criticism on a character of Garrick's—he was once playing a gentleman disguised as a valet—Johnson furnished not only Garrick, but all players too, with an invaluable principle which is the foundation of all acting : " No, sir ; he does not let the gentleman break out through the footman."

A new play at the Lyceum was rarely concluded without a speech being insisted upon. Irving himself favoured this practice, but reluctantly, yielding only to the irresistible pressure of ardent and clamorous admirers. The system now obtains at every theatre where there is an "actor-manager." But there can be no question but that it is an abuse, and a perilous one. It encourages a familiarity, and often insolence, which shakes authority. The manager, when he makes his speech, seems to invite the galleries down on to his stage, and it is to be noticed that the denizens of these places are growing bolder, and fancy, not unreasonably, that they are entitled to have *their* speech, as the manager has his. [1]   It

[1] Once, at Edinburgh, during a performance of ' The Merchant of Venice,' the students of the University had been very

also impairs the mystic feeling which always attached to the figure of the actor.

The manager was always guided by the principle of alternating his greater attempts with others on a more moderate and less pretentious scale. With this view he brought out, on April 17, 1879, the ever-attractive 'Lady of Lyons'—which would seem naturally suited to him and his companion. He was himself in sympathy with the piece, and prepared it on romantic and picturesque lines. It has been usually presented in a stagey, declamatory fashion, as affording opportunity to the two leading performers for exhibiting a robustious or elocutionary passion. It was determined to tone the whole down, as it were, and present it as an interesting love-story, treated with restraint. Nothing could be more pleasing than the series of scenes thus unfolded, set off by the not unpicturesque costumes of the revolutionary era. It is difficult to conceive now of a Pauline otherwise attired. It would seem that a play always presented itself to our manager's eye as a series of poetical scenes which take shape before him, with all their scenery, dresses, and situations. As he mused over them they fell into their place—the figures moved; a happy suitable

tumultuous, and scarcely a word was heard of the first scenes. Suddenly the drop-scene descended, and the actor appeared. There was silence; then, with perfect good-humour and firmness, he said that, owing to some misunderstanding, the first portion of the piece had not been heard by the audience, and that he was now going to recommence the whole from the beginning. And so it was done.

background suggests itself, with new and striking arrangements; and thus the whole order and tone of the piece furnishes him with inspiration.

Indeed, it must be confessed that there are few plays we should be less inclined to part with than this hackneyed and well-worn drama. The " casual sight " of that familiar title on the red-brick corner wall in some country or manufacturing town—it may be weeks old, the old paper flapping flag-like— always touches a welcome note, and the names of the characters have a romantic sound. In the story there is the charm of simple effects and primitive emotion; it is worked out without violence or straining, and all through the ordinary sympathies are firmly struck, and in the most touching way. Tinselly or superficial as many have pronounced the piece, there is depth in it. So artfully is it compounded that it is possible to play the two characters in half a dozen different ways; and clever actors have exerted themselves to gloss over the weak spot in Melnotte's character—the unworthy deception, which involves loss of respect. Pauline, however, is a most charming character, from the mixture of emotions; if played, that is, in a tender, impulsive way, and not made a vehicle for elocutionary display. The gracious, engaging part of the heroine has been essayed by our most graceful actresses, after being created by the once irresistible Miss Helen Faucit. For over six years this drama has held its ground, and is always being performed. The young beginner, just stepping on the boards, turns fondly to the effective " gardener's son," and is all but certain that he could deliver the passage ending, "*Dost like the picture?*"—a burst often smiled at, but never failing to tell. Every one of the characters is good and actable, and, though we may have seen it fifty times, as most playgoers have, there is always a reserve of novelty and attraction left which is certain to interest. In Irving's Claude there was a sincerity and earnestness which went far to neutralise these highly artificial, not to say "high-flown," passages which have so often excited merriment. Miss Terry, as may be conceived, was perfectly suited in her character—the ever-charming Pauline; and displayed an abundance of spontaneousness, sympathy, and tenderness.[1]

The public was at this time to learn with interest that the actor was to accompany Lady Burdett-Coutts, with whom he was in high favour, on a voyage to the Mediterranean in her yacht *The Walrus*, and all was speculation as to the party and their movements. But this party of pleasure was to be fruitful of some romantic results, for a young American found favour in the eyes of his hostess—who shortly after married him. Unassisted by this alliance, Mr. Bartlett—now Mr. Burdett-Coutts, M.P.—has fashioned for himself a distinguished career. During this pleasant voyage *The Walrus* directed her course to Venice and various Italian cities—all new and welcome to our actor, who was

[1] The late Earl of Lytton once told me many interesting particulars of his father's popular play. It was really an adaptation from a French story called "The Bellows-mender."

at the same time taking stock of the manners, customs, dresses, &c., of the country, and acquiring, as
it were, the general flavour and *couleur locale*.   His
scene-painter had also found his way there, and was
filling his sketch-book with rich " bits of colour,"
picturesque streets, and buildings.   The manager
was, in fact, pondering over a fresh Shakespearian
venture—an Italian play, which was to be produced
with the new season.   He was about to set on the
stage ' The Merchant of Venice,' with every aid that
money and taste could supply.   The moment this
selection was known, it was felt almost universally
that it was exactly the piece that should have been
chosen.   Every one anticipated by a sort of instinct
what entertainment was in store for them : for here
was the part and here was the actor.   Notwithstanding the elaborate character of the preparations,
the whole was "got up" in some four weeks, though
this period did not comprise the long course of
private study and meditation during which the
scheme was gradually matured in his mind.   When
on his yachting expedition he had taken advantage
of a hasty visit to Tangier to purchase Moorish
costumes to be used in the Shakespearian spectacle
he was preparing.

To fill up the interval he got ready Colman's
drama ' The Iron Chest,' produced on September
27, 1879.   This powerful but lugubrious piece has
always had an unaccountable attraction for tragedians.   Sir Edward Mortimer belongs, indeed, to
the family of Sir Giles Overreach.   The character
offered temptation to our actor from its long-

sustained, mournful, and poetical soliloquies, in which the state of the remorseful soul was laid bare at protracted length; but, though modified and altered, the piece was hopelessly old-fashioned. It is impossible in our day to accept seriously a "band of robbers," who, moreover, live "in the forest"; and the "proofs" of Sir Edward's guilt, a knife and blood-stained cloth, carefully preserved in an old chest which is always in sight, have a burlesque air.

Irving very successfully presented the image of the tall, wan, haggard man, a prey to secret remorse and sorrow. Wilford, the secretary, is by anticipation, as it were, in possession of the terrible secret of the murder, and is himself a character of much force and masterful control. He was really the complement of the leading personage. But Norman Forbes—one of the Forbes Robertson family, *ingenuus puer*, and likewise *bonæ indolis*—made of this part merely an engaging youth, who certainly ought to have given no anxiety in the world to a conscience-stricken murderer. The terrors of Sir Edward would have had more force and effect had he been in presence of a more robust and resolute personage—one who was not to be drawn off the scent, or shaken off his prey. This piece well served its purpose as "a stop-gap" until the new one was ready.

CHAPTER VII

1879

'THE MERCHANT OF VENICE'

THIS great and attractive play was now ready ; all was anticipation and eager interest. The night of its production—November 1, 1879—was a festive one. The house was most brilliant : and indeed this may be accounted the first *regular*, official Lyceum *première*. I recall that among the audience were Tom Taylor and Henry Byron, names that now seem ghost-like, so rapidly do literary shadows depart. Like some rich Eastern dream, steeped in colours and crowded with exquisite figures of enchantment, the gorgeous vision of the pageant seems now to rise in the cold, sober daylight. As a view of Venetian life, manners, and scenery, it has rarely been matched. The figures seemed to have a grace that belonged not to the beings that pace, and declaim upon, the boards. Add the background, the rich, exquisite dresses, the truly noble scenery—a revel of colour, yet mellowed—the elegant theatre itself crammed with an audience as elegant,

ELLEN TERRY AS "PORTIA."
Photo by Lock & Whitfield, Ealing, W.

To face p. 103.

and it may be conceived what a night it was. The scenery alone would take an essay to itself, and it is hard to say which of the three artists engaged most excelled. The noble colonnade of the ducal palace was grand and imposing ; so was the lovely interior of Portia's house at Belmont, with its splendid amber hangings and pearl-grey tones, its archings and spacious perspective. But the Court scene, with its ceiling painted in the Verrio style, its portraits of Doges, the crimson walls with gilt carvings, and the admirable arrangements of the throne, &c., surely for taste, contrivance, and effect has never been surpassed. The whole effect was produced by the painting, not by built-up structures. The dresses too—groupings, servants, and retainers —what sumptuousness! The pictures of Moroni and Titian had been studied for the dove-coloured cloaks and jerkins, the violet merchant's gown of Antonio, the short hats—like those of our day—and the frills. The general tone was that of one of Paolo Veronese's pictures—as gorgeous and dazzling as the *mélange* of dappled colour in the great Louvre picture. There was a judicious reserve too, and none of that overloading of illustration without *a propos*, which was such a serious blemish in later productions.

Shylock was not the convential usurer with patriarchal beard and flowing robe, dirty and hook-nosed, but a picturesque and refined Italianised Jew, genteelly dressed : a dealer in money, in the country of Lorenzo de' Medici, where there is an aristocracy of merchants. His eyes are dark and piercing, his face is sallow, his hair spare and turning grey; he wears a black cap, a brown gaberdine faced with black, and a short robe underneath. [1] And, at the same time, it must be said that this system of reviving the tone of the era seems quite *un*-Shakespearian. These revels and Venetian dances and gondolas, put in for "local colour," have really little to do with high tragedy and dramatic interest : persons of our day, when involved in an acute crisis, have no thought of such material things about them. You must "come to the 'osses." Everything else seems trivial and interruptive. But this "overloading" of the Bard is a fertile theme and almost requires a treatise to itself.

The "Trial scene," with its shifting passions, must have stamped Irving as a fine actor. See

---

[1] Sometimes one of his richer revivals would cost eight or ten thousand pounds. Further, as he was easy and magnificent in his dealings, he was charged always the full or fullest price. How unlike the worthy old " Colonel " Bateman ! I was once with the latter when a traveller in stuffs was shown in and unfolded his cheap wares, blue, green, crimson, which the Colonel felt and tested all ways, and got his own price too ! Everybody had their " pull " at the " Chief." He was always splendid in his private transactions. Any book that he desired at an auction he bought without limit of price. After one visit to Mr. Quaritch in search of a book of German costumes for 'Faust,' he came away having paid £80 for a number of volumes ! I was once with him in Birmingham at Christmas-time, when he brought me to Elkington's to choose handsome presents for the company. It was fine to see in what stately style he selected—pointing to this and that piece of silver, "Send up that!" I was not forgotten. All which was to have its natural sequel.

IRVING AS "SHYLOCK"
Photo by Lyddell, Sawyer, & Dunn.

To face p 105.

him as he enters, having laid aside his gaberdine and stick, and arrayed in his short-skirted gown, not with flowing but tightened sleeves, so that this spareness seems to lend a general gauntness to his appearance. There he stands, with eyes half furtively, half distrustfully following the Judge as he speaks. When called upon to answer the appeal made to him "from the bench," how different from the expected conventional declaration of violent hatred! Instead, his explanation is given with an artful adroitness as if *drawn* from him. Thus, "If you deny it" is a reminder given with true and respectful dignity, not a threat; and when he further declares that it "is his humour," there is a candour which might commend his case, though he cannot restrain a gloating look at his prey. But as he dwells on the point, and gives instances of other men's loathing, this malignity seems to carry him away, and, complacent in the logic of his illustration of the "gaping pig" and "harmless necessary cat," he bows low with a Voltairean smile, and asks, "*Are you answered?*" How significant, too, his tapping the bag of gold several times with his knife, in rejection of the double sum offered, meant as a calm, business-like refusal; and the "I would have my bond!" emphasised with a meaning clutch. Then the conclusion, "Fie upon your law," delivered with folded arms and a haughty dignity; indeed, a barrister might find profit here, and study the art of putting a case with adroitness and weight. But when Antonio arrives his eyes follow him with a certain uneasy distrust, and on Bellario's letter

being read out he listens with a quiet interest,
plucking his beard a little nervously.   As, however,
he sees the tone the young lawyer takes, he puts on
a most deferential and confidential manner, which
colours his various compliments: "O wise young
judge," "A Daniel," &c., becoming almost wheedling.   And when he pleads his oath—

> "Shall I lay perjury upon my soul?
>   No, not for Venice!"

there is a hypocritical earnestness, as if he were
given his reason privately to the counsel, though
there is a strange, indescribable sneer conveyed in
that "not for Venice."   Then the compliment to
Portia, "How much more elder art thou than thy
looks!" which he utters, crouching low, with a
smiling, even leering, admiration, but admiration
given for what is on his own side.   And what
follows opens a most natural piece of business,
arising out of the sort of confidential intimacy
which he would establish between them—

> "Ay, his breast,
> So says the bond;—Doth it not, noble judge?
> *Nearest his heart*, those are the very words";

the latter words pronounced with canine ferocity,
his eyes straining over the other's shoulders, while
he points with his knife—secure, too, that the other
will agree with him.   He fancies that he has
brought over the counsel to his side.   And it may

be added that this knife is not flourished in the butcher's style we are accustomed to; it is more delicately treated, as though something surgical were contemplated. When bidden to "have by some surgeon," nothing could be better than the sham curiosity with which he affects to search the bond for such a proviso, letting his knife travel down the lines, and the tone of "I cannot find it," in a cold, helpless way, as if he had looked out of courtesy to his "young judge," who appeared to be on his side. The latter at last declares that there is no alternative, but that Antonio must yield his bosom to the knife; then the Jew's impatience seems to override his courtesies, his gloating eyes never turn from his victim, and with greedy ferocity he advances suddenly with "Come, prepare!" When, however, Portia makes her "point" about the "drop of blood," he drops his scales with a start; and, Gratiano taunting him, his eyes turn with a dazed look from one to the other; he says slowly, "Is—that—the—law?" Checked more and more in his reluctant offers, he at last bursts out with a demoniac snarl—"Why, then, the devil give him good of it!" Finally he turns to leave, tottering away bewildered and utterly broken. As may be imagined, this new Shylock excited a vast deal of controversy. The "old school" was scornful; and here again it would have been worth hearing the worthy Jack Ryder—whom we still must take to be the type of the good old past—on the subject.

Nothing was more remarkable than the general

effect of this fine and thoughtful representation upon the public. It was a distinct education, too, and set every one discussing and reading. Admittedly one result was the great increase in the sale of editions of Shakespeare's works ; and the ephemeral litera-ture engendered in the shape of articles, criticisms, and illustrations of all kinds was truly extraordinary. Here again was heard the harsh note of the jealous and the envious. But there was plenty of fair and honest dissent as to the interpretation of the play, with some reasonably argued protests against the over-abundant decoration.[1]

The hundredth night of the run of this pro-digiously successful revival was celebrated in hospitable fashion by a supper, to which all that was artistic, literary, and fashionable—*tout Londres* in short—was bidden. The night was Saturday, February 14, 1880, the hour half-past eleven. As soon as the piece was terminated a panto-mimic change was accomplished. In an incredibly

[1] As I write, there is being performed a very meritorious and interesting revival of the play, by Mr. Bourchier, at the Garrick Theatre. It is a thoughtful, and even sufficient, rendering. But it must be said, there is a wide gulf between it and Irving's version. The Bourchier representation is practical and prosaic. Irving's was full of poetical suggestion : of a sort of pulsating feeling which stirred the spectators. Improving on the hint given by Irving, of Shylock being shown returning to his house after the flight of his daughter, Mr. Bourchier "works it up"—pauses before his door, knocks, and knocks again. After all, we had seen his daughter carried off by her young man, which disposed of the business. As we depart further from the date of Irving's death we shall come to recognise his merits.

short space of time—some forty minutes—an enormous marquee, striped red and white, that enclosed the whole of the stage, was set up ; the tables were arranged and spread with "all the luxuries of the season" with magic rapidity. An enjoyable night followed. The host's health was given by that accomplished man, and man of elegant tastes, Lord Houghton, in what was thought a curiously *mal à propos* speech. After conventional eulogiums, he could not resist some half-sarcastic remarks as to "this new method of adorning Shakespeare." He condemned the system of long "runs," which he contrasted with that of his youth, when pieces were given not oftener than once or twice in the week. He then praised the improvement in the manners of the profession, "so that the tradition of good breeding and high conduct was not confined to special families like the Kembles, or to special individuals like Mr. Irving himself, but was spread over the profession, so that families of condition were ready to allow their children to go on the stage. *We put our sons and daughters into it.*" I recall now the genuine indignation and roughly-expressed sentiments of some leading performers and critics who were sitting near me at this very awkward compliment. He then proceeded to speak of the new impersonation, describing how he had seen a Shylock, formerly considered a ferocious monster, but who had, under their host's treatment, become a "gentleman of the Jewish persuasion, in voice very like a Rothschild, afflicted with a stupid servant and wilful and pernicious daughter, to be eventually foiled by a very charming woman. But there was one character Mr. Irving would never pervert or misrepresent, and that was his own," &c.

Never was the power and good-humour—the *bonhomie*—of the manager more happily displayed than in his reply.   As was said at the time, it showed him in quite a new light.   Taken wholly unawares— for whatever preparation he might have made was, he said, " rendered useless by the unexpected tone of Lord Houghton's remarks "—he was thrown on his impromptu resources, and proved that he really possessed what is called debating power. He spoke without hesitation, and with much good sense and playful humour put aside these blended compliments and sarcasms.

Some time before the manager, who was on friendly terms with the gifted Helen Faucit, determined to revive a piece in which she had once made a deep impression, viz., ' King Réné's Daughter.' This poem, translated by her husband, set out the thoughts and feelings of a young girl in the contrasted conditions of blindness and of sight recovered. With a natural enthusiasm for his art, Irving persuaded the actress, who had long since withdrawn from the stage, to emerge from her retirement and play her old character "for one night only."   This news really stirred the hearts of old playgoers, who recalled this actress in her old days of enchantment, when she was in her prime, truly classical and elegant in every pose, playing the pathetic Antigone.   But, alas! for the old Antigone dreams;

we could have wished that we had stayed away!
The actress's devices seemed to have hung too long
a "rusty mail, and seemed quite out of fashion."
Irving did all he could, in an almost chivalrous
style, and it was certainly a kindly act of admiration
and enthusiasm for his art to think of such a
revival. Such homage deserved at least tolerance
or recognition.

Miss Terry herself had always fancied the character of Iolanthe, and it was now proposed to give the
play as an after-piece to 'The Merchant of Venice,'
a substantial meal for one night. Our heroine made
a tender, natural, and highly emotional character of
it. A new version or adaptation from the Danish
had been made, for obvious reasons, by the trusty
Wills: the piece was set off by one really lovely
scene, which represented the heart of some deep
grove, that seemed almost inaccessible to us, weird
and jungle-like. A golden, gorgeous light played
on the trees capriciously; there was a rich tangle of
huge tropical flowers; while behind, the tall, bare
trunks of trees were ranged close together like
sentinels. Golden doors opened with a musical
chime, or clang; strange, weird music, as of æolian
harps, floated up now and again. With this background, knightly figures of the Arthurian pattern
and ethereal maidens were seen to float before us.
Miss Terry's conception of the maid was not Miss
Faucit's, which was that of a placid rather cold
and elegant being. She cast over the character
a rapture, as though she were all love and
impulse, with an inexpressible tenderness and

devotional trust, as when she exclaimed, "I *go*
to find the light!" This sort of rapture also
tinged the hero's character, and the audience
were lifted into a region where emotion reigned
supreme.

CHAPTER VIII

1880

'THE CORSICAN BROTHERS' AND 'THE CUP'

WITH his usual tact the manager had determined on a change of entertainment which should offer a marked contrast to the classical success just obtained, and was now meditating a revival of the once popular romantic drama, 'The Corsican Brothers,' with all its spectral effects—certainly one of the best of many admirably-constructed and effective French pieces. To such a group belong the absorbing 'Two Orphans,' 'Thirty Years of a Gambler's Life,' 'Victorine,' and others. 'The Lady of Lyons' is the only one of our *répertoire* that can be put beside these ingenious efforts. Some thirty years ago, when it was produced at the Princess's, the horny-voiced Charles Kean performing the Brothers, it took hold of the public with a sort of fascination—the strange music of Stöpel, and the mysterious, gliding progress of the murdered brother across the stage, enthralling every one. There was a story at the time that the acts, sent over from Paris in separate parcels for

9

translation, had become transposed, the second act being placed first, and this order was retained in the representation with some benefit to the play. This may be a legend; but the fact is that either act could come first without making any serious difference.

Magnificent and attractive as was the mounting of this piece at this time, it was far excelled in sumptuousness on its later revival in 1891. The experience of ten years had made the manager feel a certainty in the results of his own efforts; his touch had become sure; the beautiful and striking effects were developed naturally, without that undue emphasis which often disturbs the onward course of a piece. Hence that fine, unobtrusive harmony which reigned in all his pictures. Even now the wonderful opera house, the forest glades, the *salon* in Paris, all rise before us. Nor was there less art shown in the subdued tone of mystery which it was contrived to throw over the scenes. The scenes themselves, even those of reckless gaiety, seemed to strike this "awesome" note. Much as the familiar "ghost tune" was welcomed, more mysterious, as it always seemed to me, was the creepy variation on the original theme, devised by Mr. H. Clarke, and which stole in mournfully at some impending crisis all through the piece. There was some criticism on the D'Orsay costumes of the piece; the short-waisted waistcoats, the broad-brimmed opera hats, and the rich cravats—*Joinvilles*, as they used to be called. These lent a piquancy, and yet were not too remote from the present time. Terriss, it must be said, was lacking in elegance and "distinction." There always lingers in the memory the image of the smooth grace and courtesies of Alfred Wigan, who really made a dramatic character of the part—sympathetic and exciting interest. It is in these things that we miss the style, the bearing which is itself acting, without utterance of a word, and which now seems to be a lost art. One result of this treatment, as Mr. Clement Scott truly pointed out, was the shifting of sympathies. "Château-Renaud was, no doubt, a villain, but he was one of the first class, and with magnetic power in him. He had won for himself a high place. He was cold as steel, and reserved. For him to deal with Louis was child's play. And yet all this was reversed: it was Louis that dominated the situation; no one felt the least apprehension for his fate." A judicious criticism.

Familiarity has now somewhat dulled the effect of the gliding entrance of the ghostly Louis, which at first seemed almost supernatural. The art was in making the figure rise as it advanced, and an ingenious contrivance was devised by one of the stage foremen. It was a curious feeling to find oneself in the cavernous regions below the stage, and see the manager rush down and hurriedly place himself on the trap to be worked slowly upwards.[1]

[1] Arthur Matthison, a quaint, clever American, who had written some successful dramas, was chosen to play "the double" of the leading actor: that is, after passing behind the "practicable" tree, he was to emerge, taking care to keep his back to the audience. Unluckily for stage effect, no known art will help "to dodge

The use of intense light has favoured the introduction of new effects in the shape of transparent
scenery ; that is, of a scene that looks like any
ordinary one, but is painted on a thick gauzy
material.   Thus, in the first act, the back of the
scene in the Corsican Palace is of this material,
through which the tableau of the Paris duel is
shown, a fierce light being cast upon it.   In the
original representation the whole wall descended
and revealed the scene.   The upper half ascending,
the other offers something of a magic-lantern or
phantasmagorian air.   The same material is used in
the dream in 'The Bells,' when the spectral trial is
seen going on, made mysterious and misty by the
interposition of the gauzes.

In the duel scene one of the swords is broken by
an accident ; the other combatant breaks his across
his knee, that the duel may proceed "on equal
terms."   It is not, of course, to be supposed that a
sword is broken every night.   They are made with
a slight rivet and a little solder, the fitting being
done every morning, so that the pieces are easily
parted.   But few had noted how artfully the
performer changed his weapon ; for in the early

Nature" in such points.   She has no *replicas* in her store : makes
everything distinct.   And it is significant of the strong individuality which belongs to the whole body as well as to the face, that
the eye will at once note the difference of expression in the *back*
outline of the figure, arms, &c.   I believe no two people could be
found so alike in their general appearance as to be indistinguishable—thus illustrating the late Mr. Carlyle's quaint phrase when
speaking of some one whose character he had interpreted un-
favourably, "*I knew it by the twist of the hip of him.*"

stages of the duel the flourishings and passes would have soon caused the fragments to separate. It is done during the intervals of rest, when the combatants lean as on the seconds to gather strength for the second "round," and one gets his new weapon from behind a tree, the other from behind a prostrate log.

But it is in the next act that the series of elaborate set scenes succeeding each other entails the most serious difficulties, only to be overcome in one way —viz., by the employment of an enormous number of persons. Few modern scenes were more striking than that of the opera house lit *à giorno*, with its grand chandelier and smaller clusters running round. The blaze of light was prodigious; for this some five thousand feet of gas-tubing had to be laid down, the floor covered with snake-like coils of indiarubber pipes, and the whole to be contrived so as to be controlled from a single centre-pipe. There were rows of boxes with crimson curtains, the spectators filling them—some faces being painted in, others being represented by living persons. Yet nothing could be more simple than the elements of this opera house. From the audience portion one would fancy that it was an elaborately built and costly structure. It was nothing but two light screens pierced with openings, but most artfully arranged and coloured.[1]

---

[1] This was followed by the double rooms of the supper party, a very striking scene: two richly-furnished rooms, Aubusson carpets, a pianoforte, nearly twenty chairs, sofas, tables, clocks, and a supper-table covered with delicacies, champagne bottles, flowers, &c. It was succeeded almost instantly by a scene occupying the

At its close, down came the rich tableau curtains, while behind them descended the cloth with the representation of the lobby scene in the opera house. It used to be customary for the manager's friends to put on a mask and domino and mingle with the gay throng of roysterers in the opera house scene, or to take a place in one of the practicable boxes and survey the whole—and a curious scene it was. A cosy supper in the Beef-steak-room, and a pleasant *causerie* through the small hours, concluded a delightful and rather original form of a night's entertainment.

As we call up the memories of the Lyceum performances, with what a series of picturesque visions is our memory furnished—poetical Shake-spearian pageants; romantic melodramatic stories, set forth with elegance and *vraisemblance;* plays of pathetic or domestic interest; exhilarating comedies;

same space—that of the forest, requiring the minutest treatment, innumerable properties, real trees, &c. This is how it is con-trived. The instant the tableau curtains are dropped, the auxiliaries rush on the scene; away to right and left fly the portions of the Parisian drawing-room : tables, chairs, piano, sofa, vanish in an instant. Men appear carrying tall saplings fixed in stands ; one lays down the strip of frozen pond, another the pros-trate trunk of a tree—every one from practice knowing the exact place of the particular article he is appointed to carry. Others arrive with bags of sand, which are emptied and strewn on the floor ; the circular tree is in position, the limelights ready. The transformation was effected, in what space of time will the reader imagine ? In thirty-eight *seconds*, by the stage-manager's watch ! By that time the tableau had been drawn aside, and Château-Renaud and his friend Maugiron were descending into the gloomy glade after their carriage had broken down.

A curious little controversy arose as to the authorship of the

with highly dramatic poems, written by the late Poet Laureate, Wills, and others. Indeed, who could have conceived on the opening night of the Lyceum management, when 'Hamlet' was to be brought out, that this was to be the first of a regular series—viz., nine gorgeous and ambitious presentations of Shakespearian pieces, each involving almost stupendous efforts, intellectual and physical, that we were to see in succession 'The Merchant of Venice,' 'Romeo and Juliet,' 'Much Ado About Nothing,' 'Othello,' 'Twelfth Night,' 'Macbeth,' 'Henry VIII.,' and 'King Lear'? What a gift to the public in the shape of the attendant associations, in the glimpses of Italian and other scenery, the rich costumes, the archæology!

The late Laureate, not contented with the popularity which his poems have won, always "hankered" after the entrancing publicity and excitement of the

Ghost Melody. It was claimed for Mr. Stöpel, who was acting as *chef d'orchestre* at the Théâtre Historique when the play was originally produced. Another claim was made for Varney, author of the stirring hymn, *Mourir pour la patrie.* Oddly enough, Stöpel, who was then at the Adelphi, could not be got "to say yes or no." "He was amused," he said, "at the importance attached to such a trifle, and could, if he chose, set the matter at rest in a few words." But he did not. But there used to be a pianoforte piece by one Rosellen— a *Reverie*—which certainly began and went on for many bars in the same fashion. However, a copy of the music of the *Ghost Melody*, arranged for the pianoforte, and published in 1852, was unearthed, which bore on its title the words: "Composed by M. Varney, of the Théâtre Historique: arranged by R. Stöpel, director of the music at the Princess's Theatre." This settled the point, and it explained the ambiguous declaration of the arranger. We must assuredly give the credit of this air to Varney.

theatre.[1] He made many an attempt in this direction,
and his list of performed dramas is a fairly long one ;
few, however, have enjoyed any signal success, save
perhaps the last, recently produced in the United
States.   To one indeed—witness the unlucky ' Promise of May '—the regular "first-nighter," as he is
called, was indebted for an amusing and enjoyable
evening's entertainment.[2]   It must be conceded,
however, that there is a dramatic tone or flavour
about his pieces which is attractive, in spite of all
deficiencies, and any one who could not see a touching grace and elegance in such a piece as ' The
Falcon,' weak as it is in treatment, must have little
taste or feeling.   So with ' Queen Mary,' which had
a certain grim power, and, above all, local colour.
His own striking success in the character of King
Philip was an agreeable recollection for Irving ; and
he now lent himself with much enthusiasm to a project for bringing forward a new drama by the poet.
The preparations for this elegant play were of the

[1] Tennyson s dramatic "baggage" is really important, for a poet.
He can count no less than six pieces.
[2] This was one of the most hilarious, enjoyable nights that it
was possible to conceive.   The richest Palais Royal farce could
not compare.   I " assisted."   It was a great event.   The great
Gladstone came specially to see his friend's triumph, and "duly
emboxed," glared portentously round the house.   The hero of
the piece was a flagrant Socialist, uttering periodically the
most shocking doctrines, on which the gallery became by and
by inflamed, uttering cries and booings.   The point of the jest,
however, was that the bard intended to hold up the character to
odium ; but unluckily the crowd took this to be the author's repel-
lent creed, and so the tumult increased.   The gloom gathered on
the brow of the great politician, who yet seemed persuaded that
all would be well.   But it went from bad to worse.

most lavish and unstinted kind.   Nothing, literally, was spared in the outlay of either study, thought, money, or art.   The manager usually followed an eclectic system, choosing his *aides* and assistants as they appear suited to each play.   Thus an architect of literary tastes, Mr. Knowles, was called in to design a regular Temple-interior, which was the principal scene, and which was to be treated, *secundum artem*, in professional style.   And so it rose with all its pillars and pediments "behind the scenes."

> "No ponderous axes rung;
> Like some tall palm the mystic fabric sprung."

The name of the new piece was 'The Cup,' a fine "barbarian" story, strangely interesting and even fascinating.   It was, of course, diffuse and expanded to inordinate length.   And there were many pleasant stories afloat of the poet contending "for the dear life" for his "ewe lambs," and for every line of his poetry; the manager, in his pleasant, placid way—but firm withal—quietly insisting on the most abundant compression.

The night of performance was that of January 3, 1881, when the beautiful play-poem was at last set before the audience in all its attraction.   It still lingers in the memory with an inexpressible charm, breathing poetry and romance.   We shall ever look back fondly to 'The Cup,' with its exquisite setting, and lament heartily that others did not so cordially or enthusiastically appreciate it.   There was something so fascinating about the play, something so refining, and also so "fantastical," that though lacking the strong thews and muscles of a regular drama, it satisfied eye and ear. As it floated before us, in airy, evanescent fashion, it seemed to recall the lines that wind up the most charming of Shakespeare's plays, when the revels now had ended, and all had "melted into air, into thin air." The noble Temple, with its rich mouldings, was destined too soon, alas! to pass away into the same dark grave of so many noble creations. On the two chief characters, both full of tragic power, the eye rested with an almost entrancing interest. Never did Irving *act* better— that is, never did he convey by his look and tones the evidence of the barbaric conception within him. There was a fine, pagan, reckless savagery, yet controlled by dignity. Miss Terry's Camma returns to the memory like the fragment of a dream. The delightful creation was brought before us more by her sympathetic bearing and motion than by speech; but what music was there in those tones, pitched in low, melodious key, interpreting the music of Tennyson! Her face and outline of figure, refined and poetical as they were, became more refined still in association with the lovely scenery and its surroundings. She seemed to belong to the mythological past. There was a strange calm towards the close, and all through no undue theatrical emphasis or faulty tone of recitation to disturb that dreamy sense.

Mr. Gladstone always affected a particular interest in our actor—even an enthusiasm; and used to sit in the wings, his hand to his ear listening to the Tennyson and other plays. This must have been an amiable affectation, for what he saw could not

THE LYCEUM LION.

" A SCORE OF DOGS GNAWED AT HIS ANKLES; AT LAST HE FELT THE TROUBLE OF HIS FEET—PUT FORTH ONE PAW, SLEW FOUR AND KNEW IT NOT."—" THE CUP."

[To face page 122.

have been after his taste. Indeed, none of "the old school," I always noted, could understand or tolerate Irving. When he went to Windsor to play 'Becket' before her late Majesty, the performance was not found suited to her old-fashioned taste.

It was not a little disheartening to think that this "entire, perfect chrysolite" was received with a rather cold admiration, or at least not with the enthusiasm it richly merited. The apathetic crowd scarcely appreciated the too delicate fare set before it, we scarcely know why. I suppose that it had not sufficient *robustness*, as it is called. After some weeks the manager found it needful to supplement the attraction of the play by the revived 'Corsican Brothers.' It may be conceived what a strain [1] was

---

[1] One agreeable night which was spent behind the scenes enabled me to study the admirable arrangements by which this complicated operation was carried out with smoothness and success. "No sooner has the drop-scene fallen—and a person always 'stood by' to see that the huge roller was kept clear of careless spectators—than a busy scene set in. Instantly men emerge from every side; the hills and banks, the slopes leading down the hill, the steps and massive pedestal that flank the entrance to the Temple on the right, are lifted up and disappear gradually; the distant landscape mounts slowly into the air; the long rows of jets are unfastened and carried off—in three or four minutes the whole is clear. At this moment are seen slowly coming down from aloft what appear to be three long heavy frames or beams— two in the direction of the length, one across the whole breadth of the stage. These make a sort of enclosure open on one side, and form the pediment or upper portion of the Temple meant to rest on the pillars. Soon busy hands have joined these three great joists by bolts and fastenings; the signal is given, and it begins to ascend again. Meanwhile, others have been bringing out from the 'scene dock' pillars with their bases, and arranging them; and as the great beams move slowly up to their place, they

here on the resources, not merely of the actors, but
even of all who were concerned with the scenery
and properties.   Two important pieces had to be
treated and manipulated within an incredibly short
space of time.

hoist with them the columns, attached by ropes which pass
through.   By this time all the columns are swinging in the air ;
another moment and they have dropped into their places in the
pedestal.   The place of each pedestal is marked on the floor.   In
a few moments everything is fitted and falls into its place, with
an almost martial exactness.   Then are seen slowly descending
the other portions of the roof, sky-borders, &c., all falling into
their places quietly and with a sort of mysterious growth.   We
have glimpses in the galleries aloft of men hauling at ropes and
pulleys, or turning 'drums.'   Finally the whole is set and complete, and men bear in the altars and steps and the enormous idol
at the back—over twenty feet high.   It is worth while looking
close even at the sound and effective modelling of the raised
classic figures that encircle the lower portions of each column, all
in good relief, such as we see in Mr. Alma Tadema's pictures.
The variety and richness of these are surprising, and they fairly
bear a close inspection.   They are coloured, too, with that ivory
tone which the older marbles acquire.   All this was wrought in
the property-room, and worked in clay ; the figures were then
plastered over with paper, or *papier-mâché*, a material invaluable
to the scenic artist as furnishing relief and detail so as to catch
the lights and shadows, having the merit of being exceedingly
light and portable, of bearing rough usage and knocking about,
which carved wood would not.   The idol, now looming solemnly
at the back, is formed of the same material.   It is curious to find
that the pillars and their capitals are all constructed literally in
the lines of perspective, as such would be drawn on a flat surface ;
they diminish in height as they are farther off, and their top and
bottom surfaces are sloped in a converging line. Thus the " building " stood revealed and complete, and round the pillars ran an
open space, enclosed as it were by the walls.   What with the
gloom and the general mystery, the whole would pass, even to
those standing by, as a very imposing structure."

CHAPTER IX

1881

'OTHELLO' AND 'THE TWO ROSES' REVIVED

AT this time there came to London an American
actor whose reputation in his own country was
very high, and for whom it was claimed that, as a
legitimate performer, he was superior to all rivals.
This was Edwin Booth. He was welcomed with
cordiality and much curiosity, and by none was
he received with such hearty goodwill as by the
manager of the Lyceum. Unluckily, he had made
his arrangements injudiciously, having agreed to
appear under a management which was quite
unsuited to the proper exhibition of his gifts. The
Princess's Theatre was a house devoted to melodrama of the commoner type, and was directed by
commercial rather than by æsthetic principles. In
fact, we had seen *horses* on this stage! This
mistake proved fatal. The manager, finding that
there was no likelihood of success, was not inclined
to waste his resources, and, no doubt to the anguish
of the actor, brought out the pieces in a meagre,

starved fashion that was fatal to the American's chances.

In this disastrous state of things the manager of the Lyceum nobly came to the rescue of his *confrère* with a suggestion as delicate as it was generous. He offered him his theatre, with its splendid resources and traditions, his company, and—himself. He proposed that a Shakespearian play should be produced on the customary scale of magnificence, and that he and Booth should fill the leading characters. This handsome offer was, of course, accepted with gratitude, and 'Othello' was selected as the play.

The arrangements for this "Booth season," as it might be termed, were of an unusual and certainly laborious kind. The manager, however, was never disposed to spare himself. The programme began on May 2, 1881, when Booth was to appear as Othello, performing on Monday, Wednesday, and Friday, the manager playing Iago. On the other nights of the week, 'The Cup,' with the lively 'Belle's Stratagem,' was to be performed. In the following week there was the same arrangement, except that Irving took the part of Othello.[1]

---

[1] One morning, during the preparations, I found myself in the painting-room, where Mr. Craven was busy with one of the interesting little models of scenery by which the effect can be tested. The reader may not know that the scenic artist has his model theatre, a foot or so wide, but made "to scale." He has also ground-plans of the stage, showing all the exits, &c., also done to scale. By these aids the most complicated scenes can be designed and tried. I was struck with the careful, conscientious fashion in which the manager discussed a little Venetian scene,

RIVAL HAMLETS.

Box *(An English Hamlet)*—Who are You?

Cox *(An American Hamlet)*—If it comes to that, Who are *You?*

[*To face page* 127.

The night of May 2 was an exciting one, even in the list of exciting Lyceum nights. The Americans were, of course, there in tremendous force. Irving —Booth—Ellen Terry : this surely formed, in theatrical phrase, a galaxy of talent, and the cynosure of a crowded, brilliant audience. It was, indeed, a pleasing performance—intellectual, highly-coloured, and treated in the romantic fashion which the age seems to demand. The old days of lusty-throated, welkin-splitting declamation, emphasised with strides and lunges, are done with.

Of Irving's Iago it would be difficult to say too much. There have been always the two extremes : one portraying the Ancient as a malignant, scowling, crafty villain, doing much work with his eyes ; the other as a kind of dapper, sarcastic, sneering personage, much after the model of Mephistopheles, this tone being emphasised by an airy, fashionable dress, as though he were some cynical Venetian "about town." In Irving was seen the man of power and capability. There was breadth of treatment—the character was coherent throughout. The keynote was found in his *humour*. In " I hate the Moor ! "—one of those secret, jealous, morbid broodings which belong to human nature,

rudely painted in water-colours, which had just been set. He saw it in connection with the entrances of the actors, and was not quite satisfied with the arrangement. He tried various devices, and proposed a gateway ; but this entailed making a new design, all which he suggested to the painter with pleasant persuasion and kindly, apologetic courtesy, but was, as always, firm in his purpose. If a second experiment did not satisfy, it must be tried again. *Suaviter in modo*, &c., was certainly his maxim.

and an admirably delivered soliloquy—he strives to find some reasonable excuse for this suggestion; 'He has done my office' is merely accepted as a suitable pretext. The mode in which this was, as it were, *chased* through the turnings of his soul; the anxious tone of search, " I know not if 't be true"; the covering up his face, and the motion by which he let his hands glide, revealing an elated expression at having found what would " serve," was a perfect exhibition of the processes of thought. All this was set off by a dress of singular appropriateness and richness : a crimson and gold jerkin, with a mantle of dull or faded green, sometimes alternated with a short cloak and a red mantle worn on one arm. This striking impersonation deeply impressed the judicious and reflecting—from its extraordinary *cleverness.* It was so intelligent : the meaning of passages was so distinctly brought out. Yet, strange to say, he never thought of it again or reverted to it. This was really curious, as he thus lost what might have proved a great success and one of his striking characters. But then—the Manager Actor interposes—what of the *Othello ?*

In Booth's Othello there appeared to be a lack of vigour, and the elocutionist was too much present. There was a system of "points." Some critics were rude enough to say that " his make-up suggested at times an Indian juggler, while about the head he seemed a low-cast Bengali." He was never the " noble Moor." " He had a tendency at times to gobble like a turkey." This was rather hard measure. But in the scene with Iago, and, above all, in the scenes with Desdemona, the frantic bursts of jealousy, the command of varied tones, the by-play, the fierce ordering of Emilia and his wife—all this was of a higher class, and stirred us. Miss Terry's Desdemona was pathetic, and her piteous pleadings and remonstrances went straight to the heart.

At the next performance the parts were interchanged. A figure arrayed in a flowing amber robe over a purple brocaded gaberdine; a small, snow-white turbine; a face dark, yet not "black"—such was Irving's conception of Othello, which, indeed, answered to our ideal of the Moor. His tall figure gave him advantage. His reading of the part, again, was of the romantic, passionate kind, and he leant more on the tender side of the character than on the ferocious or barbaric. In the scene of Desdemona's death or murder, there was now another and more effective arrangement: the bed was placed in the centre of the stage, and the whole became more important and conspicuous. When it was at the side, as in the Booth arrangement, it was difficult to believe in the continued presence of the lady after her death, and there was an awkwardness in the efforts to keep in sight of the audience during the struggle.

Booth's Iago had been seen before, and was much praised. It was on the old "Mephistopheles" lines. The dress, indeed, strangely meagre and old-fashioned, scarcely harmonised with the rich costumes about him. I remember Lord Houghton,

10

on his return from the United States, telling me, on my asking him his opinion, that " Booth was a really fine actor—quite so." But it struck me and many others that he was of an old fashion, and about twenty years behind Irving.

The whole of this transaction, as I have said, did honour to the English actor. Nothing more cordially hospitable could have been imagined. But at the time there was a " Booth party," who gave out that their favourite had not had fair play, and that on a stage of his own his superiority to all rivals would be apparent. These and other insinuations were scattered about freely. Irving might have passed them by with indifference. It was certainly not his duty to share his stage with a stranger and a rival. At the same time we may give him credit for a certain delicate *finesse*, and he may have later thought, with a smiling, good-humoured complacency, that, owing to his allowing the experiment, the issue had turned out very differently from what " good-natured people " had hoped. He had not been " played down." The mortification for the American must have been the greater from the disadvantage of the contrast, which brought out in the most forcible way the want of " distinction," the stock of old, rather faded, devices with which he came provided, and which he tried on his audience with an antique gravity. Audiences have, unfortunately, but little delicacy. In their plain way they show their appreciation of whom they think " the better man " in a business-like manner ; and I remember how they insisted that the encouraging applause which they gave to the new actor should be shared by his host.[1]

When the actor took his benefit—how strange the phrase reads, for the new generation knows nothing of "benefits"!—at the close of this laborious season, the theatre presented an opera-house appearance, and was filled to overflowing with a miscellany of brave men and fair women, the latter arrayed in special splendour and giving the whole an air of rich luxury and magnificence befitting the handsomest and best-appointed theatre in the kingdom. Bouquets of unusual brilliancy and dimensions were laid in position, clearly not brought for the enjoyment of the owners. The entertainment consisted of the stock piece of 'The Bells.' Mr. Toole performed Mr. Hollingshead's farce, 'The Birthplace of Podgers,' a happy subject, which showed that the "germ" of the æsthete "business" existed twenty years before. The feature of the night was a well-known scene from 'The Hunchback,' in which Modus is so pleasantly drawn into making a declaration. Sheridan Knowles is often ridiculed for his sham Elizabethan situations; yet it may be doubted if any living writer could treat this incident with such freshness or so naturally. It is a piece of good wearing stuff, and will wear even better. When the scene drew up, the handsome curtains, festooned in rich and abundant folds,

[1] It should be mentioned that the prices on this engagement were raised to the opera scale—a guinea in the stalls, half a guinea for the dress-circle. It is sad to think that later when Irving went to the States Booth studiously kept aloof.

revealed a new effect, throwing out, by contrast, the pale greenish-tinted scene, and heightening the light so that the two figures were projected on this mellow background with wonderful brilliancy. It was played in sparkling fashion by Irving and his partner. Miss Terry's performance was full of animation and piquancy. Most remarkable, indeed, was the new store of unexpected attitudes and graces revealed at every moment—pretty stoopings, windings, sudden half-turns, inviting "rallyings"—so that even a Modus more insensible to her advances must have succumbed. But in truth this wonderful creature "adorns all she touches." There was a Jordan-like vein of comedy. Irving's Modus was full of a quaint earnestness, and his air of helplessness in the hands of such a mistress was well maintained. Modus is generally made to hover on the verge of oafishness, so as to make it surprising that there should be any object in winning such a being. Irving imparted a suitable air to it, and lifted the character into pure comedy.

At the end came the expected speech, delivered with a pleasant familiarity, and dwelling on past successes and future plans. It was a pleasant and remarkable season to look back upon : the enchanting 'Cup,' which lingers like a dream, or lotus-eating fancy ; the 'Corsican Brothers,' so sumptuously mounted ; the splendid 'Othello,' the meeting of the American and the English actor on the same stage, and their strangely opposed readings of the same characters.

The performance of ' The Belle's Stratagem,'
which supplemented the attraction of ' Othello,' was
interesting, as it introduced once more to active life
that excellent and sound old actor, Henry Howe,
who was then, perhaps, the only link with the
generation of the greater actors. It was a graceful
and thoughtful act of Irving's to seek out the
veteran and attach him to his company. In the
years following he always treated him with a kindly
and courteous consideration. Every one who knew
Howe could testify to his pleasant, lovable qualities. He had not a particle of that testy discontent
which too often distinguishes the veteran actor, who
extols the past and is discontented with the present,
because it is discontented with *him*, or thinks that
he lags superfluous on the stage. As we have talked
with him of a summer's afternoon, in his little retreat
at Isleworth, the image of many a pleasant hour
in the old Haymarket days has risen up with his
presence. With him rose Buckstone, Mrs. Fitz-
william, Miss Woolgar, and so many more. It was
always pleasant to encounter his honest face in the
Strand, where he lived, as he was hurrying to his
work. [1]

[1] This performer was associated with the best traditions of the
good old school ; and is linked with many interesting associations. It is curious, too, to think that he belonged to the Society
of Friends. We have, and have had, a good many Jews upon the
stage, but a Quaker is a rarity. When he was in America, he
related the story of his life to an inquirer : "I was attending a
public school in Yorkshire. It was a Quaker school at Ackworth,
although boys not of Quaker parentage attended it. Somehow
I was always selected to recite some piece for the visitors—some of

In January, 1882, our manager revived a piece in which he had achieved one of his earliest triumphs —'The Two Roses.' Miss Terry was at this time busily preparing for what was to be her great effort, in Juliet, and this interruption to her labours was judicious policy on the manager's part. Much had occurred during the long interval of twelve years since the play had been first performed, but many still recalled with enjoyment Irving's masterly creation. When he was casting the characters for the piece, he had counted on the original Caleb Decie— Thorne—who held the traditions of the play. Owing to some sudden change—I think to his entering on management—this arrangement had to be given up, and the manager was somewhat perplexed as to who he could find to fill the character. He happened to be in Glasgow at this time, when the local

those old pieces, you know, such as 'The Roman Gladiator,' or 'Paul before Agrippa.' In this way I acquired my first liking for the stage. One night I went with my cousin John to the Old Drury Lane Theatre to see Kean, who was then creating a *furore* by his magnificent acting. In those days, you know, they sold good seats in the gallery for a shilling ; so I and my cousin Jack paid our shilling—the usual half-price—and went into the gallery. I shall never forget that night. The playing opened, I think, with the third act. I see Kean as plainly as if it were only yesterday. There he sat, a small man, upon his throne in the middle of the stage. Well, after leaving the theatre, Jack and I had to cross a bridge on our way home. I sat down in the recess of the bridge, almost overcome by my emotion, and said, 'John, I am going to be an actor.' He tried to dissuade me, and laughed at the folly of the idea, but my mind was made up." One of the most striking incidents of 'King Lear' was the "ovation," as it is called, which greeted the veteran as he presented himself in a small character.

manager said to him, "There is a young fellow here who, I think, would exactly suit you; he is intelligent, hard-working, and anxious to get on. His name is Alexander." Irving listened to the advice, and secured an actor who was of his own school, of well-defined instincts and much elegance, and exactly suited to be *jeune premier* of the Lyceum. It may be conceived with what delight, as he himself has told me, this unexpected opening was received by the then obscure youth; and at a pleasant supper the new engagement was ratified. Now the young Glasgow candidate is the prosperous manager of the St. James's Theatre, a position which many years of conscientious work has placed him in. Far more rough and thorny was the path along which Irving had to toil, during a score of years, before he found himself at the head of a theatre. But in these *fin de siècle* times, both days and hours have doubled their value.

The piece was well mounted and well played, and there was much interest felt in comparing the new cast with the old. In a pleasant, half-sad meditation, my friend the late Clement Scott called up some of the old memories; the tyrant Death, he said, had played sad havoc with the original companies that did so much for this English comedy. "Far away, leagues from home, across the Atlantic sleep both Harry Montague and Amy Fawcitt. We may associate them still with Jack Wyatt and Lottie—who seemed the very boy and girl lovers that such a theme required—so bright and manly and noble, so tender, young, and handsome." David James

had taken the place of the oleaginous Honey, and
for those who had not seen the latter, was an
admirable representative of the part. The "Roses"
were Miss Helen Mathews and Miss Emery.

The manager, in his old part, received much
praise from the entire circle of critics. Some considered it his most perfect creation, and likened it
to Got's 'Duc Job' and Regnier's 'Annibal.' It
was certainly a finished and original performance; but it must be confessed that the larger
stage and larger house had its effect, and tempted
the actor into laying greater emphasis on details of
the character. It was much "coarsened," even overdone; for Irving now was beginning to lose that
delicate comedy touch, which once so distinguished
him—and I really think fancied he could be farcical
when he chose. But an actor cannot stand still, as
it were. Repetition for a hundred nights is one of
the vices of the modern stage, and leads to artifi-
ciality. Under the old *répertoire* system, when a
piece was given for a few nights, then suspended to
be resumed after an interval, the actor came to his
part with a certain freshness and feeling of novelty.

At the same time, it should be said that the play
itself was accountable for this loss of effect. It was
of but an ephemeral sort, and belonged to an old
school which had passed away. It was written for
a particular moment and season. Other players
besides Irving, conscious of this weakness, have
felt themselves constrained to supplement it by
such broad touchings. The average "play of
commerce" is but the inspiration of the time,

and engendered by it—authors, manager, actors, audience, all join, as it were, in the composition. Every portion, therefore, reflects the tone of the time. But after a number of years this tone becomes lost or forgotten ; the fashions of feeling and emotion, both off as well as on the stage, also pass away: it seems flat, and must be supplemented.

When closing his season and making the important announcement of the selection of 'Romeo and Juliet' for the new one, the manager promised alterations and improvements in the theatre. These were duly carried out, and not only added to the comfort of the audience, but also to the profits of the management. The corridor at the back of the dress-circle was taken in, and supplied some sixty or seventy new seats ; while below, on the pit floor, place was found for some two hundred additional persons, by including the saloon.[1] Further, the arch of the gallery which impeded the view was raised, padded seats were furnished for the pit, and the manager was willing even to supply " backs," an unusual luxury—to the seats in the gallery ; but the Lord Chamberlain interposed, on the ground that in any panic or hurrying down the steep ascent, these might be found an obstruction. Other alterations were made in the exits and entrances—though these were merely in the nature of makeshifts. The manager was not content until,

[1] It was amazing in the pre-County Council days how such shifts could be tolerated. The Lyceum pit was always a terrible cavern, and in case of panic there would have been terrible scenes.

many years later, he had purchased the adjoining houses and thoroughly remodelled the whole.[1]

In the interval he took his company on a provincial tour to the leading towns. At Glasgow it was proclaimed to be "the greatest engagement ever witnessed in that city." As he told his audience on the last night, the receipts for the twelve nights amounted to over £4,000—an average of £334 per night. But the extraordinary "drawing" power of our actor was never exhibited more signally than during the engagement at Edinburgh, at Mr. Howard's theatre, which produced results that were really unprecedented. On his last appearance Irving told the audience that this "engagement—and you must not take it for egotism—has been the most re-

---

[1] For a time the house was "on crutches," as it is called, an operation of considerable architectural delicacy. In the great "cellarage" below the stage, huge storehouses filled with the rubbish of half a century, were discovered masses of decayed peacocks' feathers, which much perplexed the explorers and everybody else, until it was recalled that these were the antique "properties" used by Madame Vestris in one of her Planché burlesques. The labour was herculean, and the indefatigable Bram Stoker threw himself with heart and soul into the business. We might lament, however, that the beautiful interior suffered somewhat in these later alterations. The elegant contour was disturbed ; the double pillars, which recurred periodically in the dress-circle, were reduced to a single one. The fine entrance-hall lost its symmetry from being enlarged. But such sacrifices are absolutely necessary, and are not the first that have had to be made under "the form and pressure of the time." The alterations cost a very large sum indeed, but our manager has always been an improving tenant, and has periodically laid out vast sums on the improvement and decoration of his house.

markable one played for any twelve nights in any theatre, I should think, in Great Britain, certainly out of London, and there are some large theatres in London. I may tell you that there has been taken during the engagement here £4,300, which is certainly the largest sum ever had before in any theatre during the space of time, and I believe it is perfectly unprecedented in any city." This was a tribute to his attraction. On his departure a gold repeater watch was presented to him.

CHAPTER X

1882

'ROMEO AND JULIET'—BANQUET

BY March 8, 1882, the great revival of 'Romeo and Juliet' was ready. For this performance the manager drew upon all the resources of his taste, purse, study, and experience. The fascinating play, indeed, offered opportunities for adornment only too tempting. Those glittering, bewitching pictures still linger in the memory of the playgoer, though so many years have elapsed since the opening night. "Among the restorations will be found that of Romeo's unrequited love for Rosaline, omitted, among other things, in Garrick's version."

Those who came away from the Lyceum on that opening night must have had a sense almost of bewilderment, so rich and dazzling were the scenes of light and colour that had for hours passed before their eyes. According to a true illusive principle of this stage, the lights were lowered as every scene was about to change, by which a sense of mystery was produced, and the prosaic mechanism of the movement shrouded. Hence, a sort of richness of effect and surprise as the gloom passes away and a gorgeous scene steeped in effulgence and colour is revealed. Since this sentence was written the darkening has become a familiar, almost necessary custom, though the darkening has been overdone. Irving, perhaps, did not know that it was Goethe who first indicated this method. It would take long to detail the beautiful views, streets, palaces, chambers, dresses, groupings, that were set before the audience, all devised with an extraordinary originality and fertility of resource; though this was the third of these Italian revivals. When it is considered that there were twenty-two scenes, and that most of these were "sets," it is amazing with what rapidity and smoothness the changes were contrived. All was glitter and jewels and colours, and all bathed in floods of light; Shakespeare seemed altogether lost and drowned. Not the least pleasurable part of the whole was the romantic music, written in a flowing, tender strain by Sir Julius Benedict, full of a juvenile freedom and spirit, thoroughly Italian in character, and having something of the grace and character of Schubert's 'Rosamunde.' In the exquisite garden, with it, depths of silvered trees glistening in the moonlight, viewed from a terrace, the arrangement of the balcony was the only successful solution seen as yet. It has always been forgotten that Juliet has to act—is, as it were, "on the stage"—and should not be perched in a little wobbling cage. Here it was made a sort of solid loggia, as much a part of the stage as that upon which her lover was

standing. I fancy this was the scenic triumph of
the night.

When we consider that Romeo and Juliet are
characters almost impossible to play so as to
reach the Shakespearian ideal, it becomes easier to
"liberate one's mind" on the subject of the performance of the two leading characters. The chief
objection was that they scarcely presented the ideal
of superabundant youth—boyish and girlish—required by the play. I have always thought this
a point to be but little insisted upon; it is much the
same as with strictness of costume, which is overpowered, as it were, by the acting. It is the *acting*
of youth, not the appearance of youth, that is
required; and a case is conceivable where all the
flush of youth with its physical accompaniments
may be present in perfection, and yet from failure
of the acting the idea of maturity and age may be
conveyed.[1] In the dramatic ball-room scene, when

---

[1] Mr. Labouchere, a shrewd observer, a friend and admirer of
the actor's abilities, always speaks out his opinions in plain, blunt
terms: "An actor must, in order to win popularity, have mannerisms, and the more peculiar they are, the greater will be his
popularity. No one can for a moment suppose that Mr. Irving
could not speak distinctly, progress about the stage after the
fashion of human beings, and stand still without balancing to
and fro if he pleased. Yet, had he not done all this, he
would—notwithstanding that there is a touch of real genius
about his acting sometimes—never have made the mark that he
has. He is, indeed, to the stage what Lord Beaconsfield was to
politics. That exceedingly able man never could utter the
resonant clap-trap in which he so often indulged, and which
made men talk about him, without almost showing by his manner
that he himself despised the tricks which gave him individuality.

he was moving about arrayed as a pilgrim, the unbecoming dress and rather too swarthy features seemed to convey the presentment of a person in the prime of life. The critics spoke freely in this sense.

It was, indeed—if we must speak the truth— a most grotesque exhibition, and when he became the passionate lover, his frantic gestures and extraordinary gamut became truly comic. The youthful antics combined with an elderly face, even now provokes a smile. But such experiments are pardonable and natural too. It was really the fault of the assiduous flappers and flatterers. "Oh, Mr. Irving, you would be an ideal Romeo!" I heard some ladies say at a dinner; "you *must* act Romeo." But in the latter, more tragic portion of the play, the very intensity of the emotion seemed to add maturity and depth to the character of Romeo. Nothing could better supply the notion of impending destiny, of gathering gloom, than the view of the dismal, heart-chilling street, the scene of the visit to the apothecary. Our actor's picturesque sense was shown in his almost perfect conception of this situation. The forlorn look of the houses, the general desolation, the stormy

Were Mr. Irving at present to abate his peculiarities, his fervent worshippers would complain that their idol was sinking into mere common-place. Therefore, as I sincerely hope that, for his sake, the idolaters will continue to bow down before him and fill his treasury, I trust that he will never change." There is a cynical flavour in this, and it is not very flattering to the audience, but underlying it there is much truth.

grandeur in keeping with the surroundings, the properly subdued grotesqueness of the seller of simples (it was the grotesqueness of *misery* that was conveyed), filled the heart with a sadness that was almost real. In Miss Terry's case there was a division of opinions, some thinking her performance all but perfect, others noting the absence of "girlishness." All agreed as to its engaging character and its winning charm. Terriss was the Mercutio, which he gave with his favourite blunt impetuosity. One of the most perfectly played characters was Mrs. Stirling's Nurse. This accomplished woman represented all the best traditions—high training, admirable elocution, with the art of giving due weight and breadth to every utterance. And yet—here was a curious phenomenon—the very excellence of the delineation disturbed the balance of the play. The Nurse became almost as important as the leading pair, but from no fault of the actress. She but followed the due course. Such is a blemish which is found in many exhibitions of Shakespearian plays, where the inferior actor works up his Dogberry, or his Gravedigger, or his Bottom the Weaver, or his melancholy Jacques, to the very fullest extent of which they are capable. But there should be subordination; these are merely humours exhibited *en passant*. With an actress of Mrs. Stirling's powers and rank, the manager no doubt felt too much delicacy to interfere; nor would perhaps the audience have placidly accepted any effacing of her part. But as it was, the figure of this humble retainer became unduly prominent.[1]

'Romeo and Juliet' was witnessed one night by the impetuous Sarah Bernhardt, who afterwards came behind the scenes to congratulate the performers. "How can you act in this way every night?" she exclaimed to Ellen Terry. The latter, in her simple, natural way, explained: "It is the audience—they inspire me!"

Such was this refined, elegant, and brilliant spectacle, which, as usual, furnished "talk for the town," and stirred its interest. The hundredth night of performance was celebrated by the usual banquet on the stage, on Sunday night, June 25, 1882. Here assembled critics, dramatists, artists, *e tutti quanti*; there were many admirers, friends, and sympathisers present, most of whom have since passed away. There is a sadness in thinking of these disappearances.

But among the guests at the banquet was Mr. Abbey, the American manager, well known for his many daring and very successful *coups* in management. His appearance excited much interest and speculation. In the course of the night there were rumours circulated as to the motives of his presence in town; but an allusion in Irving's speech, when he said pointedly that he hoped next year to have good experience of the cordiality of American audiences, set the matter at rest. This

[1] A rapturous article from a Liverpool critic, Sir E. Russell, appeared in *Macmillan's Magazine*, which was, indeed, too undiscriminating in its praises.

scheme had long been in his thoughts; and, indeed, already many invitations and proposals had been made to him to visit the United States. There was something dazzling and fascinating in this prospect of going forth to conquer a new great kingdom and new audiences. There was the chance, too, of riches "beyond the dreams of avarice." No wonder, then, that the scheme began to take shape, and was presently to be decided upon.

After one hundred and thirty nights' performance of 'Romeo and Juliet,' the season was brought to a close, the manager taking "a benefit" on his last night. Some ungracious folk objected to this old-established form of compliment, but he defended it in a very modest and judicious way.

CHAPTER XI

'MUCH ADO ABOUT NOTHING '—AMERICAN VISIT
ARRANGED

IN his speech at the close of the season, the manager announced the new piece selected for the next season. With the judicious view to contrast or relief which directed all his efforts, he had settled on a true comedy—the effective 'Much Ado About Nothing.' To this piece many had long since pointed as being exactly adapted to the special gifts of the two performers. Here was the fourth Shakespearian play of an Italian complexion and atmosphere, which entailed accordingly a fresh exhibition of Italian streets, manners, and costumes. A happy impression was produced by the very note of preparation, the air was filled with the breath of the coming piece ; all felt, in anticipation, the agreeable humours and fancies of Benedick and his Beatrice. This feeling of comedy, it may be said, is ever a delightful one ; it spreads abroad a placid, quiet enjoyment and good-humour with which nothing else can compare.

On Wednesday, October 11, 1882, the delightful piece was brought out. From the excellent acting of the two principal performers, and the beautiful "setting" of the whole, it was destined to become one of the most popular and acceptable of the Lyceum *répertoire*. By a curious delusion, owing no doubt to the recollection of the lavish splendours of 'Romeo and Juliet,' some critics pronounced that it had been brought out with but a moderate display of scenic resources. The truth was that the play had been " mounted " with as much state as it would properly bear. Some scenes were equipped in an unusually lavish and superb style. The general effect, however, was harmonious ; indeed, the happy tact of the manager was never displayed to such advantage as in seizing on what might be termed the proper key of the piece. When we recall, with a pleasant enjoyment, these various Lyceum spectacles, we find that there is no confusion of one with the other, that each has a special, distinct note, and thus was started a train of impressions, delightful for their variety, which enrich the chambers of the memory.

There was one scene which, for its splendour and originality, was to be talked of for many a day, viz., the beautiful interior of a church at Messina—the "Church Scene," as it was called. The art displayed here, the combination of "built-up" scenery with "cloths," the rich harmonious tintings, the ecclesiastical details, the metal-work, altars, &c.,

made an exquisite picture.[1] The well-known passage of the interrupted bridal was "laid out" with extraordinary picturesqueness, much emphasis being given to the religious rites. It was felt, however, that the genuflections before the altar were introducing rather too awful a suggestion, though the intention was, no doubt, reverent. It must be admitted by all whose memories wander back to that performance, that the vision of this "Church Scene" rises before them with an almost pathetic significance, owing in some part to the touching, sympathetic acting of Miss Millward. One of the most typical instances of Irving's dealings with Shakespeare was found in this effective ecclesiastical panorama. Still the critic is compelled to say that this "Church Scene" unhappily exhibits the worst vices of the new Shakespearian illustration. The stage directions are large and general: as here, "A Church." By this is meant simply the precincts of a church—somewhere within the walls. All Catholics know that in great cathedrals the average wedding takes place in a side chapel— a clergyman comes out and ties the knot; there is no procession, incense, boys, or trains of priests. The familiarity of the talk and lack of reverence shows that it took place somewhere in aisles when folk talk freely. The idea of Benedick and Beatrice making love in front of the high altar is not to be thought of.

[1] Mr. Forbes Robertson, who is painter as well as actor, depicted this striking scene on canvas, giving portraits of the performers. It has been engraved (or rather "processed") with very happy result.

All eyes, as it may be conceived, were drawn to the figures of Benedick and Beatrice, as portrayed by Irving and Ellen Terry. Their scenes were followed with a delighted interest, and their gay encounters of wit and flirtation gave unalloyed pleasure. Irving threw a Malvolian gravity over the character, alternated by a certain jocoseness.

He also imparted to the character a sort of pragmatical air—but somewhat lacked the gay, impulsive, irresponsible feeling. Self-consciousness, to a certain degree, was always present. At the same time he did it far better than any one else could do it: and his own strong personality neutralized defects.

These two characters, Benedick and Beatrice, are so much the heritage of all lovers of true comedy, that every one seems to have fixed a standard for himself, which he will critically apply to every representation. This partiality does not make us particularly *exigeant*, but we have each our own fancies. There is nothing more interesting, entertaining, or fruitful in speculation than the discussion of how favourite characters in comedy should be represented. It is as though they were figures in real life. For myself, I confess I should have preferred that the actor had taken the character into still higher realms of airy comedy, and had less emphasised the somewhat farcical passages. Benedick was a man of capacity, a soldier, a gentleman, and though he was likely to be so imposed upon, he would not have given his friends the satisfaction of seeing him in this de-

jected condition, almost inviting laughter and rude
"rallying." [1]

During all this time, preparations for the great
American visit were being carefully matured.
There is supposed to be a sort of hostility between artistic gifts and business-like habits; but
Irving always showed great capacity where organisation and arrangement were in question—he had
the clearest vision, and the firmest, most decided
purpose. In this he has often suggested a surprising
likeness to the departed novelist Dickens, who was
also remarkable for his business power and decision
of character, and whose motto it was to do even a
trifle in the best way that it could be done. Anything worth doing at all, he would say, was worth
doing well.

Nothing then was left undone to ensure success.
Everything was "thought out" beforehand with

[1] It was an unusual tribute to the interest excited in every
direction by the actor's personality, that the lady students at
University College should have chosen him for the subject of a
formal debate, under the presidency of the clever Miss Fawcett.
The thesis set down was, "That Henry Irving has, by his
dramatic genius, earned his place as foremost among living
actors," and the discussion was begun with much spirit and
fluency by Miss Rees, who proceeded to give an analysis of
his Hamlet and other characters, contending that his extraordinary *success* was a proof of his merit. The opposition was
led by Mrs. Brooksbanks, who fairly and unsparingly attacked
the actor for his mannerisms and various defects. After a reply
from Miss Rees, the original motion was put to the ladies, and
was carried by a slender majority. The actor must have read
these proceedings, which were flattering enough, with much
enjoyment.

the greatest care and deliberation. The American manager, Abbey, who had undertaken the direction of the venture, and had a vast store of experience and skill at command, planned, of course, the arrangements of the visit; but the purely theatrical details were thrown upon the English actor, who had to equip completely some dozen plays with scenery, dresses, and properties. A following of from seventy to a hundred persons— including actors, actresses, secretaries, scenic and music artists, dressers, supernumeraries—was to be taken out.[1]   Further, with a view to making the company thoroughly familiar with the *répertoire*, for months beforehand a sort of continuous rehearsal went on before the regular Lyceum audiences; that is, all the stock-pieces were revived one after the other, and performed with much care.

The honours and flattering tributes that were now lavished on the departing actor would have turned the head of one less sensible or less unspoiled. The town seemed really to have " run horn-mad " after him, and could talk of nothing but of him and his expedition.   As was to be expected, the compliment of a public dinner was the smallest of these tributes.   Presents and invitations were lavished upon him.   In a caricature he was shown as being

[1] An idea of what a "tremendous" business this was may be gathered from a single detail. A well-known experienced wig-maker from Covent Garden, with two assistants, was engaged to look after the *coiffures* of the company, and these "artists in hair" had under their charge a collection of wigs, entirely new, no fewer than eleven hundred in number. On a later visit there were fifteen hundred!

profusely anointed, by critics and others, from a tub filled with a composition labelled "butter." In another the Prince of Wales is obsequiously presenting an invitation, which the actor excuses himself from accepting owing to "my many engagements." The most famous portrait-painter of the day begged to be allowed to paint his picture, which he wished to offer as a present to the Garrick Club.[1] Rumours were busily circulated— and contradicted—that a knighthood had been offered and declined.

The public dinner at St. James's Hall was fixed for July 4—a compliment to the American people. The list of stewards was truly extraordinary, comprising almost every one of mark in the arts and the great professions. The Chief Justice, Lord Coleridge, who was himself setting out for a tour in the States, was to take the chair. Mr. Gladstone and some Cabinet Ministers were on the committee. There were three thousand appli-

---

[1] Where it now hangs over the chimneypiece in the Guests' Room. It is not so successful as many others of Millais' works ; it is rather sketchily painted, and lacks force and expression. The late Mr. Long painted the actor as Hamlet and Richard III. They are not very striking performances, but they are refined and interesting portraits. Mr. Whistler produced an extraordinary one of him as Philip II., strangely "shadowy" but powerful, and of preternatural length. A number of artists of less pretension have also essayed to limn the actor ; but all have failed to sketch the mobile, delicate expression of the lips. Boldly daring, I myself have fashioned a bust of him in terracotta. For this he gave me sittings in the year 1876, when he was only 37. There is an ugly bust of him also done about this time.

cants for the five hundred possible seats, all that Mr. Pinches, the secretary—a relation of the actor's old master—could contrive to supply. Two Bishops excused their attendance in flattering terms, and Mr. Gladstone would gladly have attended, but was compelled by his duties to be absent.[1] At this banquet, beside the Chief Justice and the Lord Chancellor of Ireland, there were five other judges present, together with all that was distinguished in the professions and arts.

The Chairman, in a thoughtful and studied speech, delivered perhaps one of the best *apologias* for the actor that is ever likely to be offered. The skill and moderation of the accomplished advocate was shown to perfection; he did not adulate, but gave the actor a graduated and judicious measure of praise for all he had done in the improvement in the general tone, morals, and methods of the stage. Irving acknowledged these compliments in grateful and heartfelt terms, addressed not so much to the diners present as to the kingdom in general.

After these metropolitan honours, he passed to Edinburgh, Glasgow, and Liverpool. At each city

---

[1] It is said that the origin of the acquaintance between Irving and this statesman was an accidental encounter in the street, when the latter, with a sympathetic impulsiveness, stopped Irving and introduced himself. Later, he was an assiduous frequenter of the Lyceum, and in his eighty-third year was seen in the stalls or behind the scenes, in a little special corner, near the prompter's box, following the course of 'Henry VIII.' with unabated interest.

he was greeted with complimentary banquets. At Edinburgh he opened a new theatre, named in compliment to his own, the Lyceum. He was invited to Hawarden by Mr. Gladstone, and also to Knowsley by Lord Derby.

On October 10, 1883, the chief members of the company—over forty in number—sailed for New York, under the conduct of Mr. Bram Stoker. Tons of scenery, dresses, properties, &c., had been already shipped. The following day Irving and Miss Terry embarked on board the White Star liner, *The Britannic*. Up to the last moment telegrams and letters containing good wishes (literally by hundreds) were being brought in. Even while the vessel was detained at Queenstown, the Mayor and Corporation of Cork seized the opportunity of saluting him with a parting address. The incidents have been all described by my friend Mr. Joseph Hatton, who attended the party as "historiographer"; and I may refer the reader to his interesting volumes.

The visit was to prove one long triumph, and the six months' progress a strange, wonderful phantasmagoria of receptions, entertainments, hospitalities of all kinds. Novel and original, too, were the humours and fashions that greeted them everywhere, and the eyes of the two players must have often turned back with pleasure to that odd pantomime.

'The Bells' was selected for his first performance, which was on October 29, 1883. Though his reception was overpowering and tumultuous, there was some hesitation as to the success of the play itself, and the critics seemed to be a little doubtful as to whether it fairly represented the full measure of his gifts. 'Charles I.', however, followed, and the two great artists made the profoundest impression. But when 'Louis XI.' and 'Much Ado About Nothing' were presented, all doubts vanished. Such things were all probably new to them. Miss Terry won all hearts; her sympathetic style and winsome ways made conquest of every audience. It might be almost said that *she* was his loadstar. Nothing struck the Americans with such astonishment as the exquisite arrangement and "stage management" of the Shakespearian comedy, the reserved yet effectively harmonious treatment of all the details being a complete revelation. The actor's consummate taste was recognised; in fact, the result of the visit was a complete revolution in all the American stage methods. The extraordinary record of lavish hospitalities, tributes of all kinds, with the adventures, is set forth fully in the story of the tour. But it is only by consulting the American journals that we can gather a notion of the odd "humours," often grotesque, by which the American public displays its enthusiastic approbation.[1] The "interviewers," as may be imagined, were rampant, and extracted from the genial and courteous actor opinions on everything connected with his profession. One immortal criticism deserves to be recorded here.

[1] These newspapers were sent to me without interruption during all his tours by Irving's direction.

'He has rung," said a newspaper, "*the knell* of *gibbering* GOSH!"[1]

The party remained in the country until the May of the year following. The receipts exceeded every forecast, a quarter of a million dollars having been taken in the first four weeks. But the expenses were enormous. The substantial profit was found in Irving's securing a new, vast, and prominent audience in the West; in his winning the suffrages of Americans abroad as well as of those at home, who became his most fervent adherents.

The following is an amusing scene. "Irving had been invited to the Journalists' Club, and after the close of the performance of 'Louis XI.,' the actor

---

[1] A description of a "first-night" at the Opera House is worth quoting:—

"Ladies took their place in line and waited for hours to get tickets for the opening performance. The face of the tall and genial Bram Stoker, Mr. Irving's agent, wore a broad smile as, standing in the vestibule, he noticed the swelling crowd passing between the continually swinging doors. The array of regular first-nighters was up to the notch, and all the familiar faces, not only those most looked for with the lorgnettes, but those that vanish between the acts, were there. Tall Tom Donaldson, one of Blaine's lieutenants, whose wife and daughter were in one of the boxes, was leaning against the wall talking to Judge William Haydon, formerly of Nevada, one of the oldest theatre-goers in the United States, who saw Edmund Kean play Hamlet, and thinks Irving the best actor he has seen since. Joseph F. Tobias, ruddy, genial, and Chesterfieldian as ever, was shaking hands at every turn, and L. Clark Davis, in immaculate evening dress and pearl studs, but with the inevitable Bohemian hat, was the centre of a chatty group. Charles E. Cramp and Horace Warding were talking to Dr. Thomas H. Andrews, who has the largest theatrical practice of any physician in Philadelphia, and has been called to

had come round to the club, where he partook of a supper tendered to him by a few members in a private room. He had been in the building three-quarters of an hour before he made known his presence by coming upstairs, escorted by several gentlemen. The guest of the evening then held an informal reception.

" After he had said something pleasant to almost every one, he volunteered to do his share towards entertaining those present. It had been slightly hinted to him that something of the kind was looked for, and he entered into the spirit of the occasion. Then the great tragedian turned from

attend half the stars who have appeared here in recent years. Almost every well-known first-nighter was on hand, and the invariable sentiment was that this was the big event of the present year. There were many well-known people who are not often seen at the theatre, notably Daniel M. Fox, Director of the Mint, who sat in the centre aisle, near the stage, with a party of friends, and appeared to enjoy the performance very much. Just back of him was a large party from Bethlehem, Pa. John R. Jones, the Bible publisher, had with him Miss Jones, in a stunning grey imported costume, one of the most artistic in the theatre. Robert W. Downing had quite a party. There were several large theatrical parties. The most noticeable was the one given by Miss K. N. Green, which included many attractive ladies. Ex-Attorney-General Brewster was the centre of quite a large party in the orchestra, including several ladies. A very beautiful bevy was the party given by Miss Hattie Fox, daughter of George S. Fox, which numbered thirty-five. They all had seats in the orchestra circle. Some of the most fashionable people had to be content with seats upstairs, and there was one party of young ladies in the family circle who were in full dress and went direct in carriages, at the close of the performance, to the dancing-class."

the serious to the comic. He recited, in a way
that provoked roars of laughter, the funny little
poem, 'Tommy's First Love.'

"When this was over there was a unanimous
shout, which lasted several minutes. It was a
loud cry for more. Mr. Irving expressed his will-
ingness to give another recitation, and called for
a chair. After sitting down he observed that, as
all were standing, those in the rear could see but
indifferently. 'Suppose we change the stage management,' he suggested. 'Can't we all sit down?'
This was received with some merriment, as there
were few chairs in the room. Some one, however,
saw Mr. Irving's idea that those in the front ranks
should sit upon the floor, and in a moment the four
foremost lines were kneeling upon the carpet.

"Mr. Irving then recited 'Eugene Aram's
Dream.' The splendid elocutionary talents of the
actor kept the audience spellbound. Every emotion, every pang of the schoolmaster was vividly
depicted by the expressive face of the tragedian.
The scene was a remarkable one. Mr. Irving
threw himself so earnestly into the character that
at one time *he tore the white necktie from his throat*
without realising what he was doing, and, as his
features were wrought up to show the usher's
agony, similar lines seemed to show themselves
by sympathy in the faces of those present. At
the close of recitation the motionless figures, some
standing, some sitting with crossed legs upon the
floor, became moving, enthusiastic men. Those
on their feet threw their arms into the air and

cheered as if for dear life, while those on the floor bounded up simultaneously and expressed their enthusiasm. It was some time before the excitement subsided.

" ' I recited that once to a friend of mine,' said Mr. Irving, after quiet had been restored, 'and what do you think he said? Why, he seriously exclaimed: "There is one point in that story that I'd like to know about. *What became of the boy?*" ' This anecdote produced a chorus of laughter. After shaking hands all round, Mr. Irving went downstairs and out, accompanied by the club's officers. Before he left the room, ' Three cheers for Mr. Irving ' were called for and given by throats already hoarse with applauding him."

CHAPTER XII

1884

'TWELFTH NIGHT'—'THE VICAR OF WAKEFIELD'—
OXFORD HONOURS

ON July 8, 1884, a few weeks after the return
to London, 'Twelfth Night' was brought
out at the Lyceum, and, for luxury of scenery,
dresses, and mounting, fully equalled all its predecessors. Irving was, of course, the Malvolio,
which he rendered not exactly after Charles Lamb's
interpretation, but, indeed, as any one of Shakespearian intelligence would have done, never lapsing
into farce, but treating the whole earnestly. It was
a beautiful and graceful show, full of alternate sympathy and humour. Personally we look back to it
as one of the most welcome and interesting of his
revivals; all the incidents connected with Viola, so
charmingly interpreted by Ellen Terry, have an
irresistible and touching interest. The scenery was
costly and exquisite, and reflected the tone of the
piece. The audience, however, listened with a
somewhat languid interest—some said because of

12

the oppressive heat of a July night, which fretted and put them out of humour ; but I believe because they were unfamiliar with the piece, and had not been "educated up to it." When the manager came out at the close, with all the good-humour and freedom of a privileged favourite, he was confounded to find his expressions of self-congratulation and satisfaction greeted with uncouth denial and interruptions. He was not accustomed to such coarse reception, and with much spirit he administered this well-deserved chastisement : " I can't understand how a company of earnest comedians and admirable actors, having these three cardinal virtues of actors — being sober, clean, and perfect — and having exercised their abilities on one of the most difficult plays, can have given any cause for dissatisfaction." But there are curious idiosyncrasies in audiences, one of which is, as I have noted, that they must be in some way familiar with the piece and its incidents ; and there must be broad, comprehensive types of character. Now, Malvolio, one of the most delicately exquisite of conceptions, it could be seen, was quite unintelligible to "the general": they took him for some "crank," or half-cracked being, appearing in his nightcap, &c. Sir Toby and Sir Andrew and their rollickings were actually thought "low" or vulgar, on the same principle that Tony Lumpkin's alehouse friend could not abide anything low. So much for the ignorant, ill-mannered section of the audience.

It was argued, indeed, by critics that Irving's

Malvolio was somewhat *too* much in earnest, and therefore was liable to be accepted by the audience as a serious person, actually in love with his mistress, and this, with his eccentricities and oddities, became an impertinence. Whereas, as Lamb says, by imparting a quaint humorousness the audience sees the absurdity of the jest and is amused. Elia, indeed, always insists that the actor of such " fantastical " parts should hint to the audience, slily as it were, that he is only half in earnest.

A most delightful sense of pure natural comedy was induced by the likeness between the Terrys, brother and sister, who had a sort of Shakespearian elegance in their bearing. But this did not avail much with the uncultured crowd. It was objected also that the play was set forth somewhat pedantically and too much *au grand sérieux*, many of the actors, not being comedians—witness Mr. Terriss—imparting a literal tone to all they said and did. This was not without its effect on the audience, who by the very promise of seriousness were beguiled into expecting something serious. Irving himself was not wholly free from this method; and in the strange scene of the imprisonment, so difficult to " carry off," he was deeply tragic, as if really suffering, and without any underlying grotesqueness. His exit, too, with solemn menaces, had the air of retributive punishment in store.[1]

[1] As the world knows, it was given with great effect and popularity at His Majesty's Theatre. I am afraid, owing to extreme farcical treatment, the judicious wondered and grieved as they saw Malvolio enter, preceded by half a dozen serving-men

Now followed a second expedition to the States, as well as to Canada, the details of which I pass over. On the reopening of his theatre on his return a rather disagreeable episode occurred, connected with an alteration he had made in the arrangements of his house. It was announced that places in the pit might be reserved and secured in advance, which gave rise to indignant protest and to cries of "*Give us back our Pit.*" The question was warmly discussed in the newspapers. The advantage of the debate was that it clearly established a true theatrical principle—viz., that pit and galleries are intended for the crowd, and should be free and open to the "man in the street": that the best seats here must be the prize of the strongest and most patient. The principle of numbering and booking, it was shown, would actually abolish the pit. The judicious manager understood and recognised the public discontent, and made announcement that on May 18th he would restore the old custom.

In accordance with his engagement he now proceeded to get ready Wills's pleasing and sympathetic drama, 'Olivia.' This was no doubt selected with a view to furnishing a fresh opportunity for the display of Miss Terry's magic attraction ; but it will be seen that she was not to be altogether the cynosure of the whole, and that two other accom-

stepping in time to a comic tune ! These were graduated in size so as to produce due pantomimic effect. Mr. Tree, to receive the ring, held out his long stick of office, on which it was made to slide up to his hand !

IRVING AS "THE VICAR," AND ELLEN TERRY AS "OLIVIA."
Photo by Window & Grove.

To face p 165.

plished performers were to share the honours of
the piece. It was produced on May 27, 1885, and
excited much interest. The Vicar had been admirably performed by Vezin—on the old conventional lines of the kindly but "heavy" father, and it
became interesting to contrast the two styles. The
creation of Dr. Primrose is one of the most delightful and most original of Irving's characters. It
is elaborated and finished to the very highest point,
and yet there is no lack of simplicity or unaffected
grace. The character suited him in every way, and
seemed to hold completely in check all his little
"mannerisms," as they are called. There was a
sort of Meissonnier delicacy in his touches, and
scarcely any other of his characters was so filled in
and rounded with unspoken acting—that is, by the
play of facial expression, gesture, walk, &c. It
was, indeed, a delightful performance, and always
held the audience, which attentively followed the
Vicar's successive emotions. These the actor
allowed unconsciously, as it were, to escape him,
as he pursues his little domestic course unconscious
of spectators. One reason for this complete success
was, of course, that Irving, like so many others, had
read, known, and felt this engaging character from
his childhood, altogether outside dramatic conditions, though of course it is not every play that
enjoys this advantage.

As we look back to the Lyceum, the eye rests
with infinite pleasure on the engaging figure of the
Vicar, with his powdered wig and rusted suit, and
that amiable smile of simplicity which betokened

what agreeable fancies were occupying his mind. There was he, centre of a happy family, content with the happiness of his wife and children. No picture could have been prettier. With an exquisite feeling of propriety, the quaint, antique associations were developed, and no more pleasing scene could have been conceived, nor one that lingers more in the memory, than the scene at night, when the family are singing at the spinet, Moses accompanying with his flute,[1] the Vicar in his chair, the cuckoo-clock in the corner. It was a fine instinct that directed these things.

It should be added that the piece had been somewhat altered from its first shape, and no doubt gained from the manager's suggestions. One of the most astonishing things connected with it is the admirably firm and coherent construction, it being laid out in the most effective way. The various characters are introduced with singular skill. The last act seemed, indeed, somewhat superfluous and too much drawn out; but the whole design was really admirable.

This play of Wills's was always for me an unsolved and most perplexing thing; it is so workmanlike, so artistic, so full of nature and admirable character-drawing, that it seemed incredible it

---

[1] When the piece was first given at the Court Theatre there was a bit of realism that was almost too conscientious. The little family music was accompanied on a genuine old harpsichord, which, it was gravely announced in the bill, was actually dated 1768, about the period of the novel, and was, of course, "kindly lent" by the owner.

IRVING AS " THE VICAR " IN " OLIVIA."
Photo by Window & Grove.

To face p. 167.

should have come from his hand. In his other pieces there is a sort of *incoherence*, almost childish at times, with an insistence on trivial points. Could it be that some secret coadjutor helped him, or was it some ingeniously adapted French play? If not, it was a marvel, truly, and its author deserves infinite credit.

It was poor Wills's fate to have alternating "ups and downs"—reverses and triumphs—in his playwriting. Two of his sensational pieces still keep the stage, and are constantly travelling round the country, to wit, 'Jane Shore' and that capital Napoleonic drama 'A Royal Divorce.' The success of the latter he did not live to witness. I have seen him, when he was writing to the actor's measure, take out an envelope on which he had scribbled some half a dozen verses, and recite the same to the great man, as part of an intended speech. And, strange to say, the other listened with pleasure and approbation.

Such tales as these—world-wide stories that belong to all countries and to all time—Shakespearian, in short—seem on repetition to have the air of novelty ; at least, they always interest. The situations are dramatic, and the characters even more dramatic than the situations. Miss Terry's Olivia is not only one of her best characters, but is a most touchingly graceful and varied performance. The gifted pair were indeed at their best here. In the excellently-contrived scene at the "Dragon," Miss Terry's transition of horror, astonishment, rage, shame, succeeding each other, were displayed with extraordinary force and variety. Some insisted that the part suffered from her restlessness, but, as it was happily said, " She is for ever flickering about the stage in a series of *poses*, or rather disturbance of *pose*, each in itself so charming that one can hardly account for the distrust she herself shows of it by instantly changing it for another." The other characters were no less excellent in their way. Terriss, as the Squire, was admirably suited, his very defect—an excessively pronounced brusqueness—adding to the effect. It was said at the time in the theatre that there was only the one performer for Thornhill, and that one Terriss. He—and he only—must be secured. He never performed so well as in this character.

A year later there occurred what must have been one of the most gratifying incidents in the actor's career, and one of the most pleasant to recall. The Oxford commencements, held on June 26, 1886, were more than usually brilliant. At that time the late learned and popular Dr. Jowett was Vice-Chancellor, a man, as was well known, of the largest sympathies. Though a divine, he took a deep interest in Irving and his profession. On its being proposed to confer honorary degrees on certain distinguished guests, including Mr. John Bright, the Vice-Chancellor, it is said, suggested the name of the well-known actor. There was something, as I say, dramatic or characteristic in this proposal, coming, as it did, from so expressive a personality. The University, however, was not prepared to go so far as this, though the proposal was only negatived, it is said, by a narrow majority of two votes. The vigorous purpose of the Vice-Chancellor was not to be thus baffled, and by a brilliant *coup* he contrived that the very omission of the actor's name—like the absence of one portrait from a series—should suggest that the chief performer had been " left " out, and thus supplied a fresh element in the brilliancy of his reception. He invited him to deliver a lecture on his art in the very precincts of the University, and under the patronage of its most distinguished professors and " Heads." It may be conceived that the figure of the popular player became the cynosure of attraction in the brilliant academic show.

> " For when the well-grac'd actor quits the scene,
>   The eyes of men are idly bent on him
>   That enters next."

When it became known that the actor was to give his address, every one of note and culture and importance in the place rushed to secure seats. Some fourteen hundred persons were present, with most of " the Heads of Houses," and distinguished professors. Dr. Jowett welcomed him in some warm and well-chosen phrases, telling him how much honoured they felt by his coming to them. A good English actor, he said happily enough, lived in the best company—that of Goethe and Shakespeare ; and, coming from such, he might seem to convey that he was good enough company for them.

But during the year 1892 the University of

Dublin was the first to recognise officially the actor's position, and at the celebration of its tercentenary conferred on him the degree of Doctor of Letters, in company with many distinguished men. Indeed, Irving's sympathetic temperament has always been specially acceptable to this University, and the youths of Trinity College from the beginning were eager to exhibit their appreciation and admiration of his talent. They would attend him home from the theatre in uproarious procession, and sing songs in his praise in the galleries. So early as June, 1877, he had given a reading in the University in its great Examination Hall. The Provost, the Dean, and other "dons" all attended. He gave 'Richard III.,' a chapter of "David Copperfield," and 'Eugene Aram.' An illuminated address was presented to him, and to make the day truly festive and collegiate, the actor dined in the hall, the guest of the college, and went his way covered with honours.

Later came the turn of Edinburgh, where he was much considered, and in 1881 delivered a lecture before the Edinburgh Philosophical Institute. He gave, also, an interesting lecture on Acting at the Royal Institution in London. With pleasure, too, must he have looked back to his welcome at Harvard University. The novelty of the scene, the warm welcome accorded to him in a strange land, must have made a most welcome form of honour. He delivered a lecture on the "Art of Acting"—his favourite topic—in the great Sande's Theatre, into which over two thousand persons were crowded—the usual audience was sixteen hundred. An enormous crowd blocked the doors, so that the actor on his arrival could not gain admittance, and had to be taken in by a subterranean passage. The president was in a conspicuous place, and all the professors and dons attended. Another American University, that of Cambridge, also invited him to lecture (rather to give instruction) before them, and the newspapers of the country declared that the honours with which he was welcomed were really "unprecedented." Again he discoursed on the "Art of Acting." An even more flattering and unusual compliment was the invitation to the Military Academy at Westpoint, where, with his company, he performed 'The Merchant of Venice' in Elizabethan dresses, but without scenery—to the huge enjoyment of professors and students. Here is a round of University distinctions that has never fallen to the lot of any other actor. We may see in it an instinctive recognition of a cultured and artistic feeling that has influenced the community and done excellent educational service.

Irving had long wished to display his sardonic power in Goethe's great character of Mephistopheles. He had already given proof of his quality in this line in Louis XI. and Richard III.; but there was the satirical piquancy and range in Mephistopheles which naturally offered him an attraction, from the mixture of the comic or grotesque with deep tragic force. It also offered room for a superb and almost unlimited display of scenic magnificence. It was no secret, too, that in this particular display he was resolved to surpass all his previous efforts.

To Wills was entrusted the work of preparing the adaptation, this writer having, as I said, a command of flowing and melodious versification, which, moreover, was fitted to the actor's delivery. The adapter had completed his task many years before, and the piece had long lain in the manager's desk. During this period he let his conception of the piece slowly ripen; he discussed it with scholars; thought over it; while the adapter, a German student himself, revised his work at intervals, according to the views of his chief. All this was judicious enough. It was, however, destined to be one of the last works that he was to prepare for his old friend and faithful Lyceum patron. It must be said that the latest adapter was not altogether well fitted for the task, as he was too much given to descriptions and " recitations," while Mephistopheles might have been made far more of.

The preparations made were of the most thorough kind. For months the manager's rooms were hung round with a profusion of sketches by artists of all kinds, relics of Nuremberg and the Goethe country, with old engravings of Albert Dürer, and great folios of costumes. To permeate himself with something of the tone and feeling of the piece, he travelled in Germany, accompanied by his scene-painter, Mr. Craven. Both stayed at Nuremberg, where the artist imbued himself with the whole poetry of the old city. Every one of artistic feeling

THE REVIVAL OF "FAUST" AT THE LYCEUM THEATRE.
IN MARTHA'S GARDEN AT NUREMBERG.

To face p. 172.

will recall one truly romantic scene—a simple cloth set very forward on the scene, perhaps to its disadvantage—a view of the old city, with its dull red high roofs and quaintly-peaked spires.

During the preparations, the theatre, now some eighty years old, had been redecorated afresh, but at the complete sacrifice of the old Vestris adornments, the elegant medallions or cameos, and the double gilt pillars, which were thought to interfere with the view. The outline of the dress-circle was brought forward with some gain of space, and its graceful undulations abolished. For such changes no one can be brought to account — the irresistible pressure of the time and the laws of convenience bring them about. An entirely new system of decoration was introduced, suggested by that of Raffaelle's Loggie at the Vatican, which seemed scarcely sober enough for an auditorium. More structural changes were also made in the interests of the galleries, of which the manager had always shown himself careful.

On December 19, 1886, the piece was produced. There was the now invariable excitement of a Lyceum *première*, and there were stories of frantic efforts, grovellings, implorings, &c., to obtain a seat. A peer had actually been seen in the gallery—and was more than content with his place. The Royal Family were in their box, and the Prince of Wales watched the play from behind the scenes. Mephistopheles was destined for many a night to give the keenest enjoyment to vast audiences. It was, indeed, a most original conception. With successive performances he enriched it with innumerable telling and grotesque touches; for, as I have said, the adapter had "laid out" the character on rather conventional lines. In spite of all these defects, he suggested the notion of "uncanniness" and a supernatural *diablerie*. His antic scaring of the women at the church-door will be recalled by many. Miss Terry's Marguerite was full of pathos and poetry, occasionally suggesting, as in the "Jewel" scene, the operatic heroine. But at the first performance it became plain that a serious mistake had been made in the choice of Conway for the hero, Faust. He seemed scarcely to feel or understand the part; there was a lack of passion and sympathy. It was, indeed, an overwhelming burden for a player whose gifts lay in the direction of light comedy.

But on one Saturday night the audience was somewhat astonished to see before them a new Faust, one who, moreover, came on with a book in his hand, which he continued to read aloud even after Mephisto had paid him his visit through the steam clouds. It proved that Conway was suffering from gout, and Alexander, resigning his own character to Tyars, took the *rôle* of Faust, which on the following night he assumed permanently, and "discharged" in the regular way. Considering the shortness of the notice, he performed this awkward duty *en vrai artiste*—as, indeed, might be expected.[1]

[1] It is but fair to add that Mr. Conway was suffering from the approach of a serious illness, which declared itself shortly after.

However, the cast was further strengthened by the excellent Mrs. Stirling, whose part was scarcely worthy of her. Placing a strong performer in a part that is inferior in strength, instead of improving or fortifying, only further brings out the poverty of the character.

In this piece numerous scientific devices were introduced to add to the effect, such as the clouds of steam which veiled the apparition of Mephistopheles, a device of French origin. This is scarcely illusive, as it is attended by an unmistakable "hissing" sound, as of a locomotive; it seems what it is— namely, steam. The blue electric light flashed with weird effect as the swords of Valentine and Faust crossed. But here again there was an electric wire and "contact," and a current "switched on." It may be paradoxical to say so, but these "advances" in scenic art are really retrograde steps.

Of the regular scenes or structures put on the stage, it would be difficult to say too much. The grandly-built porch of the Church of St. Lorentz Platz at Nuremberg, and the buildings grouped round it, were extraordinary works of construction, the porch being "moulded" in all its details, and of the real or natural size. Another scene that lingers in the memory with a sort of twilight melancholy is the garden scene, which again illustrated the admirable instinct of the manager. Red-brick walls of calm, quiet tones, old trees, and, above all, the sombre towers of the city, were seen in the distance. The dresses of the characters were chosen to harmonise, and the deep sunset cast a melancholy glow or tinge over all. The most striking effects were contrived by changes of the lights and "mediums."

The Brocken scene, for its vastness and ambitious attempt to suggest space and atmosphere, has never been surpassed. Most people were struck by the bewildering crowd of unearthly spirits, witches, and demons, &c. ; but the real marvel was the simulation of the chill mountain atmosphere, the air of dizziness, of mists that hover over vast crevasses and depths, and make one shiver to look at. The designing, direction, and controlling of the elements in this wonderful scene seemed a bewildering and gigantic task.

The vision of Angels in the last act seemed a little conventional. There were many objections, too, taken mostly by Germans, to the treatment of the great story, such as the fixing of the scene at Nuremberg instead of at Leipsic, the placing the drinking bout in the open air, and at the tavern door, instead of in Auerbach's cellar. These changes could not, of course, be justified, save on the ground of theatrical expediency.

For seven months, though 'Faust' continued to attract vast houses, it had really, as the manager said, "only started on its wild career." On the occasion of Miss Terry's benefit, he made an interesting, half-jocular speech announcing his plans.

The ninety-ninth night was celebrated in a remarkable and somewhat appropriate fashion. The venerable Abbé Liszt was at this time in London, followed with an eager curiosity, affecting even the "cabbies" with interest, who were heard

RAB

"MEPHISTO."

THE AC[T]

[To face pa

talking of the "Habby List." No one who had seen him at this time will forget the striking personality of this interesting and brilliant man. He was induced to visit the theatre, and to witness the performance. After the first act, the orchestra broke into his own "March," and, being presently recognised by the audience, the great virtuoso received a perfect ovation. He followed the piece throughout with singular interest, and applauded with enthusiasm. After the play was over, he was welcomed at a supper in the old Beef-steak dining-room, where there were invited to meet him a few distinguished persons. His favourite dishes—"lentil pudding, lamb cutlets, mushrooms in batter"—were prepared for him by Gunter's *chef*. He was delighted with this delicate hospitality. This is one of the many pleasant and dignified memories associated with the Lyceum.

During the performance of 'Faust' Miss Terry found the fatigue excessive, and, not being very strong at the time, had to resign her part. During these intervals, the character was supported by a clever young actress, bearing an historic name, Miss Winifred Emery, who brought much intelligence and refinement to her task. She has since "gone far," indeed. It was generally agreed that, considering her resources, she had supplied the place of the absent actress very well. The *feu sacré* was, of course, not to be expected, and cannot be supplied to order.

It was when 'Faust' was being played that the catastrophe of the burning of the French Opéra

13

Comique occurred.   This excited general sympathy, and the kindly manager of the Lyceum promised that when the proper time came he would furnish assistance.   In due course a performance of ' Faust ' was announced for the benefit of the sufferers, and a crowded audience assembled.   Every one concerned —and they were to be counted by hundreds—gave their services gratis—the manager behaved in his own liberal style—and, as the result, a sum of £419 was despatched to Paris.   This liberality was much appreciated by the French press.   The *Figaro* devoted an article to a review of the various characters played by the English actor, and in flattering terms pointed out that, notwithstanding all his detractors, Mr. Henry Irving was "the most perfect gentleman."

This appreciation of our manager-actor by the French will naturally suggest the inquiry, What is his reputation generally in that eminently theatrical country, whence we draw our chief supply of dramas and dramatic ideas, and whose school of acting is perhaps the first in Europe?   So frequent have been the visits of French companies to London, that nearly all the leading performers have had opportunities of seeing the English actor perform. Their ignorance of the language has, of course, stood in the way of a satisfactory judgment—they cannot follow the play as an average Englishman will follow a French piece ; but all have been struck by his fine faculty of imparting colour and romance to a character, and have broken into raptures over the intelligence that directs the scene, and the lavish magnificence of the *spectacle.*

The memorable visit of the French Comedians to London in 1879, and the fine series of performances in which every player of note displayed his talent, curiously coincided with the new departure on the English stage. Few will forget the deep impressions left by that season or the opportunities afforded for a liberal education in dramatic taste. With the company came the *fin fleur* of French critics, Sarcey, Claretie (since become director of the company he had so often criticised), and others of less note. These judges were glad to seize an opportunity, which under other circumstances they would never have thought of seeking, of visiting the Lyceum and witnessing the performances of the most distinguished of English actors. I recall Sarcey at this time, a coarsely-built man, with not very refined features, lounging night after night into his stall, with an air of something like arrogance. He did not relish his enforced banishment from the Boulevards, and indemnified himself by making rather free criticisms on the French players. He was induced to go and see some of the English performances, but with an amusing hauteur pleaded his ignorance of the language as an excuse for not passing any serious judgment. He wrote :

" Having weighed the matter well, I have determined to say very little regarding English actors. I have as yet seen but a few, and those only through the medium of a language imperfectly understood. I should be placing myself in a ridiculous position if I had the impertinence to touch upon matters which I am thus incompetent to deal with. I may remark, however, that Mr. Henry Irving appeared to me a remarkable actor, notwithstanding a wilful tendency to exaggeration.   Possibly, in this latter respect, he followed rather the taste of his audience, whom his instinct judges, than his own deliberate choice."

To these brilliant and gifted strangers, however, the new manager did the honours of his craft and extended to them a kindly hospitality.   Indeed, since that day, no distinguished artist has visited these shores without being welcomed with rare hospitality.[1]

The most accomplished of French comedians is Coquelin *ainé*, an extraordinary performer, from the versatility and even classical character of his talents. This gifted man, who never appears without impart-

---

[1] I recall a Sunday morning during this visit, when a message arrived from the manager asking me to join a festive party to Dorking, to which he had invited some members of the French Comedy.   At the Garrick Club, the favourite coach, " Old Times," was waiting, and presently it was " Buzz !—here come the players."   A delightful drive it was, and a truly enjoyable day.   There was Mounet Sully, the fervent stage lover—then, it was whispered, the prey of a hopeless attachment to the gifted " Sarah "—the *spirituel* Delaunay, still a *jeune premier* in spite of his years; with two or three others of the *corps*.   Of the party were also my friend Mr. Walter Pollock, with his genial, well-cultured father, the late Sir Frederick ; Campbell Clarke, and Mr. Bartlett, now Mr. Burdett-Coutts.   There was the drive down to the inviting little town, with a lunch at the old inn, some wanderings about its leafy lanes, and a return in the evening to the club, where the host gave a banquet, at which speeches in French and English were delivered.   The interesting strangers took away with them the lasting impression that he was " a truly sympathetic personage, with a great deal of French grace and *bonhomie* in his nature."

ing intellectual enjoyment of the highest kind seems to have always been attracted to the English actor, though exhibiting his feelings in an oddly mixed fashion, compounded of admiration and hostility. Analysis of the workings of character is the most entertaining of pastimes, and is, of course, the foundation of theatrical enjoyment ; and the public has much relished the controversies between two such eminent personages. In 1886 Coquelin, during a supper at Mrs. Mackay's, was invited in a very flattering way by the Prince of Wales to play in London under Mr. Mayer. At this time, in obedience to the very natural " force and pressure " of gain which was beginning to dissolve the great company of the French Comedy, he had begun to " star it," as it is called, in the various capitals of Europe, and having found himself appreciated in London at private houses, as well as on the stage, he seems to have nourished a feeling that he was contending for the suffrages of the public with the English actor ! Not that he was conscious of any actual " jealousy," but something of this impression was left on those who were watching the incident. In matters of art, however, such contentions are healthy, and pardonable enough.

An early token of this curious feeling was offered in an article published in *Harper's Magazine* in May, 1887, where the French actor discussed with some acuteness the different systems of acting in England and in France, particularly in the matter of what is called " natural " or materialistic acting. He dwelt on the question how far the gifts of the comedian will enable him to exhibit tragic characters, contending that the practice of minute observation would materially aid him.

What was in Coquelin's thoughts all this time would appear to have been a sort of eagerness to measure himself with the English actor in 'Le Juif Polonais,' which he looked upon as his own, and which had made a reputation for Irving. With some lack of taste or tact, Coquelin later challenged an English audience to decide between the two readings of Mathias. He performed it, I think, on two different occasions. It was an interesting and instructive experiment, for it proved that two artists of eminence might legitimately take directly opposite views of the same character. But does not character in real life offer the same varieties of interpretation? Coquelin presented a sort of comfortable *bourgeois*, a tradesman-like personage, who was not likely to reach the heroic or melodramatic place. He was not over-sensitive, nor was his remorse very poignant; and the keynote to his agitation was the desire to be thought respectable, to keep his position, and not be found out. It was agreed that the two conceptions were altogether opposed. "Irving's hero was a grave, dignified and melancholy being: Coquelin's was a stout Alsatian, well-to-do, respected by his neighbours, but still on an equality with the humble folk around him. Irving's was a conscious-stricken personage; Coquelin's had no conscience at all. Irving's was all remorse; Coquelin was not in the least disturbed. He takes delight in his ill-got treasures. The only side on which he is assailable is that of his fears, and the arrival of the second Jew, so like the first, terrifies him; and too much wine on the night of the wedding brings on the disturbed dream." The question might be thus summarised: Irving's reading was that of a tragedian; Coquelin's that of a comedian. For myself, I confess a liking for both.

A friendly and even enthusiastic appreciation of the actor was furnished by Jules Claretie, then a critic of eminence. "His reputation," he said, "would be even greater than it is if he had the leisure to extend his studies and correct his faults; but, as Mr. Walter Pollock remarks, a man who has to play six or seven times a week can hardly be expected to find much time for study. England, unlike France, does not possess a national theatre.[1]

"'Richelieu' was the first play in which I saw Mr. Irving in London. Here he is superb. The performance amounts to a resurrection. The great Cardinal, lean, worn, eaten up with ambition, less for himself than for France, is admirably rendered. His gait is jerky, like that of a man shaken by fever; his eye has the depth of a visionary's; a hoarse cough preys upon that feeble frame. When Richelieu appears in the midst of the courtiers, when

---

[1] Mr. Pollock had translated Diderot's curious and instructive piece, in which is discussed so acutely the point whether an actor should perform under actual, *real* emotion, or simulate it. Irving held, in theory as in practice, that the actor must *train* his feelings and exhibit them artificially, otherwise each performance will be worse than the preceding. It has not been noted that Bishop Butler's analysis of active and passive habits helps to supply the solution.

he flings his scorn in the face of the mediocrity that is to succeed him, when he supplicates and adjures the vacillating Louis XIII., Mr. Irving endows that fine figure with a striking majesty.

"What a profound artist this tragedian is! The performance over, I was taken to see him in his dressing-room. I found him surrounded by portraits of Richelieu. He had before him the three studies of Philippe de Champaigne, one representing Richelieu in full face, and the others in profile. There was also a photograph of the same painter's full-length portrait of the Cardinal. Before playing Louis XI. again, Mr. Irving studied Commines, Victor Hugo, Walter Scott, and all who have written of the *bourgeois* and avaricious king, who wore out the elbows of his *pourpoint de ratine* on the tables of his gossips, the skin-dressers and shoe-makers. The actor is an adept in the art of face-painting, and attaches great importance to the slightest details of his costume.

"I asked him what other historical personage he would like to represent, what face he, who excelled in what I call stage-resurrection, would wish to revive. He reflected a moment, his countenance assuming a thoughtful expression. 'Français ou Anglais?' he at length asked. 'Français ou Anglais : peu importe,' I replied. 'Eh bien!' he said, after another short pause, 'je serais heureux de créer un Camille Desmoulins.'

"Mr. Irving's literary and subtle mind leans to psychological plays—plays which, if I may so express myself, are more tragic than dramatic. He is the true Shakespearian actor. How great was the pleasure which the performance of 'Hamlet' afforded me! For a literary man it is a source of real enjoyment. Mr. Irving, as manager of the Lyceum, spends more than £3,000 a month to do things on an adequate scale. His theatre is the first in London. He would like to make it a sort of Comédie Française, as he would like to found a sort of Conservatoire to afford young English artists the instruction they stand so much in need of.

"In Louis XI. Mr. Irving has been adjudged superior to Ligier. Dressed with historical accuracy, he is admirable in the comedy element of the piece and the chief scenes with the Monk and Nemours. The limelight projected like a ray of the moon on his contracted face as he pleads for his life excited nothing less than terror. The hands, lean and crooked as those of a Harpagon—the fine hands whose character is changed with each of his *rôles*— aid his words. And how striking in its realism is the last scene, representing the struggle between the dying king and his fate!"

Another admirable French player, Got, once the glory of the French Comédie, and unquestionably the most powerful and varied performer of his day, used to come a good deal to London between the years 1870 and 1880.

It was a singular tribute to Irving that so great a player, in his day greater even than Coquelin, should have been drawn from his retirement to take up one of his characters. Got, the " Dean of the

French stage," as Irving is " Dean " of the English theatre, by and by felt himself irresistibly impelled to give his version of ' The Bells.'   He induced a Paris manager to draw forth the long-forgotten piece from its obscurity, and presented Mathias very much on the *bourgeois* lines of Coquelin.

CHAPTER XIII

1887

'FAUST'—'WERNER'—'MACAIRE'—THE ACTOR'S SOCIAL GIFTS

HE was now preparing for his third American tour, the object of which was to introduce to the audiences of the United States his splendid spectacular piece, 'Faust.' This had excited much interest and expectation, and its attractions were even magnified by distance. It was the "last word" in scenic display. The Americans had now become a section, as it were, of the audiences, and it would seem to be inevitable that at fixed intervals, and when a series of striking plays had been given in England, the manager should feel a sort of irresistible pressure to present the same attractions on the other side of the Atlantic. This expedition took place in October, 1887, and was crowned with all success. Henceforth the periodical visit to America became a necessity; a new visit was planned in concert with Mr. Abbey, and fixed for 1893.

On the return of the company, after their United

States triumphs, ' Faust ' was revived for a short period.   At the close of the first performance the manager announced his plans, which were awaited with some curiosity.   " The devil," he said, " had been to and fro on the face of the earth."   After a month of ' Faust,' he proposed to give Mr. Calmour's ' Amber Heart,' to bring forward Miss Terry, while he himself was to conclude the evening with a revival of ' Robert Macaire.'

On July 1, 1887, the manager of the Lyceum performed one of those many kindly, graceful acts with which his name is connected—an act done at the right moment, and for the suitable person.   He lent his theatre to benefit a veteran dramatist, Dr. Westland Marston, who in his day had been associated with the classical glories of the stage, and had written the interesting ' Wife's Secret' for Charles Kean.   As he now told the audience from the stage, fifty years had elapsed since he had written his first piece for Macready.   The committee formed was a most influential one, and comprised the names of such eminent *littérateurs* as Browning, Alfred Austin, E. W. Gosse, William Black, Wilkie Collins, Gilbert, Swinburne, Tennyson, and many more.   The performance was an afternoon one, and the play selected was Byron's ' Werner,' written " up to date," as it is called, by Frank Marshall.   New scenery and dresses had been provided, though the actor did not propose giving another representation.   He, however, intended to perform it on his approaching American tour.   It must be said that the play gave little

MR. HENRY IRVING
AS
ROBERT MACAIRE

[To face page 188.

satisfaction, and was about as lugubrious as 'The Stranger,' some of the acts, moreover, being played in almost Cimmerian gloom. What inclined the manager to this choice it would be difficult to say. He had rather a *penchant* for these morosely gloomy men, who stalk about the stage and deliver long and remorseful reviews and retrospects of their lives. Audiences, however, sympathise, and listen with respectful attention.

'Werner' was to illustrate once more the conscientious and laborious care of the manager in the production of his pieces. He engaged Mr. Seymour Lucas to furnish designs for the dresses, who drew his inspirations from an old volume of etchings of one "Stefano della Bella" in 1630. So patiently *difficile* was our manager in satisfying himself, that it is said the dresses in 'Faust' were made and re-made three times before they were found satisfactory. In this case all the arms of antique pattern, the dresses, quaint head-dresses, and the like, even down to the peculiar buttons of the period, were made especially in Paris under Auguste's superintendence.

'Robert Macaire,' that strange, almost weird-like drama, was familiar enough to Irving, who had occasionally played it in the early part of his course, and also at the St. James's Theatre in 1867. For all performers of genius who have taste for the mere *diablerie* of acting, and the eccentric mixture of tragic and comic, this character offers an attraction, if not a fascination. We can feel its power ourselves as we call up the grotesque figure; nay, even those who have never seen the piece can have an understanding of the character, as a coherent piece of grotesque. There is something of genius in the contrasted and yet intimate union between the eccentric pair. In June, 1883, there had been a performance at the Lyceum for the Royal College of Music, when Irving had played the character, assisted by "friend Toole," Bancroft, Terriss, and Miss Terry—certainly a strong cast. When the piece was formally brought out, the part was allotted to Mr. Weedon Grossmith, who was in the other extreme, and too subordinate.

The play was produced in July, 1888, and was found not so attractive as was anticipated. It seemed as though it were not wholly intelligible to the audience. There were some reasons for this, the chief being the gruesome assassination at "the roadside inn," which is old-fashioned, being literally "played out." More curious was it to find that the quaint type of Macaire seemed to convey nothing very distinct. All accepted it as an incoherent extravagance : which opens an interesting speculation—viz., How many such parts are there which have been the characters of the original actors, and not the author's—the former's creation, in short ? Lemaître's extraordinary success was, as is well known, the result of a happy inspiration conceived during the progress of the piece. From being a serious or tragic character, he turned it into a grotesque one. There may have been here something founded on the sort of *gaminerie* that seems to go with crime; or it may have been

a recklessness, which, together with ludicrous
attempts at a squalid dandyism, showed a mind
not only depraved, but dulled and *embêté*. This
sort of inspiration, where an actor sees his own
conception in the part and makes it his own, is
illustrated by 'The Bells,' which—in the hands of
another actor—might have been played according
to conventional laws. An English actor who
would have succeeded in the part was the elder
Robson. In Irving's case, the audience were not
in key, or in tune; the thing seemed *passé*, though
our actor had all the traditions of the part, even to
the curiously " creaking snuff-box."[1]

Among Wills's friends, admirers and associates—
of which his affectionate disposition always brought
him a following—was Calmour, the author of some
pieces full of rather graceful verse of the antique
model. Like Mr. Pinero, he " knew the boards,"
having "served" in the ranks, an essential advantage
for all who would write plays; had written several
slight pieces of a poetical cast, notably 'Cupid's

---

[1] This also seemed quite unintelligible to the audience; but
its secret was the secret of the creator or originator of the part.
Such devices are really significant of something dramatic that has
actually prompted them; they become an expression. The
revived "business," therefore, will not serve unless the original
spirit attends it. This squeaking snuff-box was a note of *diablerie*,
introduced with strange sudden spasms at unexpected moments,
and corresponded to the twitches and spasms of Macaire's mind.
For the manager I collected much of old Lemaître's business,
and those curious chants with which the robber carried off his
villainies. Jingle and Job Trotter were certainly modelled on
Macaire and his man; for the piece was being played when
" Pickwick " came out.

Messenger,' in which the graceful and sympathetic Mary Rorke had obtained much success in a "trunk and hose" character. But a play of a more ambitious kind, 'The Amber Heart,' had taken Miss Terry's fancy; she, as we have said, had "created" the heroine at a *matinée*. It proved to be a sort of dreamy Tennysonian poem, and was received with considerable favour.

'The Amber Heart,' now placed in the bill with 'Robert Macaire,' was revived with the accustomed Lyceum state and liberality. To Alexander was allotted the hero's part, and he declaimed the harmonious lines with good effect. But I fancy the piece was found of rather too delicate a structure for such large and imposing surroundings.[1]

Whenever there is some graceful act, a memorial to a poet or player to be inaugurated, it was pretty certain that our actor-manager would be called on to take the leading and most distinguished share in the ceremonial. At the public meeting, or public dinner, he deported himself with much effect. There are plenty of persons of culture who have been deputed to perform such duties; but we feel there is often something artificial in their methods and speeches. In the case of the actor, we know

---

[1] We may at least admire this writer's perseverance and intrepidity, who from that time has never relaxed his efforts to win the approbation or secure the attention of the public. One could have wished him better success with his later venture and most ambitious attempt, the management of the Avenue Theatre, where he introduced his own piece illustrative of "modern English life," with which his critics—for whom, like the sapper, "nothing is sacred"—made merry.

that there is a something genuine; he supplies a life
to the dry bones, and we depart knowing that he has
added grace to our recollections of the scene. Nor
does he add an exaggeration to what he says;
there is a happy judicious reserve. This was felt
especially on the occasion of one pleasant festival
day in the September of 1891, when a memorial by
Mr. Onslow Ford was unveiled to Marlowe, the
dramatist, in the good old town of Canterbury. It
was an enjoyable expedition, with something simple
and rustic on the whole, while to any one of poetical
tastes there was something unusually harmonious in
the combination offered of the antique town, the
memory of " Dr. Faustus," the old Cathedral, and
the beaming presence of the cultured artist, of
whom no one thought as manager of a theatre.
A crowd of critics and authors came from town by
an early train, invited by the hospitable Mayor.
At any season the old town is inviting enough,
but now it was pleasant to march through its
narrow streets, under the shadow of its framed
houses, to the small corner close to the Christ
Church gate of the Cathedral, where the speeching
and ceremonials were discharged. The excellent
natives seemed perhaps a little puzzled by the new-
found glories of their townsman; they were,
however, glad to see the well-known actor. Equally
pleasant, too, was it to make our way to the old
Fountain Inn, where the "worthy" Mayor entertained his guests and where there were more
speeches. The image of the sleepy old town, and
the grand Cathedral, and of the pretty little fountain

14

—which, however, had but little suggestion of the colossal Marlowe—and the general holiday tone still lingers in the memory. Irving's speech was very happy, and for its length is singularly suggestive. With this little expedition I was later destined to be associated in a more intimate way. From lack of funds three of the four niches were left unfilled, and I am at this moment supplying figures of my own design and workmanship to fill the spaces.

It was in October, 1887, that a memorial was set up at Stratford, a clock-tower and fountain, in memory of Shakespeare. It was the gift of the wealthy Mr. Childs, of New York, who had been hitherto eager to associate his name, in painted windows and other ways, with distinguished Englishmen of bygone times. It may be suspected that Childs's own name will not be so inseparably linked with celebrated personages as he fondly imagined. There is a sort of incongruity in this association of a casual stranger with an English poet. Irving took his part in this show.

Many a delightful night have his friends owed to the thoughtful kindness and hospitality of their interesting host. Such was, indeed, one of the privileges of being his friend. The stage brings with it abundance of pleasant associations; but there are a number of specially agreeable memories bound up with the Lyceum. Few will forget the visit of the Duke of Meiningen's company of players to this country, which forms a landmark of extraordinary importance in the history of our modern stage. With it came Barnay, that accomplished and romantic actor; and a wonderful instinct of disciplining crowds, and making them express the passions of the moment, as in Shakespeare's 'Julius Cæsar.' The skilful German stage-managers did not import their crowds, but were able to inspire ordinary bands of supernumeraries with the dramatic feelings and expression that they wanted.

It was one pleasant Sunday evening at the close of a summer's day, when Irving invited his friends to meet the German performers at the Lyceum. The stage had been picturesquely enclosed and fashioned into a banqueting-room, the tables spread; the orchestra performed in the shadowy pit. It was an enjoyable night. There was a strange mingling of languages—German, French, English. There were speeches in these tongues, and at one moment Palgrave Simpson was addressing the company in impetuous fashion, passing from English to French, from French to German, with extraordinary fluency. Later in the evening there was an adjournment to the Beefsteak-room, where the accomplished Barnay found himself at the piano, to be succeeded by the versatile Beatty-Kingston, himself half German. There were abundant " Hochs " and pledgings. Not until the furthest of the small hours did we separate, indebted to our kindly, unaffected host for yet one more delightful evening.

The manager once furnished a pleasantly piquant afternoon's amusement for his friends on the stage

of his handsome theatre.   Among those who have
done service to the stage is Mr. Walter Pollock,
lately editor of the *Saturday Review*, who, among
his other accomplishments, is a swordsman of no
mean skill.   He has friends with the same tastes,
with whom he practises this elegant art, such as
Mr. Egerton Castle, Captain Hutton, and others.
It is not generally known that there is a club
known as the Kerneuzers, whose members are
amateurs enragés for armour and swordsmanship,
many of whom have fine collections of helmets,
hauberks, and blades of right Damascene and
Toledo.[1]   Mr. Egerton Castle and others of his
friends have written costly and elaborate works on
fencing, arms, and the practice of the *arme blanche*,
and at their meetings held exciting combats with
dirk and foil.   It was suggested that Mr. Castle
should give a lecture on this subject, with practical
illustrations ; and the manager, himself a fencer,
invited a number of friends and amateurs to witness
the performance, which took place on February 25,
1891.   This lecture was entitled " The Story of
Swordsmanship," especially in connection with the
rise and decline of duelling.   And accordingly there
was witnessed a series of combats, mediæval
Italian, and others, back-sword, small-sword, sword
and cloak, and the rest.   Later the performance
was repeated at the instance of the Prince of
Wales.

[1] The quaint name of this club, "the Kerneuzers," was
suggested by a simple attendant, who actually so described the
members ; it was his pronunciation of the word "connoisseurs."

SIR HENRY IRVING IN HIS DRESSING-ROOM AT THE LYCEUM THEATRE.

THE KNIGHT OF THE STAGE.

Drawn from Life by Paul Renouard.

[*To face page* 197

Irving often contributed his share to "benefits" for his distressed brethren, as they are often called. In the days when he was a simple actor he took his part like the rest; when he became manager he would handsomely lend his theatre, and actually "get up" the whole as though it were one of his own pieces. This is the liberal, *grand* style of conferring a favour.

In June, 1876, a performance was arranged at the Haymarket for a benefit, when the ever-blooming 'School for Scandal' was performed by Phelps, Miss Neilson, "Ben" Webster, Irving, Bancroft, and others. Irving was the Joseph Surface, a performance which excited much anticipation and curiosity. Some time after he performed the same character at Drury Lane. It might naturally have been thought that the part would have exactly suited him, but whether from novelty or restlessness, there was a rather artificial tone about the performance. But what actor can be expected to play every character, and to find every character suited to him? Joseph is held to be one of the most difficult in the whole *répertoire* to interpret. It was the most extraordinary, puzzling exhibition that could be conceived; utterly unlike all idea of Joseph Surface—in fact, travelling off in lines totally opposed to any rational conception of the character. It seemed that he could make nothing of it. It was, in short, a phenomenon. At the Belford benefit—Belford and his services to the stage, such as they were, are long since forgotten—the all but enormous sum of £1,000 was received! For schools, charities,

convents even, and philanthropic work of all
kinds, some contribution from Henry Irving in the
shape of a recitation or scene was always looked
for.

Irving's vein of pleasantry was as welcome as it is
unpretentious.   I have heard him at the General
Theatrical Fund dinner give the toast of "The
Army, Navy, and Reserve Forces," when he said,
"There is an Artists' Corps—I am curious to know
why there should not be an Actors' Corps.   *We are
accustomed to handle weapons.*"   On this occasion
"friend Toole" had to leave on duty ; "whose fine
Roman visage," said his friend, "has beamed on
us during dinner—he has been obliged to go away,
fortified, I hope, for his arduous labours, but he will
return—I know him well—and he will too, I am sure,
with a most excellent donation."   He could tell a
story or relish a humorous situation with equal effect.
In company with Toole, he often contrived a droll
situation or comic adventure.[1]

[1] Once, when visiting Stratford-on-Avon with Toole, he saw a
rustic sitting on a fence, whom they submitted to an interroga-
tory.   "That's Shakespeare's house, isn't it?" it was asked inno-
cently.   "Ees."   "Ever been there?"   "Noä."   "How long
has he been dead?"   "Dunno."   "What did he do?"   "Dunno."
"Did he not write?"   "Oh yes, he did summat."   "What was
it?"   "Well, I think he writ *Boible*."   A pleasantry that both
the players once contrived in Scotland, at the expense of an old
waiter at an hotel, is of a higher order of merit than such hoaxes
usually offer.   At this country inn they had noted that the spoons,
forks, &c., seemed to be of silver, and with some artfully designed
emphasis they questioned the waiter about the property.   As soon
as he had gone out, they concealed all the plate, and, having rung
the bell, jumped out of the window, which was close to the

At one period, when he was oppressed with hard work, it was suggested to him that sleeping in the country would be a great restorative after his labours. He much fancied an old house and grounds at Hammersmith, known as "The Grange"; and having purchased it, he laid out a good deal of money in improving and restoring it. It had nice old gardens, with summer-house, a good staircase, and some old panelled rooms.

To a man with such social tastes, the journey down and the night spent there must have been banishment, or perhaps was found too troublesome. Literary men, artists, and the like do not much relish these tranquil pleasures, though practical men of business do. Most will agree, I am certain, that they leave Fleet Street and the Strand with reluctance and return to it with pleasure. After a few years he was anxious to be rid of what was only a

ground, and hid themselves in the shrubbery. The old man re-entered: they heard his cries of rage and astonishment at the robbery, and at the disappearance of the supposed thieves. He then rushed from the room to summon the household. The rest of the story is worth giving in Irving's words, as reported by Mr. Hatton. "We all crept back to the room, closed the window, drew down the blind, relighted the gas and our cigars, put each piece of silver back into its proper place, and sat down to wait for our bill. In a few minutes we heard evidently the entire household coming pell-mell to the dining-room. Then our door was flung open; but the crowd, instead of rushing in upon us, suddenly paused *en masse*, and Sandy exclaimed, 'Great God! Weel, weel! Hae I just gane clean daft?'

"'Come awa', drunken foo', come awa'!' exclaimed the landlord, pulling Sandy and the rest back into the passage and shutting the door."

useless toy, and it was offered for sale for, I think,
£4,000.[1]

---

[1] Quite a number of relics of great actors have, as we have
already shown, found their way to Irving's custody.   Thus on his
visit to Oxford he had spoken of the last days of Edmund Kean.
A few days later he received a purse of faded green silk found
in the pocket of the great actor just after his death, and found
empty. It had been given by Charles Kean to John Forster, and
by him to Robert Browning.   Edmund and Charles Kean,
Forster, Browning, and Irving form a remarkable combination.
" How can I more worthily place it," wrote Browning, "than in
your hands, if they will do me the honour to take it, with all
respect and regard ? "   At the recent sale of his effects there were
seen a vast number of these memorials.

CHAPTER XIV

1888

'MACBETH'—'THE DEAD HEART'—'RAVENSWOOD'

THE approach of the opening night of 'Macbeth'—its second revival by our actor—caused more excitement than perhaps any of the Lyceum productions. There was a sort of fever of expectancy ; it was known that everything in the way of novelty—striking and sumptuous dress and scenery, elaborate thought and study, and money had been expended in almost reckless fashion. There were legends afloat as to Miss Terry's marvellous " beetle-green" dress, and the copper-coloured tresses which were to hang down on her shoulders.[1] The scenery was to be vast, solid, and monumental. It was no surprise when it was learned that before the day of

---

[1] One of these many " snappers-up of trifles " described the nightgown worn by Lady Macbeth in her sleep-walking scene, which was all of wool knitted into a pretty design. Mrs. Comyns Carr designed Miss Terry's dresses, which certainly did not lack bold originality. There was the curious peacock blue and malachite green dress which contrasted with the locks of copper-coloured hair, from which the half American artist, Mr. Sargent, formed a striking but not very pleasing portrait.

performance some £2,000 had been paid for seats at the box-office.

While allowing due praise to the accomplishments and sagacity of our dramatic critics, I confess to looking with some distrust and alarm at a sort of "new criticism" which, like the so-called "new humour," has developed in these latter days. This amounts to the assumption of an aggressive personality—there is a constant manifestation, not of the play or performers criticised, but of the writer's own thoughts and opinions. It seems to be the fashion for a critic to devote his article to Mr. ——, an opposing critic, as though the public attached any importance to the opinions these gentlemen held of each other. The vanity thus unconsciously displayed is often ludicrous enough. The instances, however, are fortunately rare.

Produced on December 29th, the play caused considerable excitement among Shakespearian students and "constant readers"; and Miss Terry's reading —or rather the appearance of Miss Terry in the part—produced much vehement controversy. We had "The Real Macbeth" in the *Daily Telegraph*, with the usual "old playgoers" who had seen Mrs. Charles Kean. I fancy there were but three or four persons who were able to compare the performance of Miss Terry with that of Mrs. Siddons—about sixty years before.[1]

[1] It was likely that the majority of these persons were incapacitated by age from forming a judgment on this matter; but it was curious that I should have conversed with two persons at least who were capable of making the comparison. One was Mr.

Banquo's ghost has always been the difficulty in every presentation of the play ; all modern apparitions and phantasmagorian effects neutralise or destroy themselves. The powerful light behind exhibits the figure through the gauzes, but to procure this effect the lights in front must be lowered or darkened. This gives notice in clumsy fashion of what is coming, and prepares us for the ghost.

" New and original " readings rarely seem acceptable, and, indeed, are scarcely ever welcomed by the public, who have their old favourite lines to which they are well accustomed. We never hear one of these novelties without an effect being left as of something " purely fantastical," as Elia has it, and invariably they seem unacceptable and forced, producing surprise rather than pleasure. Irving rarely introduced these changes. A curious one in ' Macbeth ' was the alteration of a line—

> " She should have died hereafter,"

into

> " She would have died hereafter."

Fladgate of the Garrick Club, a most interesting man, well stored with anecdotes of Kemble, Kean, and others, who, in the library of the club, gave me a vivid delineation of the good John's methods in ' The Stranger.' The other was Mr. Charles Villiers. A most characteristic incident was a letter from the veteran Mrs. Keeley, with much generous criticism of Miss Terry's performance, thus showing none of the old narrow spirit which can only " praise bygone days." She frankly added that until visiting the Lyceum she had never witnessed a performance of the play from one end to the other, though she had seen many a great performer in it, and had herself performed in it. This recalls Mrs. Pritchard, one of the great Lady Macbeths, who, as Dr. Johnson said, had never seen the fifth act, as it did not fall within her part.

That is a sort of careless dismissal of his wife's
death, as something that must have occurred, according to the common lot.   But who could condone the
strange reading of the passage, " What, if we fail,"
&c., to which Miss Terry, in a light, pleasant way
replied, " We fail"; in other words, "Why, we fail—
that's all " ?   The true, obvious meaning being " *We*
fail!" a thing not to be thought of.   It seems incredible
that Irving should have conceived such a reading.

The irresolution and generally dejected tone of
the Scottish King, as presented by the actor, was
much criticised, and severely too.   There was something "craven," it was said, in this constant faltering
and shrinking.   This, however, was the actor's conscientious "reading" of the part : he was not bound
by the Kemble or Macready traditions, but irresistibly impelled to adopt the highly-coloured
"romantic" view of our day.   He made it
interesting and picturesque, and, in parts, forcible.
When, later, he gave readings of the play, his
conception had become firm and matured—it was
a very interesting and thoughtful performance.
Miss Terry's Lady Macbeth filled every one with
wonder and admiration ; as in the case of her
Queen Katharine, it seemed a miracle of energy
and dramatic inspiration triumphing over physical
difficulties and habitual associations.   The task was
herculean, and even those who objected could not
restrain their admiration. [1]

[1] Charles Reade's strange, odd appreciation of this gifted,
mercurial woman is worth preserving :—

"Ellen Terry is an enigma.   Her eyes are pale, her nose

The pictures set forth in this wonderful representation linger in the memory. The gloomy Scottish scenes, the castles and their halls, the fine spreading landscapes, the treatment of the witches, and Banquo's ghost, were all but perfect in tone, and were treated with a judicious reserve. There was nothing overdone. How admirably and exactly, for instance, did the scene correspond to the beautiful lines :—

> " This castle hath a pleasant seat ; the air
> Nimbly and sweetly recommends itself."

There painting and poetry went together! The banqueting-hall, the arrangement of the tables, at right angles with the audience, had a strange, barbaric effect, the guests being disposed in the most natural and unceremonious fashion.

After the run of 'Macbeth' had ceased, the manager proceeded to carry out a plan which had long been in his thoughts, and which many had

rather long, her mouth nothing particular, complexion a delicate brick-dust, her hair rather like tow. Yet, somehow, she is *beautiful*. Her expression *kills* any pretty face you see beside her. Her figure is lean and bony, her hand masculine in size and form. Yet she is a pattern of fawn-like grace. Whether in movement or repose, grace *pervades the hussy*. In character impulsive, intelligent, weak, hysterical—in short, all that is abominable and charming in woman. Ellen Terry is a very charming actress. I see through and through her. Yet she pleases me all the same. *Little Duck !*"

This suggests the old rhyme :—

> "Thou hast so many pleasing, teazing ways about thee,
> There's no living with thee or without thee."

suggested to him. This was to give "readings," in conjunction with Miss Terry, of some of his plays. This would offer some respite from the enormous outlay entailed by producing these great pieces at his theatre, and which, it is clear, were already straining his resources. For here is the penalty of this sort of dram drinking—the dose must be made stronger with each successive draught. We found ourselves gazing vacantly on some gorgeous and elaborate display which had cost time, labour, and money, but which did not excel previous efforts. All expected, as of right, that he would "go one better." One could fancy that nothing could be more attractive than such "readings," the interest in the personality of the two great performers being so generally diffused. He rearranged 'Macbeth' for this purpose, and set off on a tour in the provinces. But though everywhere well received, I think the plan did not command the full success that was expected. There was a defect somehow in the plan : two characters seemed to rob the performance of that *unity* which is the charm of a reading. Further, it was illustrated by the fine music, with orchestra, &c., and this again disturbed the natural simplicity of a reading. The actor's own vividly-coloured imagination and tastes could not, in fact, be content with the bald and *triste* mechanisms of the ordinary reader : he tried to impart what ornamentation he could. The experiment was not, however, carried out very long.[1]

[1] It was interesting to note, at a St. James's Hall performance, June 25th, the pleasant, eager vivacity of the actress, who, familiar

Some thirty years before, in the old Adelphi days, when "Ben" Webster was ruling, a drama was produced, the work of a hard-working, drudging dramatist, Watts Phillips. It was a pure melodrama, and people had not yet lost their faith in the old devices. There was an honest belief that villainy would be punished ere the end came. By the laws of such pieces, the most painful situations were always contrasted with scenes of broadest farce, which were supposed to relieve the excited feelings. I well recall these humours. On the revival, however, all this was softened away or abolished, and, I fancy, not without injury to the constitution of the old piece.

This production of 'The Dead Heart' furnished one more instance of the tact and abilities which secured the manager of the Lyceum his high position. Here was a piece of an old-fashioned kind, which, had it been "revived" at an ordinary theatre, would have been found not only flat and stale, but unprofitable for all concerned. Our manager, seeing that it had dramatic life, enriched it, brought the whole into harmony with the times, and, by the skilful *remaniement* of Mr. Walter Pollock, imparted to it a romantic grace. It is admitted that he himself has rarely been fitted with

as she was with the play, seemed to be repeating with her lips all the portions in which she was not concerned. In the more dramatic portions, it was plain she was eager to be on the scene once more. As she sat she anxiously waited for the orchestra to come in at their proper places, sometimes giving them the signal. This very natural behaviour interested every one.

a part so suited to his genius and capacities, or in which he has roused the sympathies of his audience more thoroughly. It is only the romantic actor that understands what might be called the *key* of a play.

In this picturesque part of Robert Landry were exhibited no fewer than four contrasted phases of character : the gay, hopeful young artist ; the terribly metamorphosed prisoner of nearly twenty years ; the recently delivered man, newly restored to the enjoyment of life ; and, lastly, the grim revolutionary chief, full of stern purpose of vengeance. This offered an opening for the display of versatile gifts, which were certainly brought out in the most striking contrast. But it was in the later scenes of the play, when he appears as the revolutionary chief, that our " manager-actor " exhibited all his resources. Nothing was more artistic than the sense of restraint and reserve here shown, which is founded on human nature. A person who has thus suffered, and with so stern a purpose in view, will be disdainful of speech, and oppressed, as it were, with his terrible design. Quiet, condensed purpose, without any " fiendish " emphasis, was never better suggested. Even when the drop-scene is raised, and he is revealed standing by his table, there is the same morose, unrelenting air, with an impression that here was one who had just passed through the fire, and had been executing an act of vengeance which had left its mark.

In a drama like ' The Dead Heart,' music forms a fitting accompaniment, furnishing colour and ap-

propriate illustration. It is almost uninterrupted
from beginning to end. M. Jacobi, of the Alhambra,
furnished some effective, richly-coloured strains,
alternately gay and lugubrious. More, however,
might have been made of the stirring "Marseillaise,"
which could have been treated in various disguises
and patterns as a sort of *Leitmotiv*, much as Litolf
has done in his symphonic work on the same subject. It was a strange coincidence that Dickens
was writing his "Tale of Two Cities" at the time
the dramatist was busy with his work. There were
the same incidents and the same *finale*, and charges
of plagiarism were freely made. [1]

A Scotch play—an adaptation of "The Bride of
Lammermoor"—was now prepared by Mr. Herman
Merivale, a dramatist of much poetical feeling, but
whose course was marked by piteous and disastrous
incidents. Buoyed up by the encouragement and
admiration of his friends, and of kindly critics who
found merit in all he did, he struggled on in spite
of miserable health and a too highly-strung nervous
temperament. His work showed refinement and
elegance, but it was more for the reader than the
playgoer. A gleam of prosperity, however, came
when Mr. Toole began to figure in the writer's
grotesque pieces, 'The Don,' and others—to
which, indeed, the author's wife had contributed
some share.

The new piece, which was called 'Ravenswood,'
had lain long in the manager's cabinet, where

[1] This incident will be found discussed in my "Life of
Dickens."

15

reposed a number of other MSS., "commanded" and already purchased, from the pens of Wills, Calmour, Frank Marshall, and others. The latter had fashioned Robert Emmett into a picturesque figure, the figure and bearing of the manager having no doubt much that suggested the Irish patriot; but the troubled period of Land Leagues and agrarian violence set in at the time of its acceptance with an awkward *à propos*.[1] There is a character, indeed, in one of Boz's early stories, in which, as the tradition runs, Irving formerly made almost as deep an impression as in 'The Bells.' This was Bill Sikes, and we can conceive what a savagery he would have imparted to it. It

---

[1] Another play was written for him on the subject of 'Mahomet,' which he was inclined to bring out; but here again authority interposed, and "invited him," as the French so politely have it, to abandon his purpose. It was at the end of the summer season of 1879 that our manager, after naming these pieces, spoke of others which he had in reserve, either revivals or wholly new ones. It is interesting to think that he had thought of the stormy and pathetic 'Gamester,' which has ever an absorbing attraction; 'The Stranger' also was spoken of; but their treatment would have offered too many points of similarity to Eugene Aram and other characters of "inspissated gloom." On this occasion, when speaking of "the romantic and pathetic story" of Emmett, he announced a drama on the subject of Rienzi, which his friend Wills had prepared for him, but which has never yet seen the light. Years have rolled by swiftly since that night, and Wills was often heard to bewail the delays and impediments which hindered the production of what he no doubt considered his finest performance. Another great drama long promised and long due was 'Coriolanus,' for which Mr. Alma Tadema designed scenery, and which was at last produced a few years before the manager's death.

would seem to be exactly suited to his powers and to his special style; though, of course, here there would be a suggestion of Dubosc. With Miss Terry as Nancy here would have been opened a realm of squalid melodrama, and "Raquin-like" horrors.

There are other effective pieces which seemed to invite the performance of this accomplished pair. Such, for instance, is the pathetic, heartrending 'Venice Preserved.' Though there might be a temptation here for the scenic artist—since Venice, and its costumes, &c., would stifle the simple pathos of the drama. 'The Taming of the Shrew' had been often suggested and often thought of, but it had been effectively done at this theatre by another company. 'The Jealous Wife'—Mr. and Mrs. Oakley—would also have suited well. There was 'The Winter's Tale,' and finally 'Three Weeks after Marriage'—one of the most diverting pieces of farcical comedy that can be conceived.

'Ravenswood' was produced on September 20, 1890. While its scenes were being unfolded before us one could not but feel the general weakness of the literary structure, which was unequal to the rich and costly setting; neither did it correspond to the broad and limpid texture of the original story. It was unfortunately cast, as I venture to think. Mackintosh, who performed Caleb, was somewhat artificial; while Ashton *père* and his lady, rendered by Bishop and Miss Le Thière, could hardly be taken *au sérieux*. Irving infused a deep and gloomy pathos into his part, and Miss Terry was, as ever, interesting, touching, and charming. But the characters, as was the story, were little more than thinly outlined. The scenes, however, unfolded themselves with fine spectacular effect; nothing could be more impressive than the scene of the first act—a mountain gorge where Ravenswood has come for the entombment of his father, and is interrupted by the arrival of his enemy, Ashton. The weird-like last scene, the "Kelpie Sands," with the cloak lying on the place of disappearance, the retainer gazing in despair, was one of Irving's finely poetical conceptions, but it was more spectacular than dramatic. The truth is, where there is so great a theatre, and where all arts are supplied to set off a piece in sumptuous style, these elements require substantial stuff to support them, otherwise the effect becomes trivial in exact proportion to the adornment.

It was at the Christmas season of 1891 that the manager was enabled to carry out a plan that had for years been before him—a revival of 'Henry VIII.' We can quite conceive how, as the fashion always was with him, the play ripened as it were with meditation; how, as he walked or followed the consoling fumes of his cigar in his chamber at Grafton Street, each scene fell into shape or suggested some new and effective arrangement, which again might be discarded as difficulties arose, or as something happier occurred to him. The result of these meditations was unquestionably a "large" and splendid setting of the play, which, to my mind, whatever be the value of the opinion, is certainly one of the finest, most finished, most poetical, and sufficient of the many works that he set before us.[1]   There was a greater Shakespearian propriety, and the adornments, however lavish, might all be fairly justified.   Most to be admired was the supreme elegance of touch found in every direction—acting, scenery, dresses, music, all reflected the one cultivated mind.   The truth is, long practice and the due measuring of his own exertion had supplied an ease and boldness in his effects.   To appreciate this excellence we have only to turn to similar attempts made by others, whether managers or manager-actors, or manager-authors—when we find only the conventional exertion of the scene-painter and stage-manager. They have not the same inspiration.

This play, produced on January 5, 1892, was received with great enthusiasm.   It became "a

---

[1] An American lady, a Californian artist, was the first to enter the pit for the opening performance of 'Henry VIII.' at the Lyceum.   "I and a friend went with our camp-stools and took our places next the door at ten o'clock in the morning.   We were provided with a volume of *Harper's Magazine*, a sketch-book, writing-paper, and a fountain-pen, caricatures of Henry Irving, and much patience.   A newspaper spread under the feet and a Japanese muff warmer, with sandwiches and a bottle of wine, kept us comfortable.   Two ladies were the next comers, and shortly a crowd began to collect.   Real amusing it was, but not very elegant.   After about two hours Mr. Bram Stoker came and had a look at us, and cheered our hearts by telling us that tea would be served from the neighbouring saloon (public-house). At last, at seven o'clock, we were rewarded for our patience by getting seats in the front row.   The play was superb, and the audience—well, every one looked as if he had done something."

common form " of criticism to repeat that it was
of doubtful authorship; that it was nothing but a
number of scenes strung together; that there was
no story; that Buckingham vanished almost at the
beginning of the play; and that towards the end,
Wolsey vanished also. These, as I venture to say,
are but ignorant objections; characters will always
supply a dramatic story, or a dramatic interest that
amounts to a story, and in the fate of Wolsey and
of Katharine, gradually developed and worked out,
we had surely a story sufficiently interesting.

I have little doubt that Irving kept steadily in
view the object the great author had before him,
viz., to present a page of history enriched by all
the suitable accompaniments of dress and manners
and customs. In this he was perfectly and triumphantly successful. We were taken into the great
chambers and tribunals; shown the ecclesiastical
pomp and state, so difficult to conceive of now; the
processions passing through the streets, and presented in an exceedingly natural and unconven-
tional fashion.[1] The drama was set forth fully,
with every adjunct of dress, furniture, scenes, and
numbers of auxiliaries.

The scenery, offering wonderful perspectives of

---

[1] As an instance of the manager's happy touch in a trifling
matter, we might name the State trumpets constantly " blaring "
and sounding as the King approached, which offered nothing
of the usual " super " arrangement. The men seemed to tramp
along the street as though conscious of their own dignity, warning those whom it might concern to make way for their high
and puissant lord.

IRVING AS "CARDINAL WOLSEY."
Photo by W. & D. Downey, 57 Ebury St., S.W.

ace p. 214.

Tudor halls and interiors, the arrangements of the courts and various meetings, were original and very striking. Yet here I should be inclined to suggest anew the objections often made to the modern system of large groupings compressed into the small area of a stage, which, as it seems, is opposed to the canons of scenic art.[1] These, too, seemed to acquire new force from the arrangement of the " Trial Scene," as it was called, which displayed a great hall with the daïs, seats for the Cardinal, the King, &c. This was, of course, only of the size of the stage—about a third, perhaps, of the original. The result of thus supplying a great area by the system of compression (I am speaking merely of the principle), is that the leading figures become dwindled in scale and overpowered by the surrounding crowd. The contrast with the older system is brought out by Harlow's well-known picture, where only the leading figures are grouped, and where by consequence they stand out in greater relief. The spectator stands, as it were, close beside them ; but by the modern arrangement he appears to be afar off, at the bottom of the hall, obtaining but a distant view of them.[2]

[1] It was publicly stated that the "mounting" of this play had cost £15,000, and that the weekly expenses were some £800. The manager wrote to contradict this, as being altogether beyond the truth ; though, he added, with a sigh as it were, that he heartily wished the second statement were true, and that the expenses could be put at so low a figure.

[2] According to one writer, " an emissary was sent to Rome to acquire a Cardinal's robe. After some time a friend managed to secure one of the very period, whereupon an exact copy, 'both

When we consider what are the traditions of the
two great characters, how vivid they are, from the
deep impressions left by the great brother and sister
on their contemporaries—an impression which has
really extended to our time—too much praise could
hardly be given to the performance of Irving and
his gifted companion.   Irving's Wolsey was exactly
what those familiar with his other impersonations
could anticipate—poetical, elegant, and in many
portions powerful.   He was the Churchman to
perfection, carrying his robes admirably ; in the
face there was a suggestion of the late departed
Cardinal Manning.   All through the piece there
was that picturesque acting which fills the eye, not
the ear, at the moment when speech is at rest.   It
is thus that are confuted those theorists, including
Elia, who hold that Shakespeare is to be read, not
acted.

It is, perhaps, the power of suggestion and of

of colour and texture,' was made.   A price has to be paid for
scenic splendours in the shape of the delays that they necessarily
occasion.   Thanks to the ingenuity of stage-carpenters and
machinists, these delays at the Lyceum are reduced to a minimum time.   ' Henry VIII.' being not one of the longest of
the plays—though it is one-third longer than ' Macbeth '—the
text at the Lyceum has been treated with comparative leniency.
' Hamlet,' on the other hand, which comprises nearly four
thousand lines, cannot on the modern system of sumptuous
mounting possibly be given in anything approaching its en-
tirety." As a fact, very nearly one-half the play disappears
from the modern acting copies.   My friend, Mr. W. Pollock,
in a paper in the *National Review*, has justly urged in this
connection that half a ' Hamlet ' is better than no ' Hamlet '
at all.

stirring our imagination that brings about this air
of fulness and richness. Irving, when he was not
speaking, *acted* the pomp and state and consum-
mately depicted the smoothness of the Cardinal.
When he was lost to view you felt the application
of the oft-quoted line touching the absence of " the
well-grac'd " actor from the scene ; and it was wonderful to think, as we glanced round the brilliant
salle—glittering with its vast crowd of well-dressed,
even jewelled, women (" Quite an opera pit ! " as
Ellison would say)—to the fine stage before us,
with its showy figures, pictures, and pageants,
that all this was *his* work and of his creation !

There were many diverse criticisms on Irving's
conception of this famous character ; some held that
it was scarcely " large," rude, or overbearing enough.
His view, however, as carried out, seemed natural
and consistent. The actor wished to exhibit the
character as completely overwhelmed by adverse
fortune ; witness Macbeth, Othello, and many other
characters. In the last great soliloquy it was urged
there was a want of variety. Still, allowing for all
traditional defects, it stands beyond contradiction
that it was a " romantic " performance, marked by
" distinction," and a fine grace ; far superior to the
thin theatrical clericalism of " Becket " ; and we
might vainly look around for any performer of our
time who could impart so poetical a cast to the
character. And we may add a praise which I am
specially qualified to give, viz., that he was the
perfect ecclesiastic : as he sat witnessing the revels,
now disturbed, now careless—there was the Church-

man revealed ; he was not, as was the case with so many others, a performer robed in clerical garb.

Of Miss Terry's Queen Katharine, it can be said that it was an *astonishing* performance, and took even her admirers by surprise. She made the same almost gigantic effort as she did in ' Macbeth ' to interpret a vast character, one that might have seemed beyond her strength, physical as well as mental. By sheer force of will and genius she contrived to triumph. It was not, of course, the *great* Queen Katharine of Mrs. Siddons, nor did she awe and command all about her ; but such earnestness and reality and dramatic power did she impart to the character that she seemed to supply the absence of greater gifts. Her performance at the Court and other scenes of the persecuted, hunted woman, now irritated, now resigned, was truly pathetic and realistic. There may have been absent the overpowering, queen-like dignity, the state and heroism, but it was impossible to resist her—it was her " way," and by this way she gained all hearts. It must be confessed that nothing ever supplied such an idea of the talents and "cleverness" of this truly brilliant woman as her victory over the tremendous difficulties of these parts. The performance won her the sympathies of all in an extraordinary degree.

So admirably had our manager been penetrated with the spirit of the scenes, that he was enabled to present them in a natural and convincing way, and seemed to revive the whole historic time and meaning of the situation. This was particularly shown

in the scene when Buckingham is led to execution ;
his address to the crowd was delivered with so
natural a fashion, with such judicious and pathetic
effect, that it not only gained admiration for the
performance, but brought the scene itself within
range of every-day life.   For, instead of the old
conventional declamatory speech to a stage crowd,
we had some " words" which the sufferer, on entering the boat, stopped for a moment to address to
sympathisers who met him on the way.

The music, the work of a young composer, Mr.
Edward German, was truly romantic and expressive ;
stately and richly-coloured.   How wonderful, by the
way, is the progress made of late years in theatrical
music !   We have now a group of composers who
expend their talents and elegancies in the adornment of the stage.   The flowing melodies and
stately marches of the Lyceum music still linger in
the ear, while portions, such as the dances, &c.,
have become stock pieces for orchestras.

It was in January, 1892, when he was performing
in ' Henry VIII.,' that a very alarming piece of
news, much magnified by report, reached him.   His
son Laurence was playing at Belfast in the Benson
Company, and had by some accident shot himself
with a revolver ; this casualty was exaggerated to
an extraordinary degree.   Three local doctors issued
bulletins ; " the lung had been pierced "—until the
anxious father at last sent over an experienced surgeon, Mr. Lawson Tait, who was able to report that
the wound was trivial, and the weapon a sort of " toy
pistol."   Much sympathy was excited by this casualty.

CHAPTER XV

1892

'KING LEAR'—'BECKET'

AFTER presenting so many of Shakespeare's great dramas, it was to be expected that the manager could not well pass by what has been justly styled the Titanic play of 'King Lear.' This had, indeed, always been in his thoughts; but he naturally shrank from the tremendous burden and physical strain that it entailed. It was prepared in his usual sumptuous style. There were sixteen changes of scene and twenty-two characters, and the music was furnished by Hamilton Clarke. The scenery was divided between Craven and Harker, the latter a very effective artist of the same school. There were some beautiful romantic effects: the halls, the heath, and notably the Dover scenes, were exquisite. I doubt if their presentation has been excelled by any preceding attempts. The barbaric tone and atmosphere of the piece was conveyed to perfection, without being insisted on or emphasised. It is only when we compare the ambitious attempts of other managers who would indulge in effects equally lavish and sumptuous, that we recognise the ability, ease, reserve and force of the Lyceum manager.[1] They, too, will have their "archæology" and their built-up temples, designed by painters of repute, and crowds; but there is present only the sense of stage effect and the flavour of the supernumerary. The secret is the perfect subordination of such details to the general effect. They should be, like the figures on a tapestry, indistinct, but effective as a background. Charles Lamb's well-worn dictum, that 'Lear' should never be acted, was trotted forth in every criticism. There is some truth in this exaggerated judgment, because it can never be *adequately* presented, and the performance must always fall short of the original grandeur. With his remarks on the pettiness of the stage-storm, one would be inclined to agree, even on this occasion, when every art was exhausted to convey the notion of the turmoil of the elements. The truth is, an audience sitting in the stalls and boxes will never be seduced into accepting the rollings and crashings of cannon-balls aloft, and the flashing of lycopodium, as suggesting the awful warring of the elements.

'King Lear' was brought forward on Thursday,

---

[1] To illustrate his most recent productions, the manager was accustomed to issue what is called "a souvenir," an artistic series of pictures of the scenes, groupings, &c. It may be added, as a proof of the pictorial interest of the Lyceum productions, that in little more than a week after the first performance of 'Becket' no fewer than five-and-twenty illustrations, some of great pretension, had appeared in the papers. On the first night of 'Lear' a marchioness of artistic tastes was seen making sketches, which were published in an evening paper.

November 10, 1892, and its presentation was a truly romantic one. The figure had little of the usual repulsive aspects of age—the clumsy white beard, &c.—but was picturesque. The entry into his barbaric court, the strange retainers with their head-dresses of cows' horns, was striking and original. The whole conception was human. The "curse" was delivered naturally. In presenting, however, the senile ravings of the old monarch, the actor unavoidably assumed an indistinctness of utterance, and many sentences were lost. This imperfection was dwelt on in the criticisms with superfluous iteration, and though the actor speedily amended and became almost emphatically distinct, this notion seemed to have settled in the public mind, with some prejudice to the success of the piece. Though he was thus quick to remedy this blemish, distinctness had to be secured by deliberation, and at some loss of effect. The actor's extraordinary exertions—for he was at the same time busy with the preparation of a new piece—exhausted him, and obliged him for some nights to entrust the part to another. But the real obstacle to full success could be found in the general lugubrious tone of the character; the uninterrupted sequence of horrors and distresses led to a feeling of monotony difficult for the actor to vanquish. The public never takes very cordially to pieces in which there is this *sustained misery*, though it can relish the alternations of poignant tragedy attended by quick dramatic changes. Cordelia, though a small part, was made prominent by much touching pathos and grace, and the dying recognition by the old King brought tears to many eyes.[1]

An interesting feature in Irving's career had been his long friendship with Tennyson, poet and dramatist, which lasted for some fifteen or sixteen years. The actor had shown his appreciation of the poet's gifts by the rather hazardous experiment of presenting two of his poetical dramas to the public. We have seen what sumptuous treatment was accorded to 'The Cup'; and in 'Queen Mary' the actor contributed his most powerful dramatic efforts in the realisation of the grim Philip.[2]

The poet, however, made little allowance for the exigencies of the stage. During the preparation of 'The Cup,' he contended eagerly for the retention of long speeches and scenes, which would have shipwrecked the piece. Yet, undramatic as most of his dramas are, a taste for them was springing up, and not long before his death he had the gratification of knowing that his 'Foresters' had met with

[1] One touch, which might escape the superficial, showed the fine, delicate sense of the manager. The scene where Kent is exhibited in the stocks has always suggested something grotesque and prosaic. It was here so dignified in its treatment as to become almost pathetic. I may add here that the deepest strokes of Shakespeare, not being on the surface, are apt to escape us altogether, save when some inspired critic lays his finger on them. The faithful Kent at the close is brought to his master's notice, who does not recognise him. Here Lamb points out how noble is Kent's self-sacrifice in not bringing himself to the King's recollection.

[2] As I write, Whistler's portrait of him in this character—a picture, dark, misty and colourless—was sold for over £3,000.

surprising success in America. No less than six
pieces of his have been produced, and though the
idea prevails that he has been "a failure" as a
dramatist, it will be found that on the whole he has
been successful. It may be that by and by he will
be in higher favour. But he will have owed much
to Irving, not merely for presenting his plays with
every advantage, but for putting them into fitting
shape, with firm, unerring touch removing all that
is superfluous.

So far back as the year 1879 the poet had placed
in Irving's hands a drama on the subject of Becket
and the fair Rosamund. It was really a *poem* of
moderate length, though in form a drama, and the
actor naturally shrank from the difficulties of dealing
with such a piece. The "pruning knife" would here
have been of little avail; the axe or "chopper"
would have to be used unsparingly. The piece was
accordingly laid aside for that long period; the
lamented death of the poet probably removed the
chief obstacle to its production.[1] It was repeated,
indeed, that almost one-half was cut away before it
could be put in shape for performance. On Monday,
February 6, 1893—the actor's birthday—this posthu-
mous piece was brought out with every advantage,
and before an assemblage even more brilliant than
usual. It revived the memories of the too recent
'Henry VIII.,' in which there is much the same
struggle between Prince and Bishop. The actor
has thus no less than three eminent Catholic

[1] It has been said however, that the poet learned on his
death-bed of the actor's intentions.

ecclesiastics in his *répertoire*—Richelieu, Wolsey, and Becket; but, as he pleasantly said, he could contrast with these an English clergyman, the worthy Dr. Primrose, Vicar of Wakefield. Yet he admirably and dramatically distinguished their several characters.

There is always a curiosity to have the curtain lifted, so that we may have a glimpse of a play in the throes and troubles of rehearsal. A writer in one of the magazines gave a very dramatic sketch of how things were conducted during the preparation of 'Becket':—

" After Mr. Irving has grouped the men on the benches, he steps back and looks at the table. 'We ought to have on it some kind of mace or crozier,' he says—'a large crozier. Now for the "make-up." All the barons and every one who has a moustache must wear a small beard. All the gentlemen who have no beards remain unshaven. All the priests and bishops are unshaven. The mob can have slight beards, but this is unimportant. Now, take off your hats, gentlemen, please. Some of you must be old, some young. Hair very short;' and he passes from group to group selecting the different people. 'Now, I think that is all understood pretty well. Where are the sketches for dresses?'

" The sketches are brought, and he goes carefully through them. Miss Terry and Mr. Terriss also look over the big white sheets of paper. The fox-terrier strolls up to the group, gives a glance at them, and walks back again to Miss Terry's chair with a slightly cynical look. Then Mr. Irving

16

returns to the groups by the benches. 'Remember, gentlemen, you must be arguing here, laying down the law in this way,' suiting the action to the word. 'Just arrange who is to argue. Don't do it promiscuously, but three or four of you together. Try to put a little action into it. I want you to show your arms, and not to keep them glued to your sides like trussed fowls. No; that isn't half enough action. Don't be frightened. Better make too much noise rather than too little, but don't stop too suddenly. Start arguing when I ring the first bell. As I ring the second bell, you see me enter, and stop.' The dog stands one bell, but the second annoys him, and he disappears from the stage altogether, until the people on the benches have finished their discussion.

"Mr. Irving next tries the three-cornered stools which are placed around the table, but prefers square ones. The dog returns, walks over to the orchestra, looks vainly for a rat, and retreats under the table in the centre of the stage as if things were getting really too much for him. But his resting-place is ill-chosen, for presently half a dozen angry lords jump on the table, and he is driven forth once more. After a stormy scene with the lords, Mr. Irving walks up the steps again. 'When I say "I depart," you must let me get up the steps. All this time your pent-up anger is waiting to burst out suddenly. Don't go to sleep over it.' He looks at the table in the centre of the stage, and turns to a carpenter. 'This table will never do. It has to be jumped on by so many people that it must be

[*Drawn by C. A. Buchel.*

IRVING AS " BECKET."

[*To face page* 226.

very strong. They follow me.' (To Miss Terry) 'They'd better catch hold of me, up the steps here.'

"Miss Terry: 'They must do something. They can't stand holding you like that.'

"Mr. Irving: 'No.' The door opens suddenly at top of steps, and discovers the crowd, who shout, 'Blessed is he that cometh in the name of the Lord.'

"The doors open and the crowd shout, but the effect is not good.

"Miss Terry: 'It would be better if it were done at the foot of the steps. The people needn't show their faces as they do it, and the effect will be so much better.'" 'Becket' contained thirty characters, and was set off by fine scenery and excellent music, written specially by Professor Stanford, this not being the first time his notes had been associated with the poet.

Never had Irving's efforts been greeted with such overpowering, tumultuous applause. At the end of every act there were as many as five "recalls." In such pieces, as well as in some of Shakespeare's, there is always a matter of interesting debate in fixing the era, dresses, architecture, &c.—points perhaps of less importance than is supposed. Irving's conception of 'Becket' was truly picturesque and romantic; he imported a pathetic tone, with a sort of gloomy foreboding of the impending martyrdom, conveyed by innumerable touches. The actor had the art of moulding his features and expression to the complexion of the character he was performing nightly. Thus, in 'Becket,' it could be seen that he had already assumed the meditative, wary look of the aspiring ecclesiastic.

It is evidence of the interest excited by 'Becket,' that a little discussion arose between a Benedictine Father and another ecclesiastic on the hymn, "Telluris ingens Conditor," which was played in the cathedral scene and through the piece. The Benedictine contended that it must have been some older form of the hymn before the pseudo-classification "of the Breviary Hymns in the sixteenth century." "I do not suppose," he added, "that Mr. Irving's well-known attention to detail extends to such *minutiæ* as these. The famous cathedral scene, in his presentment of 'Much Ado About Nothing,' was received with a chorus of praise as a marvel of liturgical accuracy. But I am told that to Catholic eyes at least some of its details appeared incorrect." Thus, to the monastery even, did the fame of our manager's efforts reach!

One of the most remarkable things connected with 'Becket' was the unanimous applause and approbation of the entire press.[1] Even one or two

[1] On March 18, 1893, Irving and his whole company were bidden to Windsor Castle to play 'Becket' before her late Majesty. A theatre was fitted up in the Waterloo Chamber; special scenery was painted; the Lyceum was closed; and the company, 170 strong, was transported to Windsor and brought back on the same night. The performance was given with much effect and to the enjoyment of the Queen. Some three or four years before, a no less interesting entertainment was arranged at Sandringham by the Prince of Wales, who was anxious that Her Majesty should see the two favourite performers in their most effective pieces—'The Bells' and the "Trial scene" in 'The Merchant of Venice.' The

IRVING READING TENNYSON'S ' BECKET ''
IN THE RESTORED CHAPTER-HOUSE OF CANTERBURY CATHEDRAL.
Drawn by S. Begg.

evening papers, which had spoken with a little hesitation, returned to the subject a few nights later to correct their judgment and to admit that they had been hasty. All confessed that they had been captivated by the picturesqueness of the central figure.

For Tennyson he always retained the warmest regard. " Lord Tennyson," he once observed, " was one of the greatest of men, and one of the dearest and best of friends. One of the most touching incidents which I remember occurred while he was on his death-bed. You know that some of his plays lacked playing qualities. One night before his death he turned to his physician, Dr. Dabbs, who told me of the incident, and said : ' I suppose I shall never see " Becket " ? ' ' I fear not,' said the doctor. ' When do they produce " Becket " ? ' ' I think in May,' was the reply. ' They did not do me justice with " The Promise of May," ' said the dying poet ; ' but Irving will do me justice in " Becket." ' Of that remark and confidence I was justly proud," concluded Irving. He once suggested Dante as the theme for a play. Tennyson at first seemed pleased with the subject, but after thinking for a few moments he said slowly, " Yes ; but where would

outlay of time, trouble, and skilful management to provide for all the arrangements within a short space of time can scarcely be imagined. The pecuniary cost, owing to the closing of the theatre, transport, &c., was serious. Yet the general impression, on the whole, was that Her Majesty did not relish, or perhaps did not quite understand, this new school of acting, being accustomed to more old-fashioned methods.

you find a Dante to write it?" And he thereupon gave up the idea.

Apart from his professional gifts, Irving was assuredly one of those figures that filled the public eye, and of which there are but few. This was owing to a sort of sympathetic attraction, and to an absence of affectation. He played many parts in the social scheme, and always did so with judiciousness, contributing to the effect of the situation. His utterances on most subjects were thoughtful and well considered, and contributed to the enlightenment of the case. At his examination by the London County Council, when many absurd questions were put to him, he answered with much sagacity. His views on the employment of children in theatres were truly sensible. More remarkable, however, were his opinions on the science of acting, the art of management, and of dealing with audiences and other kindred topics, which show much thought and knowledge. He has, in truth, written a great deal, and his various "discourses," recently collected in a pretty little volume, do credit to his literary style and power of expression.[1]

---

[1] An Irving "Bibliography" would fill many columns, and would include a vast quantity of controversial writing—attacks, defences and discussions. Besides his official discourses, he has written many agreeable papers in the leading "monthlies." I have already spoken of the "skits" and personalities which followed his early successes, and which he encountered with excellent temper and a patient shrug. These have long since been forgotten. At attempts at "taking him off," though a favourite pastime, he could afford to smile; though when it was carried beyond legitimate bounds, as in the instance of the late Mr. Leslie, he

There have been many laments over the fleeting, evanescent character of an actor's efforts. If his success be triumphant, it is only a dream for those who have not seen. Description gives but the faintest idea of his gifts. The writer, as it were, continues to write after his death, and is read, as he was in his lifetime. But the player gone, the play is over. The actor, it is true, if he be a personality, has another audience outside his theatre. As I have shown in these pages, he can attract by force of character the interest and sympathies of the general community. Whatever he does, or wherever he appears, eyes are turned to him as they would be to one on a stage. There was a sort of indulgent partiality in the case of Irving. He was a dramatic figure, much as was Charles Dickens. Eyes are idly bent on him that enters next. And this high position was never disturbed during his life; and though all popularity is precarious enough, he had the art and tact to adapt his position to the shifty, capricious changes of taste, and in the hackneyed phrase was

interposed with quiet firmness, and put it down in the interests of the profession. An American burlesque actor, named Dixie, with execrable taste gave an imitation of him in his presence. More curious was the unconscious imitation which was gaining in the ranks of the profession, and which has had some droll results. Thus one Hudson—when playing the Tetrarch in 'Claudian' in the States—was so strangely like him in manner and speech, that it was assumed by the American audience that he was maliciously "taking him off"! His own company caught up many of his "ways" and fashions—notably Haviland, and even Alexander. At the opening of 'Vanderdecken,' two at least of the performers were mistaken for him—from their walk— and had a "reception" accordingly.

more "up to date" than any person of his time. The fine lines in 'Troilus and Cressida'—the most magnificent in Shakespeare, as they seem to me—should ring in every actor's ear, or indeed in that of every one that enjoys public favour. Alas! it must be his lot to be ever at the oar. There is no relaxing, no repose; no coy retirement, or yielding to importunate rivalry. For—

> " To have done, is to hang quite out of fashion,
> Like a rusty mail in monumental mockery. . . .
> For honour travels in a strait so narrow,
> Where one but goes abreast: keep, then, the path ;
> For emulation hath a thousand sons,
> That one by one pursue: if you give way,
> Or turn aside from the direct forth-right,
> Like to an enter'd tide, they all rush by,
> And leave you hindmost ;—and there you lie
> Like a gallant horse fallen in first rank,
> For pavement to the abject rear, o'er-run
> And trampled on ; then, what they do in present,
> Though less than yours in past, must o'ertop yours."

CHAPTER XVI

1893

'KING ARTHUR'—CORPORAL BREWSTER—HONOURS

WHEN the theatre opened for the season, 'Faust' was revived to fill up the interval, and it drew excellent and satisfactory "houses" until a new piece was got ready. This, it was said, was rchcarscd on board the steamer on the way home. Our actor had long before him the idea of playing the "spotless king," and had the late Laureate been alive he might have been tempted to shape his great poem into a play. As it was, the versatile Comyns Carr was entrusted with the task, and, somewhat to the surprise of the public, he who had been art-critic, manager of Grosvenor and New Galleries, dramatist and designer of dresses, &c., for the Lyceum, now came forward as a poet; and a very respectable poet he proved to be, with harmonious, mellifluous lines, effective from a stage point of view. It must be said, however, that the play is altogether a literary one, and rather lacks dramatic movement. It is really a series of har-

monious recitations set off by beautiful shows, processions, and scenic views. The piece was no doubt
"written in the theatre" under inspiration of the
manager, and supplied exactly what he wanted.
The scenery was designed by Sir E. Burne-Jones,
who supplied some exquisite combinations or arrangements of colour, which were certainly new to
stage-land. The music was Sir Arthur Sullivan's,
and later there was to be the unusual and unprecedented incident of no fewer than *three* knights—a
musician, a painter and an actor—combining their
talents in a single play. Beautiful was the opening
scene with the blue waters and the swimming
maidens imported from ' Rheingold,' with the finding
of the " Excalibur" contrived most skilfully. There
were grand halls and castles, and woodland groves,
all exhibiting much originality of touch, with that
unvarying effective grace and tact which made the
most of the materials. The characters were rather
faintly outlined. King Arthur and his Queen are
comparatively colourless ; so is Elaine. Mr. Forbes
Robertson, who played Lancelot with picturesque
power, was early withdrawn, being bound by some
other engagement. His successor, a pleasing light
comedian, lacked the weight necessary for the character. Miss Terry was, as usual, touching and
pathetic. So refined, so perfect was the general
treatment that it attracted and drew larger and yet
larger houses.

That the element of scenery and decoration is
monstrously overdone to the destruction of acting
there can be no question. The elaborate repro-

duction, or reconstruction, of cities and antique
dresses on the stage is quite outside dramatic art.
In proof of this, what leaves so painful and de-
grading an impression as the passage through the
streets of a cartload of scenes and properties, all
rickety and daubed over with faded colours and
tinsel? Here we may just glance at Mr. Gordon
Craig's new system, which—though crude and
unscientific as yet—is still a step in the right
direction. His principle would seem a sort of
indistinct generality or misty treatment carried out
by the agency of dark draperies. I recall a church
interior represented in this fashion, and which, without supplying any details, suggested a vast expanse.
The objection, however, is a certain sameness
and sense of repetition. The whole system, however, is valuable as a protest against what may be
called, simulated scenery.

A striking proof of the care devoted by Irving to
the scenery of his pieces is found in the assistance
which he invoked of the leading artists of his day.
This is really unique in the annals of the stage.
Even when Garrick secured the services of De
Loutherberg, that artist was then, like Stanfield,
only a professional scene-painter, though later both
became Royal Academicians. The roll in Irving's
case was an extraordinary one. It included Sir
Alma Tadema, R.A., Sir E. Burne-Jones, R.A.,
Ford Madox Brown, Gustave Doré, J. Seymour
Lucas, and Sir J. Tenniel. Tadema supplied four
beautiful scenes for 'Coriolanus,' the small sketches
of which produced at the sale close on £800. Sir

E. Burne-Jones contributed no less than twenty-two designs and two pastels for 'King Arthur,' which realised only ninety-two guineas. For these contributions we may be sure Irving paid in his handsome imperial way; but in their application to his scenic purposes he was equally imperious if not impervious. For he would seem to have modified and adapted them according to the necessities of the case, not wholly to the satisfaction of the artists. During a long course of years Alma Tadema's designs were laid aside altogether, but Burne-Jones's had been freely altered. "Some things they have done well and some they have spoiled; and they have behaved very badly about Merlin, and drew him not as I have designed him, so I have made a row, and now they are going to alter him. They hurried the thing so that I saw nothing till it was on the stage." He was clearly dissatisfied. He also designed the armour.

It may be doubted, however, whether this system is really profitable, or is not merely a waste of precious material, for the two domains are almost opposed. The artist of the first rank cannot feel at home on the stage—its methods are so different from his. On the other hand, Irving may have pushed his system of shaping and docking too far, as he did in the instance of composers, and also in that of dramatists.

As the season went on, the manager, following his favourite policy, prepared a series of revivals on a gigantic scale. These were virtually convenient rehearsals for the coming American tour. But the

constant changes of scenes, dresses, &c., involved an
enormous strain.   The round of pieces included,
within the space of a few weeks, no fewer than
eleven plays : 'Faust,' 'King Arthur,' 'Louis XI.,'
'Merchant of Venice,' 'Becket,' 'Much Ado About
Nothing,' 'The Lyons Mail,' 'Charles I.,' 'Nancy
Oldfield,' 'Corsican Brothers,' 'Macbeth.'   A new
short piece, 'Journeys End in Lovers Meeting,'
by George Moore and John Oliver Hobbes, which
was to introduce Miss Terry, was also announced.
The burden of "staging" all these great works, in a
short time, must have been enormous.   But it was
only in this fashion that the revivals could be done
justice to.

It is a wonderful proof of our actor's ability that,
after so many years of experiment in characters of
all kinds, he should in almost his latest attempt have
made one of his most signal successes.   I doubt if
anything he had hitherto tried had more profoundly
impressed his audience than the little cabinet sketch
of Corporal Brewster in Conan Doyle's 'Story
of Waterloo.'   This he had first presented to a
provincial audience at Bristol, with such extraordinary effect that the general audience of the kingdom
felt instinctively that a great triumph had been
achieved.   Every one at a distance at once knew
and was interested in the old corporal.   A second
trial was made in London, for a charity ; and at last,
on May 4, 1893, it was formally brought forward
in the regular programme.   There was what is
called "a triple bill," consisting of Mr. Pinero's
early drama, 'Bygones,' this 'Story of Waterloo,'

and some scenes from 'Don Quixote,' Wills's work. [1]

This sketch of the old soldier was a noble piece of acting, highly finished, yet natural and unobtrusive, full of pathos and even tragedy. The actor excelled himself in numerous forcible touches, now humorous, now pathetic. He gave the effect of its being a large history in little; we had the whole life of the character laid out before us. It was original, too, and the oddities were all restrained with a fine reserve. The figure will always be present to the memory— a satisfactory proof of excellence. There was one mistake, however, in giving the female character to Miss Hughes, a bright and lively *soubrette*, who could not, therefore, supply the necessary sympathetic interest, though she did her best. Taking it all in all, Corporal Brewster was, in its way, one of the most masterly things the actor had done, and it can be praised—ay, extolled—without the smallest reservation.

It was followed by some scenes from 'Don Quixote,' and here, again, we must admire that admirable power of conceiving a character in which Irving excelled, and in which all true actors should excel. It was admitted that the piece was but a sketchy thing. Still here was supplied the living image of the hapless and ever-interesting "Don," who lived, moved, and had his being before us, in the most perfect way. There was a general dreaminess

[1] This "triple bill" is an unmeaning term, for a triple bill means, if anything, three bills in one, and not, as is supposed, a single bill in three parts.

over him ; his soul was so filled with high chivalrous
visions that he was indifferent to the coarsely prosaic
incidents going on about him.   He filled the stage ;
the rest were mere puppets.   The character, in
spite of the shortcomings of the piece, might have
been made one of his best.   The Don, in Irving's
hands, was a very fine specimen of the Spanish
noble.   He was the exact picture of the hero—
dignified and chivalrous—stately in bearing, though
grotesque ; always in grim earnest—even intense ;
with somewhat of a reminiscence of his Malvolio.
Yet here, again, was success missed.   The dull
public seemed to think that it was a sort of *mauvaise
plaisanterie*, or bit of pantomime.   It was really
above them.   So it ran but for a short time.   This
was disheartening enough.   And here was thus
one more sign of decay in the failure of that once
marvellous hold on public admiration.   He seemed
also to be losing the power of judicious selection.
And yet for years he had been listening to the
flattering compliments showered on him—that he
was "the ideal Don Quixote."   Critics, fair dames,
and all joined in the cry : "You would be the ideal
Don Quixote !"   And so he was.   But the crowd
could not see it.

And here it may be said that this long connection
of Wills, author of this piece, with the Lyceum
tended somewhat to the sacrifice of brisk dramatic
action, always enfeebled by an excess of poetical recitation.   There were still left many fine subjects and
fine dramas which would kindle all the actor's powers
afresh and stir his audiences.   What a fine piece,

for instance, might be made of Victor Hugo's " Notre Dame"!   We could call up our actor as the mysterious and romantic monk—one more addition to his ecclesiastical gallery.   What opportunities for scenery and music !   One of the most picturesque of stories is that of Theodore of Corsica, he who dreamed of being a king and actually became one, and who died in the King's Bench Prison in the most piteous state of misery.   We should have liked to have seen him, too, as Rodin, in Sue's 'Wandering Jew,' and, better still, in ' Venice Preserved,' or in ' Mlle. de Belleisle.'

After his twenty years' fruitful work at the Lyceum—twenty years and more of picturesque labour during which a new interest was created in the stage—an official recognition was to be given of our actor's high position.   The year 1895 will henceforth be notable as the year of the first tardy honour ever bestowed on an English actor by the Crown. We have had titled players in abundance on the stage, but they have not owed their honours to the stage.   It has been said that Sir Richard Steele and Sir Augustus Harris were the only two titled managers.   When, in May, the usual list of what are called "birthday honours" came out, the public was delighted to find their favourite knighted, in company with a poet, a novelist, and a successful traveller.   Few Government acts have given such general satisfaction.   There was a general chorus of appreciation.   Already a lecturer before the Universities and a doctor of Letters, the leading player of his time was now officially recognised.

On the lamented death of the actor, Mr. G. Bernard Shaw made a rather reckless statement, to the effect that the actor had actually applied for his knighthood on the ground that it was due to his profession, which ought to be honoured in that way just as much as were the arts and sciences. This singular contention was put forward in an Austrian paper,[1] and was promptly challenged by Mr. Stephen Coleridge in a letter, which is a graceful and effective tribute to the memory of the actor :—

"In 1883 I asked my father to broach the matter of making Irving a knight to Mr. Gladstone, who was then Prime Minister. He did so, and Mr. Gladstone intimated that, before considering the matter, and before making any recommendation to the Queen, it was essential that he should know whether Irving would accept the honour. On the 28th of June, 1883, I went and saw Irving and asked him whether in the event of a knighthood being offered him he would accept it, and I now quote from my diary written at the time :

"'He would not accept it; he said that an actor differed from others, artists, musicians, and the like, in that he had to appear in person every night appealing directly to the public for their favour. That being so, it was of paramount importance that an actor should do nothing that could possibly be misconstrued. That there was a fellowship among actors of a company that would be impaired by any elevation of one member over another; that his

---

[1] *Neue Freie Presse*, October 20, 1905.

strength as a manager and power as an actor lay far more in the suffrages of the plain folk of the pit than in the patronage, however lofty, of great people ; that he knew instinctively that large numbers of those same plain folk would be offended at their simple Henry Irving accepting decorations of a titular kind. He disclaimed any false pride in the matter, he did not affect to despise such an honour, and was very grateful to my father for his kind desires.'

" This is not the language of a man who would vulgarly ask for honours for himself. I believe that in 1895 Lord Rosebery, as Prime Minister, sent Irving's name to the Queen with a recommendation for a knighthood, and Irving received an intimation that this had been done and an instruction to repair to Windsor to receive the honour."

Mr. Shaw defended his assertion by pointing to certain appeals of Irving's, claiming a recognition for the stage exactly equivalent to that of the other artistic professions. He insisted that they should receive the same honours ; but he did not claim them for himself. Mr. Labouchere had the same design in view, and he also went to Mr. Gladstone to suggest that Irving should be knighted. A little staggered at the proposal, the Premier answered that he must first consult Lord Granville, and having done so, he offered the honour to the actor, who, however, declined it—thinking, so Mr. Labouchere says, that it would make him look absurd. Labouchere always treated with ridicule his friend's crude fancy for the Municipal Theatre as an utterly impracticable thing in this country.

There was always an adroit modesty in Irving's disclaimer of his new rank. In vain you looked in his bills for the showy "Sir Henry"; nothing but plain "Henry Irving" met the eye. And there was the suggestion from the reader, "Why does he not give himself his proper designation?" Some might think it a sort of ostentation, but it was far from that; he really wished not to raise himself above his comrades. However, propriety is its own reward, like honesty, and this simple stroke brought him more distinction than if he had flourished away in all his full-blown honour. Sir Charles Wyndham now follows the same precedent.

To no class of the community was the honour more acceptable than to his own profession. A meeting of actor-managers and others was held to take some step "in recognition," it was said, of the distinction. Mr. Bancroft presided, and a provisional committee was formed, consisting of Mr. Toole, Mr. Pinero, Mr. Beerbohm Tree, Sir A. Harris, Mr. Hare, Mr. Wyndham, Mr. G. Alexander, Mr. Terry, Mr. Forbes Robertson, Mr. Terriss, Mr. Howe, Mr. Brough, Mr. G. Conquest, and some others. Mr. Bashford acted as secretary. Another meeting with the same end in view was called of "proprietors, authors and managers." All this was very gratifying. Not less striking was the feeling with which the news was received abroad, and his *confrères* of the French Comedy—the "House of Molière" as it proudly and so justly

boasts itself—lost not a moment in calling a meeting and sending him a formal "act" of congratu-
lation. This important document ran :—

"Paris, May 28, 1895.

"Dear Sir Henry Irving,—The committee of
the Comédie Française and the *sociétaires* of the
House of Molière desire to send you their cordial
congratulations, and to signify the joy they feel at
the high distinction of which you have lately been
made the recipient. We are all delighted to see a
great country pay homage to a great artist, and we
applaud with all our hearts the fitting and signal
recompense paid to an actor who has done such
powerful service and profound honour to our calling
and our art. Accept, then, dear Sir Henry Irving,
the expression of the deep sympathy as artists and
the sincere devotion which we feel towards you.—
(Signed) Jules Claretie, administrator-general and
president of committee ; Mounet Sully, G. Worms,
Silvain, Georges Baillet, Coquelin cadet, Proudhon,
&c., of the committee ; S. Reichemberg, Bartet,
B. Baretta Worms, Paul Mounet, Mary Kalb,
Blanche Pierson, A. Dudlay, &c., *sociétaires*."

Looking back over this long period of nigh thirty
years, we are astonished to find this laborious and
conscientious performer hardly ever absent from his
stage. Night after night, year after year, he was still
found at his post, defiant of fatigue or ill-health. Only
on one occasion, I think, owing to some affection of
his throat, had a substitute to take his place. The

pressure and constant struggle of our time, it may
be, takes no account of weakness or failure ; no
one dares relax, and as Mrs. Siddons declared the
player's nerves must be made of cart-ropes, so must
he have a constitution of iron or steel.

Sir Henry thus expressed himself to an interviewer : " My 'watchword,' as you term it, must
needs be an old one—an old ideal. It is the one
word, *Health !* It is of all things essential that we
keep our drama sane, and sound, and sweet, and
wholesome. For my part, I can say that I have
always endeavoured never to produce or take part
in any play that a young fellow might not take his
sweetheart or sister to see." "You do not then
approve of Ibsen ?" "No. Frankly speaking, I most
distinctly do not. What life do such plays render ?
What lesson of good do they convey ? The
playgoing public of England have not altogether
tired of Shakespeare, or of the wondrous lessons
that he teaches. But do you know I am a little
afraid that my son "—and here Sir Henry smiled
across at Mr. Laurence Irving—" has become at
least slightly infected by the ' blight from the
North.' "

" I can have no hesitation in saying," he added,
" that I look hopefully for the time when the English
municipalities shall do something for the stage as
they do in France and Germany. All such innova-
tions are warmly opposed in a country like ours—
take, for example, the simple opening of museums
and picture-galleries, which in certain quarters was
bitterly resented. This insensate opposition must

be held to account, at least in part, for the lamentable lack of healthy and intellectual enjoyment which one notices as one passes through many country places. It is not as if we were even consistent in Great Britain—for do we not find the municipal authorities helping to give the people music and outdoor recreations while neglecting to assist the theatres?"

CHAPTER XVII

SOCIAL GIFTS

IRVING always showed himself eager to plead for his profession, to urge its claim as a wholesome and instructive moral influence that will implant in the community elevating instincts of even a religious kind. All our great actors have been forward in this way, notably Garrick, Kemble, and Macready. The former's reply to the bishop as to the success and failure of their different styles of preaching is well known. Our actor was very earnest, and fondly believed that the day is approaching when the stage, and its ways and works, will be recognised by the Church, and by good people generally, as healthy, useful agents in the work of reforming men and women. He was fond of repeating the bishop's remark to him, when he asked why, with such a taste for the theatre, he did not frequent it—" My dear Irving, I am afraid of the *Rock* and the *Record*."

In his paper, addressed to the Church of England Temperance Society, and read on March 3, 1876, Irving very valiantly pressed for the formal recognition of his profession by the Church. " Make the theatre respected by openly recognising its services. Let members of religious congregations know that there is no harm, but rather good, in entering into ordinary amusements, so far as they are decorous. Use the pulpit, the press, and the platform to denounce not the stage, but certain evils that find allowance on it. Change your attitude towards the stage, and, believe me, the stage will co-operate with you," &c.

It must be said, however, as regards this friendly invitation, that this idea of the Churches cordially recommending the stage and of the clergy being seen in the stalls, and of bishops who would go to the theatre but for fear of the *Rock* and the *Record*, seems but a pleasant delusion. Some few stray clerical visitants there are, no doubt ; but in all ages and climes the Church has found itself opposed to the stage, on the ground that in the majority of theatres is found what is destroying and corrupting. As I have said, the pieces in which anything instructive, or even elevating, is set forth are but few.

In his numerous addresses at institutes, and before the Universities, he urged the same plea. With this skilful and loyal advocacy, we have an instinct that the stage can have but small effect on the masses, and does little beyond making them acquainted with certain refining ideas and situations. As for its fostering moral or religious impressions, by exhibiting " virtue triumphant and vice defeated," that seems to be rather fanciful. It is probable that the playwrights, managers, actors, and audiences use the theatres for profit and for amusement, not for self-improvement in religion or morals. Even the great classical works, such as those of Shakespeare, are set forward with so much magnificence, show, and spectacle, that the teachings are overpowered in the spectacle and general entertainment. But even granting the contention that it may become a pure leaven in the profession, or sweetening salt to purify the rest, who can maintain that the stage as a whole, with its burlesques, "grotesques," frivolities, fooleries, and license of speech and manners, can be considered an edifying school for morality and religion? The thing is Utopian — hopeless in these days of 'Spring Chickens' and 'Mr. Popples.' What a deep impression, on the other hand, leaves such a piece as 'The School for Scandal'!—what a genuine disgust for deceit and insincerity! How it shows the danger of "playing with fire"! What a pleasant sympathy is aroused with the natural, manly virtues! Here is a certain sort of teaching if you will, and here, too, is there an elemental morality. But in these days we unhappily not only lack the talent to supply such comedies, but the public taste is debauched and gorged with grosser dishes.

As I have said, Irving collected his addresses in a little volume, "The Drama," 1893. Here, in an exceedingly persuasive and graceful style, he expounded the principles of his art. On every point he has something to say, and all is marked by judiciousness and a temperate reserve.

How true, for instance, is this: "Nor do I think that servility to archæology on the stage is an unmixed good. Correctness of costume is admirable and necessary up to a certain point, but when it ceases to be 'as wholesome as sweet' it should, I think, be sacrificed. The nicest discretion is needed in the use of the materials which are nowadays at the disposal of the manager. Music, painting, architecture, costume, have all to be employed, with a strict regard to the production of an artistic whole in which no element shall be obtrusive." When 'Much Ado About Nothing' was produced, there was a scene representing a cedar walk, and a critic discovered that there were no cedars in England until fifty years later, on which he comments—"Absolute realism on the stage is not always desirable, any more than the photographic reproduction of Nature can claim to rank with the highest art."

A little bit of pleasant comedy was found in a speech of his at a dinner of the Cab-drivers' Benevolent Association. He had always a friendly feeling for this hardworked body of men, as he told his audience autobiographically: "I have spent a great part of my life in cabs. There was a time, indeed, when a hansom, by a slight stretch of the picturesque, might have been described as my address. That was in the days of youth and high spirits. But there comes a moment in the experience of all of us when the taste for adventure is satiated, when we are no longer eager to sit under the charioteer of the sun, and snatch a

fearful joy from sharp corners and a sudden con-
gestion of the traffic. So when the decisive
moment came for me I dropped the hansom and
took up with the growler. I remember that my
first appearance in that staid and unambitious
vehicle excited a certain amount of feeling amongst
my old friends the hansom cabmen. There were
letters of remonstrance. One correspondent, as
genial a humorist as Gentleman Joe, hinted that to
be seen in a growler was equivalent to being dead,
and I think he offered to paint my epitaph on the
back. I must say that I am very comfortable in a
growler, except when the bottom drops out almost
as suddenly as if it were a gold mine. That
accident once happened to a friend of mine whose
professional business compelled him to make a
quick change of dress in the cab, and as it was
a light summer evening the passers-by were
astonished to see a pair of white legs running
under the vehicle, and not apparently connected
with the horse."

Again a pleasant sketch: "Taking them as a
body, the cabmen are as industrious and deserving
a class as you can find in the community. There
still lingers amongst them, perhaps, some of the
old spirit which prompted the cabmen to expostulate
rather forcibly with Mr. Pickwick. And considering
the vast area in which these public servants have to
work, and the elasticity of the four-mile radius
in the minds of some citizens, the friction is
surprisingly small. Not a few of us have known
cabmen whom we held in special regard. There

was one affable driver that I invited to the Lyceum,
giving him the money for admission. The next
time I saw him I said, 'Well, and how did you like
the play?' He hesitated for a moment, choosing,
as I thought, the most grateful words to express his
pleasure and admiration, and then he said, 'Well,
sir, I didn't go.' 'You didn't go! Why not?'
'Well, sir, you see, there's the missus, and she
preferred the Waxworks.'

"A friend of mine, a great ornament of the
medical profession, used to tell a story of the
cabman who drove him regularly on his rounds,
for some years, and always spoke of him with
affectionate familiarity by his Christian name. The
time came for the rising surgeon to set up a
brougham, and with much reluctance he broke this
news to his good friend the cabby, who responded
with cheerful alacrity, 'Oh, you're going to get rid
of me, are you? Not a bit of it—I'll drive that
brougham.' And drive it he did, till he became too
old and infirm for the duty. 'Ah, well, I must give
it up,' he said one day; 'I ain't fit for it any longer.'
'Dear me,' said the doctor, in great concern, 'I am
very sorry, very sorry indeed. And what are you
going to do?' 'What am I going to do? What
are *you* going to do for me? Don't you fear—I'll
never leave you!' And he spent the rest of his
days on a pension. That story has always seemed
to me to put the spirit of charity and goodwill in a
thoroughly practical light. You can scarcely get
through life in this town without a sense of your
dependence on cabby's skill and endurance, and

"Don Quixote."
Drawn by Phil May.

To face p. 253

with as grateful an obligation to him as that of the
voyager to the pilot amidst the reefs in a storm.
In this labyrinth of London, it is rare for cabby not
to know his way. I have never ceased to wonder
at the cabman's dexterity of eye and hand—
unrivalled, I venture to say, in any other capital in
Europe. And when you consider how small is the
proportion of accidents in this vast business of
locomotion, you may cheerfully grant that cabby
has some claim upon your respect and generosity."

I think the whole "key" of this is admirably
appropriate, and the touch of the lightest.[1]

Instances of his boundless generosity have been
often quoted. These were of an impulsive, lavish
kind springing from the moment. He would
engage an old actor who was of little use for his
purposes simply to furnish a retreat and support—
such as, for instance, of "Old Howe," who once
almost complained to me of his patron's generosity
and "princely" salary, for he said: "I had sooner
he gave me something to do," the veteran being
always allotted some rather minor character. Irving
would meet an old actor in the street and send him

[1] In this connection there is a characteristic story told of our
actor. He was driving in a hansom one night to the Lyceum
when the 'Merchant of Venice' was running. In a fit of absence
of mind he tendered a shilling for his fare, whereas it should have
been eighteenpence or two shillings. Whereupon the cabby,
who had recognised his man, burst out: "If yer plays the Jew
inside that theayter as well as yer does outside, darned if I won't
spend this bob on coming to see yer." It is said he was so
delighted with the retort that he promptly gave the man half a
sovereign.

on his way rejoicing with cash and stalls; or, operating more delicately, if he were an old comrade, he would find a small part for him. Once after such an engagement, the man was taken ill in the Isle of Wight. Irving actually journeyed down to see him, comforted him, kept his place open, and left £100. But by this system he overburdened his company considerably.

CHAPTER XVIII

'CYMBELINE,' produced in September, 1896, was an attempt to open up the mine of less known Shakespearian drama ; a hopeless task, as Irving found it on a former occasion. The public will condescend to interest itself only in such pieces as it knows or has heard of. As in the case of the lovely 'Twelfth Night' revival it turned its stony ears to the melodic poetry and closed its eyes to the exquisitely devised scenes. The "one and only" Miss Terry showed all her tender graces in Imogen, and her comrade contented himself with Iachimo instead of Posthumus. This was a surprise. As one of his warmest admirers said naïvely, " The result was Posthumus is no longer a very striking personage." This distorting of a character Irving was rather partial to.

Réjane's unique performance of 'Madame Sans Gêne' had made a striking success in London, where every one talked of the buoyancy, and sentiment combined, of the actress. Equal praise could be accorded to the play, an admirable piece

of work of Sardou's. Irving, always eager to
show his gifted partner at her best, saw that here
was a character to fit her, though this proved
somewhat of a miscalculation. It was translated
by his son, mounted in the usual tasteful style,
and produced in April, 1897. He himself took the
trifling part of Napoleon, to which his stature was
a serious impediment. This difficulty he contrived
to surmount by some of the ingenious resources of
stagecraft. He made the part impressive and
interesting—with certainly a deep suggestion of the
Corsican's character and gifts. The piece was
beautifully "staged" as it is called, and was
followed with much interest. Some years later it
became an English opera of extraordinary attraction and success. It was to be lamented that
Sardou, when later employed to write for the
manager, did not make the same exertion, and
could only supply very inferior work—no doubt
owing to a national contempt for the English stage
as compared with the Parisian—a contempt shown
by his never crossing the Channel to see how his
"commissioned" pieces were produced and acted.
In another view this play was of ill omen—as at
this period occurred the first symptoms of incom-
patibility between the actor-manager and his gifted
partner, which was speedily to lead to separation.

Miss Terry was a little of a disappointment : the
character was that of a French woman, whereas
she seemed to portray an English woman of a
type very familiar. Neither was she as coarsely
exuberant as Réjane. The piece was hardly enthusi-

astically welcomed, and there were perhaps signs of indifference.

Five and twenty years of almost uninterrupted prosperity was, perhaps, as much as the most popular actor could desire. It seemed, indeed, that about this time fortune seemed to tire of her favourite. The tide was about to turn. He was now to meet a series of rebuffs, and even disasters, which led to what was almost a catastrophe. He had revived, I think, ‘Richard III.’ with new scenery, effects, &c., and was revelling in his grim and grotesque personation of the King. The insolent ignoring of Buckingham’s earnest petition, the rage at being interrupted, the malignant pause between each word, the sort of snarl with which he said, “I’m not in the vein”—nothing could be finer. This piece excited little enthusiasm, and yet it was admirably done. On the first night it was coldly received in spite of all the lavish outlay.

My old friend, that admirable and measured critic, Mr. Knight, says justly enough of ‘Richard III.’—and it applies equally to many other of his performances—that the tragic and conventional element was dismissed from the character : instead of the villainous, crooked-backed tyrant, we had a laughter-moving personage. It is “a character part.” The reason of the change was that the realistic was substituted for the old conventional treatment. This raised a serious speculation, and so important a change in treatment should make us doubt; for the modern rendering of Richard seemed equally composed of Louis XI. and Mephisto.

18

This, with the unmerited treatment of 'Twelfth
Night,' might be considered the only checks he had
received—everything had been triumphant.   But
still things began to go wrong.   Looking back, it
seems to me that there was a feeling that little
more could be expected.   All were familiar with
what he could do: he was not likely to produce anything novel.   They had "travelled over his mind,"
as Johnson once said.   But now was to come the
most serious blow, the dissolution of the partnership
with the gifted Ellen Terry, which had so increased
the public stock of harmless pleasure.

This came about after the production of ' Madame
Sans Gêne,' and though the pair were to play
together hereafter, the partnership, as I said, was
dissolved for good.   It was said that Irving wished
to introduce some girlish performer who might be
more adapted to the playing of *ingenue* heroines.
This was not unnatural, but whatever the cause the
separation could not be averted.   One result of this
dearth of material was the growing tendency to fall
back on the old productions, and from this time we
find him constantly reviving "old favourites."
When he went "on tour" this was found very convenient—he went back to the days of 'The Bells'
and 'Merchant of Venice,' and these with 'The
Lyons Mail,' 'Louis XI.,' and later, 'Becket,'
became his regular "stock-pieces."[1]

---

[1] The old scenery and properties for these, and other pieces,
were stored away in a special warehouse.   In his later days one
of his sore trials that I have alluded to was the total destruction
of this emporium by fire, entailing the greatest loss and incon-
venience.   His troubles, indeed, came in battalions.

The secession of Miss Terry was a serious loss indeed. Half the interest of his own exhibitions was gone with her, for it was notorious that many admirers held that her's was the secret attraction of the theatre—that her magic charm, vivacity, and versatility, were what drew the audience; that, though nominally his assistant, her talent almost overpowered his. We might amend this unflattering view and contend that each was necessary to the other, and from constant companionship had come to draw unsuspected gifts and charms. A great actor and greater actress thus furnishing entertainment did not quite amount to "actor management"—it was nearer to the ideal of the evenly-balanced company. But here was Irving now left alone and unsupported—the Melpomene was gone. We were now likely to have unrelieved, "inspissated gloom" and declamation.[1]

It is remarkable what a dearth of talent is found nowadays, and after what long intervals it shows itself. It seems to take about forty or fifty years to produce original gifts. Then follows a long reign of mediocrity. With all his blemishes, Irving had no one near him; no one has surpassed him. No one in the same period has approached Ellen Terry. The springs, indeed, seem dried up now. It is near forty years since Dickens's death, and no one approaching him has appeared.

[1] The sparkling, incompressible Beatrice has for some years been working on her own resources, first as manageress, with new plays of an unpractical kind and offering Mr. Gordon Craig an opening for his scenical experiments, and later in characters of middle age, as in Mr. Barrie's piece, "Alice sit-by-the-Fire."

This feeling of being a little tired of their hero was not an unnatural one, considering the long period his sway had endured. People began to repeat, "Oh, here is the same thing over and over again!"—as indeed it was, and was obliged to be. He was eager to secure novelty could he find it. The wonder was that during the almost thirty years no rival had risen, nor has any risen since, though the Shakespearian decorator and upholsterer has.

While we are lamenting the eminent and amiable actor's loss, we should recollect that there was coming on with advance of years a decay, not only in his strength and health, but in his methods. Nothing was more obvious during the last few years of his life, than the gradual weakening of his voice, with indistinctness of utterance. He seemed also to be careless of stage discipline, and would, during his own or other persons' speeches, introduce strange sounds of dissent, exclamations, which was literally no more than "gag." This, he seemed to think, imported a sort of spontaneous and *degagé* tone to his part. His new reading of the Mephisto had too much of this would-be "buffoonery," he making jocose comments *sotto voce* on what was going on before him.

One of the cries most frequently heard, and tediously iterated, even by friendly advisers, was his persistent neglect of the "native talent." True, there was not much "native talent" about, but why not call to his side the Pineros, Henry Arthur Jones' —beside others of the respectable rank and file? He was warned—even threatened, with disastrous

consequences, if he were still to cling to the
old dramas. Nothing could be more unfair. A
Lyceum drama was and should be *sui generis*.
The house required a largeness of treatment, broad
lines, great force in the characters, and, above all,
the piece was to be constructed—in an easy natural
way—*round* the two main characters.

Irving's admirers were now to be rather surprised
at his next proceeding. It is rather an uncommon
thing to find the distinguished manager of a distinguished theatre allowing his son to furnish a play,
he himself taking a leading part. This was ' Peter
the Great,' produced in January, 1898, an ambitious
effort, not without promise. It was, indeed, more a
descriptive poem than a play. Irving did his best
with the hero and worked laboriously, reciting many
a lengthy speech ; but he excited little interest in
spite of a good deal of barbaric show and local
colour.

During its short run the oddity was witnessed of
the young author's taking his father's place in the
leading part. This was hardly judicious policy ; as
it showed either too much parental indulgence, or
some indifference to what the public might think.
Indeed, it was hardly a compliment to the audience
to ask them to accept a substitute. The choice of
this piece betrayed, as I believe, the anxiety he felt
at this critical stage of his course. Troubles and
difficulties were gathering about him, and to these
difficulties, the failure of several plays in succession
made a serious addition. And yet he was about to
strive and repair all by a very doubtful cast—he had

accepted a play by Messrs. Traill and Hichens. This was called " The Medicine Man," which was at least to furnish a topic of wondering speculation how so sagacious a judge could have so deliberately chosen perhaps the weakest and most unsuitable of all the pieces sent to him for perusal. It turned on the "antics," as they may be called, of an odd physician—half serious, half grotesque. But the audience were determined not to take it seriously, and before the close mixed laughter and disapprobation greeted him. Nothing was more mortifying than the way this was displayed. They dared not boo or hoot, but there was something contemptuous in the opposition. They put the whole thing aside, as who should say, " You are trying a joke on us!" The pampered crowd was also nettled that he had not gone to the usual expense and extravagance. He was bound to ruin himself, they thought, in entertaining them. It was plain that these unexpected insults wounded him grievously. It is painful to think of such things. But the public is often thus brutal, even to its old favourites. Still, apart from its merits or demerits, every one thought that such a class of piece was unsuited to the Lyceum. It was withdrawn almost at once, and something from the "stock" substituted.

But this was to prove the *coup de grâce*—his own illnesses and accidents, with the failure of three plays in succession, were rude shocks too strong for him to encounter. His sensitive temperament, long accustomed to the tides of success, had no fibre

with which to encounter disaster. He was *au bout*
—and in truth he was at the end of his resources—
without money put by for a rainy day. He had
lived always in handsome style.

Accordingly who shall forget the surprise, when
one day it was asked mysteriously, *"Had you heard
any rumours about Irving?"* It was soon spread
about that money was short—that large sums were
owing for salaries, &c. An index of this sad state
of affairs was the sudden appearance at auction of
many of his prized books, collections, rarities, all
which brought wretched prices. The name and
book plates, &c., had not been removed. It was
presently openly said that he could no longer carry
on the theatre.

It has always seemed to me that this crisis in his
affairs was rather clumsily handled. Had a few of
his wealthy friends been called into council, and all
matters placed in their hands, they would have
devised a scheme for his extrication ; money would
have been found to satisfy a large portion of his
creditors. But no doubt his own lofty pride stood
in the way. I never learned how much was the
sum for which he was indebted—perhaps thirty or
forty thousand pounds—but it is certain that no
one would have pressed him unduly, and that he
would have found as indulgent creditors as did Sir
Walter Scott before him. What was he to do now
—go round the provinces or set off for America?

But now his old friend, Mr. Comyns Carr, came
to his rescue with a bold scheme. It was agreed
that, considering his health and resources, the theatre

was no longer to be relied upon.   A company was to be formed, the shares to be taken up, Mr. Comyns Carr was to be secretary or managing-director, and Irving was to accept a number of shares for his interest while contributing a "short season" during the year of about four months—the rest of his time to be at his own disposal and for his own profit.   It must have been a wrench thus to have his kingdom taken from him ; but from what a burden was he released!   Henceforth he was a free man and could roam where he willed.   He had soon arranged his debts and formed a modest travelling company to go round the kingdom and later to the States.   Through this trial, which was also a serious mortification, Irving comported himself with a dignity and resignation that were quite admirable.   He did not advertise his sorrows, or make claims for assistance or sympathy on the ground of past service.   He bore all like a man, and did his best to extricate himself.   He determined to undertake the dull round of provincial touring, visiting places where he had not been seen, and thus work a fresh mine of interest.   He made a most successful visit to the United States, where he was received with all the old enthusiasm and affection.   It was remarkable how constant were the Americans to him, they never seemed to tire of him and his plays.   He came and yet came again.

He had, now, however, to cast about him for some suitable actress of not much pretension to play the supporting female characters.   He thus

ROBESPIERRE REFLECTING.

By Harry Furniss. From an original drawing lent by the Artist.

[To face page 265.

adopted Miss Cissie Loftus, "Miss Cecilia" she became for the Lyceum dignity; Miss Feely, an American actress; Miss Mabel Hackney, later wife of his son Laurence; and finally that most interesting and graceful performer, the creator of 'Everyman,' Miss E. Wynne-Mathieson. This absence of a first-class female performer obliged him to discard some of the more important pieces, and henceforward he contented himself with playing such old favourites as 'The Lyons' Mail,' 'Merchant of Venice,' 'Faust,' 'Becket,' 'The Bells,' and others, where the whole burden was thrown upon his single self.

In April, 1899, the new Lyceum Company having got to work with a piece by Wills's brother ('The Only Way,' another variation of the "Tale of Two Cities"), we find Irving fulfilling his part in the contract, by appearing with his "Travelling Company"—for such it was—in a new piece.

The expropriated manager was now to bring forward a Shakespearian play under the old conditions. It is to be presumed that he was given a free hand. The play chosen was the long-deferred and often-announced 'Coriolanus.' He had lying by him the scenery designed and executed long before by a celebrated artist, but which seemed ineffective. This last of the Shakespearian revivals was destined, owing to the ill-fortune which seemed to pursue Irving, to be comparatively unsuccessful, perhaps from the feeling that this was not "the old Lyceum."

Irving, always original and enterprising, was led

on by the success of 'Madame Sans Gêne,' to
enter into treaty with Sardou, to adapt a drama
to his own measure, suggesting the subject of
Robespierre. To this he was drawn by his own
fancied resemblance to the great " sea green," to a
certain reserve and grotesqueness found in both
characters. He, as it were, " felt " the man before
him. Then there was the poetic *entourage*, the
crowds, red caps, procession, "*Marseillaise*," and the
rest. But had not these things been presented in
' The Dead Heart,' which, indeed, offered the same
topics and opportunities. Sardou, as is his wont,
fashioned a story of his own, without any regard to
historical or biographical accuracy. There was an
illegitimate son introduced, whose parent Miss
Terry was to enact. Hence some movingly
pathetic scenes : the mother pleading for the
son, the " sea green " stern for a while, yet
moved himself and softened. Indeed, there were
scenes when the great man was shown at home,
relaxing, with a tender heart, and enjoying the
placid joys of the domestic fireside!

The play was produced on April 15th, and Miss
Terry, who had a rather conventional part, rejoined
the company. It must be said, Robespierre was
one of Irving's most striking " character " parts; the
general figure and bearing, with a sort of quaintness,
still live in the memory, and are revived in Mr.
Harry Furniss' spirited sketch of him, where the
half grotesque expression of the actor is caught to
the very life.

One of the attractions at the Irving sale was a

ACT III.
The nervous and suspicious Robespierre.

By kind permission of Mr. Harry Furniss and the Proprietors of the " Daily Telegraph."

[To face page 267.

huge volume overflowing with prints and illustrations all dealing with the period of the French Revolution. There were costumes, portraits, and everything connected with the subject.   These Irving had diligently collected when he was preparing this play. This showed his earnest conscientiousness.   Yet surely this seems so much waste and misspent labour, expended, moreover, in the wrong direction. The costumiers, property men, and scenic artists are all fully equipped with the conventional types of the period quite sufficiently to set forth the piece. All minute archæological details are thrown away upon an audience who, moreover, have not sufficient knowledge to appreciate or even notice them.   But all this is associated with a false and rather corrupt principle of stage illustration—which would make of the stage itself a sort of old curiosity shop and historical panorama.   The effect is, as of those museums at Amsterdam and other cities, where we are shown rooms filled with figures in national costumes of different periods.   The *spirit* of the time is what is required, and a close study of Carlyle's glowing book—written in letters of fire—would have helped far more.   We wanted the Revolution acted rather than shown.   Nothing, as a *spectacle*, could have been finer than the Procession of the Supreme Being, but it was really no more than a costly *show*. Antoine, that strange and remarkable actor and organizer, once gave a realistic, lurid sketch of the trial and execution of the Duc D'Enghien—any one who witnessed it could never forget the perfect impression it left of the Napoleonic era; it was all so

vivid and concentrated and distilled to the very
essence. Yet there were only a couple of scenes
and scarcely any *decors*. But all were permeated
with the spirit.

In the spring of the year 1904 our actor was to
" produce "—*c'est le mot* [1]—the very last of all his
long line of pieces—'Dante.'

" How like Dante ! it would be an *ideal* part !"
again exclaimed, in rapture, admirers and adulators ;
and certainly the two faces were strangely alike.
Irving no doubt fancied himself parading the stage
with slow strides, and gazing dreamily at the pit.
He dreamed that they would associate him somehow
with all the genius of poetry and romance—exhibiting the poet in his work. This poetical notion, I
am convinced, was the reason of his choice. Did
he say ever so little, his fine features would still
discourse for him ! Yet it was to prove an utterly
disappointing business. Sardou completely failed,
and that true trader in plays did not seem to have
exerted himself. It was a poor, skimpy, story-
less, passionless thing — likely enough what is
familiarly called "a pot-boiler," very different from
the powerful things he fashioned for the "divine
Sarah," and which have gone round the world.
The shrewd Parisian, who received a good price for

---

[1] The American managers now among us use a strange jargon
of their own, by way of securing credit for what is done off the
stage. They now "present" Mr.—— or Miss—— in a new
play, which is " produced " by some one else, "stage-managed "
by another, and written by one less important than the rest.
Thus there is the manager, stage-manager, producer, under the
direction of the " presenter."

IRVING WITH MISS LENA ASHWELL IN "DANTE,"
AT DRURY LANE THEATRE (1903).

To face p. 269.

his work, also took care to benefit his compatriots, and "recommended" a painter for the scenes, with a special composer for the music.   This scenery, though pretentious, was scarcely so good or effective as would have been furnished at home, while the music was of the crude "advanced" sort, which was too deep for the audience.   The composer overflowed in his abundance, and was confounded when the ever-tranquil and smiling manager proceeded to "cut out" wholesale and hew in all directions, throwing over all top hamper.   There was much indignation in the Parisian journals. But if the piece were bad and uninteresting, it could hardly have been redeemed by Irving's acting. He was, indeed, the great poet for the first few minutes, as he stood or moved about, gazing from beneath his cowl and toga, which he was perpetually draping on his arm, or throwing over his shoulder.   His voice was at this time weak and thin ; his speech slow and monotonous—it was more a recitation than acting.   In fact he was not Dante.   There was little or no passion or action. The character made no impression and seemed to be overpowered by the noisy, riotous crowds that overflowed the piece.   At the more dramatic, or perhaps less dull, moments of the piece, he became almost extinct, looking on in a sort of helpless fashion at what was going forward.   Irving, it may be noted, never could dominate the crowd as the great classical actors could do.   He must have his stage to himself, he and his audieuce.   This was shown in ' Robespierre,' where though he raved and

shrieked at the mob, he seemed overpowered ; quite
a cypher.   So with the " I banish *you* ! " in his
' Coriolanus.'   The faithful, however, saw none of
these blemishes, but thought all good.   It was the
man—the personality, they loved to look on—their
old friend.   In the country when it was taken on
tour, it was hardly tolerated.

But in spite of these efforts it was presently
rumoured that all was not going well with the
Lyceum Company.   The rosy forecasts of success
were not being justified—there were protests and
clamours from dissatisfied shareholders.   At the
meetings even the late manager was not spared,
until the faithful Stoker had to announce that he
had suffered more than the rest.

But presently was to fall a swinging stroke, which
completely wrecked the unlucky company.   This
was a peremptory summons from the inquisition of
the London County Council to put their house in
order, at the tremendous cost of nearly £20,000.
Their coffers were empty.   They might raise the sum,
but the charge would swamp the enterprise.   One
could understand how the immense prestige of
Irving should have kept off so long the inspecting
intruders, but it seemed strange how the Paul Prys
of the Council, busy with all the theatres, should
have overlooked it.   Nor was this requisition un-
reasonable or made too soon.   The wonder was
that things had been allowed to go on so long, for
it was a simple death-trap.   Who will forget the
appalling *tunnels* that led to the stalls, where only
two could pass, and where a cry of fire would have

IRVING AS "DANTE."

face p. 270.

been destruction ! Every portion of it was honey-combed with contrivances to secure extra room. The back portion of the pit was like a cellarage. When the demand was presented the unhappy shareholders saw no issue before them save that of getting rid of the whole concern. It was accordingly sold to a Music Hall Company, and razed to the ground! But before this catastrophe Irving had dissolved his connection with the place. He had given his final performance there in July, 1903—'The Merchant of Venice,' the last as it was the first and best of all his delineations in the famous old house. As he quitted the Doge's Court with his famous scowl, I wonder did he think of that night, some twenty-four years before —one of tumultuous rapture and enjoyment and which set the very seal to his fame ; or could he have divined that within a couple of years the theatre would be levelled and he himself borne up the aisles of Westminster Abbey ?

CHAPTER XIX

RING DOWN THE CURTAIN

WE have now to contemplate the closing scene of this strenuous and romantic career. After his long and brilliant course, it was a rude shock to find that he had, as it were, to begin the world anew, and this feeling, no doubt, disheartened and perhaps weakened him. He must have had a strong constitution to stand the strain of his nigh fifty years' hard work, but these latter failures must have made him despondent, while his irregular fashion of turning nights into days, kept up for years, must have laid the foundation of illness or disease. A constant strain of work and responsibility without recuperation by sleep is sure to work on the nerves and on the heart, and this proved to be the case in Irving's instance. Scott, Dickens, Irving, all three became victims to this overwork— a sad warning! Dickens fancied that he could strain the machine just "one little bit more," and then would relax and retire. Irving wished to make something for his old age from these final performances in the provinces, but miscalculated his strength.

SIR HENRY IRVING.
From a late photograph by Histed.

To face p. 273.

For a year before his death there were symptoms of a breakdown in health. At one of the Boz Club's dinners, where I had prevailed on him to take the chair, he looked sadly aged, quite an old man, his hair whitening rapidly. He made a speech which seemed rather of a rambling sort, chiefly about "Crummles and his pumps," which he reiterated again and again, as though the mere sound of the words was sufficiently comic. But a few weeks before his death a well-known personage, who had been dining in his company and sitting beside him, told me how shocked he was by his condition. Nothing better shows the almost appalling change in his features than a photograph taken only a few weeks before his death for the *Sphere*.

Before he set out on his last provincial circuit in 1905, it was understood that he was to make one farewell visit to the States. But as the progress went on, he seems to have shrunk from the task, and it appears to have been debated whether this should not be abandoned. More significant was the notice issued a week or so before the event, withdrawing 'The Bells' from his programme as too exhausting. These things ought to have supplied warning; but who heeds such warning? However, he pursued his drudging course from town to town, receiving addresses and civic honours as he went on—compliments which naturally pleased him and took off his thoughts from his state. On this—his last as it proved—tour, Irving came to places where he had never visited before, and found novelty and tumultuous encouragement. At Cardiff

19

particularly he made a deep impression.   After the
play had concluded, the Welsh enthusiasts broke
out into the hymn, "God be with you till we meet
again."   Surely never before in the annals of the
stage has an actor been greeted thus—with a hymn.
It was a remarkable sight, Sir Henry standing
reverently on the stage listening with bowed head
to the sacred song, charged as it was with affectionate
regard.

And thus as the days went by he felt the ligatures
coiling tighter about his heart.   Each night worn and
sinking, he must have returned spent and exhausted.
The same old weary routine—'The Bells,' Brewster,
Shylock and Becket—"Backet" as he would call it
—who could stand the wearing grind of that stage
machinery going on from eight till eleven?   And
this—all this for a poor frail being such as he
was!

This ending of one of the most successful and
admired of his generation was sad enough.   But
there was present an almost tragical element to add
to the poignancy of his state—the alarming precariousness of his position.   When he had announced
his retirement, no doubt dictated by the condition
of his health, he reckoned that the enthusiasm of
his friends, and the general rush to see him for the
last time, would enable him to make a sufficient
provision for his declining years.   And many, indeed,
made certain that this provision had been in part
secured.   But a number of disastrous accidents
were to frustrate these plans—the failure of the
Lyceum Company, the breakdown of his health,

which entailed the withdrawal of his most effective characters as being too agitating, and, above all, the abandonment of the American tour, which he counted on as a perfect mine of gold. All that was left was the touring from town to town—an expensive business, as he carried round with him his company, scenes, properties, &c.[1]

What, then, was to become of him when he finally took leave? All he could hope for was a few thousand pounds to be gathered during the last few weeks of his appearance. To one of his taste and habits a few hundreds a year would be beggary.

It will be said, however, that he left behind him a substantial sum, nigh twenty thousand pounds, result of the sale of his collections. But by an odd perverse fate this sum could not have existed during his lifetime, for he had to die to give it existence. It was his prestige as a dead actor that enhanced the price to four or five times its value.[2]

So, in addition to his physical sufferings, there was added the poignant feeling of anxiety as to the future. What was to become of him with no income—nothing saved?

Add to this that he had to carry a smiling, triumphant face, to make a brave, imperial show, to be liberal and lavish as was his wont, to receive his honours; while all the shouting lookers-on assumed

---

[1] At the time of his death he had been "on the road" some months, yet it does not appear from his will that profits were made, or if they were they had been expended.

[2] This is no mere speculation as a portion of these effects was sold in his lifetime, and brought prices far below their value.

he was the most fortunate of men, and "coining money." All the while the broken actor had this weight at his heart—mental as well as physical.

Now let us think of the poor, harassed creature, suffering in body, filled with gnawing anxieties, and hopeless for the future, and see how deep was the tragedy of it all! In vain the doctors bade him take care. Go forward he must; though his heart sank and failed, money must be got, for he was committed to engagements. And how chilling for him was the thought that looming ahead was the serious business of the whole—the "Farewells" in great cities, the packed masses, the shoutings, the call for exertion. How should he face that? Finally we must think of him as he appeared on that last night, when he sank down virtually alone. There was none near him, no friend or relative near to comfort, soothe, or give hopes. He had indeed his trusted lieutenants, but they had their serious work. Disdainfully he shut up his sorrows within himself.

It was while he was playing at Wolverhampton, in February, some eight months before his death, that he had a serious premonitory warning of what was impending. He had already learned that he was suffering from enlarged heart—a grave and serious danger—and as rest and absence of violent excitement was absolutely necessary for his safety, he should have withdrawn from work, just as Dickens, on a premonition of another kind of attack, at once suspended his readings, though, like Irving, he unhappily resumed his labours. If ever there was

Theatre Royal, Bradford.

Lessee   JOHN HART.

MONDAY, OCTOBER 9TH, 1905, FOR SIX NIGHTS.

⚞ FAREWELL ⚟
OF

HENRY IRVING
AND HIS COMPANY.

TUESDAY and FRIDAY NIGHTS, Oct. 10th and 13th, at 7.30

⚜ BECKET ⚜

By ALFRED LORD TENNYSON.

ADAPTED FOR THE STAGE BY HENRY IRVING.

Thomas Becket { Chancellor of England, afterwards Archbishop	....	HENRY IRVING
Henry II. (King of England)	....	Mr. GERALD LAWRENCE
King Louis of France	....	Mr. H. B. STANFORD
Gilbert Foliot (Bishop of London)	....	Mr. H. ASHETON TONGE
Roger (Archbishop of York)	....	Mr. WILLIAM LUGG
John of Salisbury } Friends of Herbert of Bosham } Becket	....	Mr. MARK PATON Mr. JAMES HEARN
John of Oxford (Called the Swearer)	....	Mr. T. REYNOLDS
Sir Reginald Fitzurse } The Four Knights of Sir Richard de Brito } the King's Household, Sir William de Tracy } Enemies of Sir Hugh de Morville } Becket	....	Mr. FRANK TYARS Mr. G. GRAYSTONE Mr. L. BELMORE Mr. LESLIE PALMER
Richard de Hastings (Grand Prior of Templars)	....	Mr. J. ARCHER
The Youngest Knight Templar	....	Mr. STEVENS
Lord Leicester	....	Mr. VINCENT STERNROYD
Philip de Eleemosyna (The Pope's Almoner)	....	Mr. W. J. YELDMAN
Herald	....	Mr. H. R. COOK
Monk	....	Mr. A. GURNEY
Geoffrey (Son of Rosamund and Henry)	....	Master TONGE
Retainers	....	{ Mr. A. FISHER Mr. HAYES
Countrymen	....	{ Mr. CHARLES DODSWORTH Mr. R. BRENNAN
Servant	....	Mr. W. MARION
Eleanor of Aquataine { Queen of England, divorced from Louis of France }	....	Mrs. CECIL RALEIGH
Margery	....	Miss GRACE HAMPTON
Rosamund de Clifford (Fair Rosamund)	.... Miss EDITH WYNNE MATTHISON	

Knights, Monks, Heralds, Soldiers. Retainers, &c.

[To face page 276.

a play likely to bring on a crisis it was surely the tempestuous 'Bells,' and even 'Becket' was trying enough. His doctor had specially interdicted the former piece, but the actor felt that half his attraction would be gone without it.

"He promised me not to play in 'The Bells' again," said Dr. Davis to a Wolverhampton correspondent, "but when I heard of his death I was much afraid that he had been doing so. He has died from practically the same thing from which he suffered at Wolverhampton. Sir Henry, however, always thought of the public, and though unfit to go on the stage, he persisted in playing Becket on the second night at Wolverhampton. An armchair was placed for him in the wings, and at the conclusion of the more severe parts he fell into the chair utterly exhausted. It was impossible to remove him from Wolverhampton for many days, but complete rest and quiet, combined with his determination to get into harness again, enabled him to continue his tour, though the American trip had to be abandoned and many other important engagements cancelled."[1]

And now was to arrive the fateful closing scene—almost on the scenic boards—on the night of October 14, 1905, when he, worn, weary of heart, was to "crack" under its burden. It was at the Theatre Royal, Bradford, where was welcomed with civic honours—"freedom of the city," Guildhall lunch, Mayor in the chair, &c. Here is the bill—the very last bill of that long fifty years' struggle. The

[1] *Daily Mail*, October 16.

first has been given—and how much between.[1] Here is the usual " Henry Irving "—not the " Sir Henry."

I take the following account of the last incidents from the *Daily Mail* of October 16th :—

" None of his company at the Bradford Theatre Royal had observed during the performance on Friday night anything in the bearing of their chief to warrant the belief that he was ill. If anything, Sir Henry's portrayal of his favourite character was more powerful than usual.

" His comrades now recall that once or twice his step seemed to falter and his hand steal out to support himself. But the first premonition of anything serious did not come until the end of the last scene, where Becket dies. As a rule, Sir Henry fell prone on the stage. On Friday night, however, he sank on the altar steps.

> " I do commend my cause to God. . . .
> Into Thy hands, O Lord—into Thy hands."

" These, the last words of Becket, were the last to be uttered on the stage by the great actor.

" For some moments after the curtain had fallen Sir Henry lay on the altar steps. An attendant hurried to his assistance, and touching his hands, found that they 'felt quite cold.' To the inquiry

---

[1] I have an extraordinary collection of Lyceum bills—one for every night of performance—so most are mere repetitions. As they are all well bound in volumes, I fancy they had belonged to the actor himself.

whether he was ill, Sir Henry Irving made no reply.

"The curtain was raised and lowered several times. Struggling to his feet in a confused way, Sir Henry turned to Mr. Belmore, his assistant stage-manager, who offered his hand to pilot him.

"'What now?' said Sir Henry.

"'They are calling for you,' answered Mr. Belmore. 'You must make a speech, sir.' He hesitated for a moment, then slowly went before the footlights and spoke a few words of thanks.

"In his room he dressed slowly. He was tired and exhausted, but not worse than he had been on two or three previous occasions.

"In this condition the great actor performed a characteristically kind act. A Bradford boy, aged fifteen, named Frederick C. P. Mobbs, employed in a shipping house, had two nights previously made a sketch of Sir Henry and left it at the stage door with the request that the actor might be pleased to attach his autograph to it. The youthful artist again visited the theatre on Friday night, and after the conclusion of the performance timidly inquired of the manager if Sir Henry had yet complied with his request. He was instructed to wait until the drawing had been signed. It was returned to him with the desired autograph at 11.15. A few minutes later the dying actor was being assisted into a cab by his valet.

"As Sir Henry entered the cab, he remarked to him, 'Are you not coming in to-night?' The attendant thereupon accompanied him to the Midland Hotel, where Sir Henry had engaged a suite of rooms. His secretary also occupied a seat in the cab. During the drive Sir Henry rested his feet on the seat opposite, and seemed in pain, but made no remark.

" He alighted from the cab without assistance and walked into the hotel, but as he entered the hall he stumbled and lurched forward. Mr. Shepherd, however, who was immediately behind, caught him before he could fall." He then asked faintly for a chair, and when he was seated almost instantly expired.

There is something pathetic and tragic about this scene. It was often noted that his last words on the stage were, " Into Thy hands, O Lord." *R.I.P.* But those who are too accustomed to " visualise " find it hard to shut out the thoughts and dreams that must have visited him that long and arduous night. The constricting, deadly grip— the sinking—the purpose to get through to the end—the strange feeling between the acts as he strove to " pull himself together "—what if he had heard a whisper—" Before midnight the curtain will have fallen for *you*, for ever, as well as for Becket."

The remains of the actor were cremated, according to his desire, and at the funeral in the Abbey were carried in a coffin to their resting-place. In this there seemed something of the usual make-believe or simulation of the stage.

The supreme honours of the Abbey were really paid to the exceeding personality of the man, for it could not be contended that his professional merits reached the highest standard. The *Spectator*, I think of all the journals, was alone in disapproval of the place of burial. Much could be said on both sides of the question, and a man of sterner fibre than the present Dean—such as Dean Stanley—would not have yielded his consent, save under the greatest pressure. I give no opinion on the point, save this, that when public opinion unanimously and tumultuously calls for the privilege it would be ungracious and perhaps impossible to resist. Even serious objection or discussion in presence of the unburied is thought scarcely decent; neither is there time to discuss, and so the matter is hurried through. Most impressive was the ceremonial in the Abbey, the solemn music, the gathering of distinguished persons, and the stately procession. One of the pall-bearers was a noble lord, the Earl of Aberdeen; yet one could not but feel a little surprise that on such an occasion more of that company of noble and distinguished people whom he so often *fêtèd* were not in attendance. This may be but a fanciful notion. But, after all, he was followed to the grave by the most distinguished of his own profession, which was the right thing. The French Comedy sent a deputation, who brought with them a wreath, and also, it is believed, a prepared *éloge*, which, as might be expected, was not delivered.

Few can imagine what a personage Irving was in the eyes of both French and Germans. His romantic course and methods, his noble and

generous hospitalities to foreigners of his profession, his intimacy with the leading performers,
these things made him quite familiar abroad.
To the leaders—to the immortal Sarah, Coquelin,
Mounet Sully—he was overwhelming in his atten-
tions. The two latter bewailed his loss sincerely,
and were lavish in their praises. Mounet Sully said
of him : " I cannot speak so soon after his death
without emotion of Irving, my brother tragedian
and the master of us all. As a man, as an actor,
and as a manager he stands out as one of the
great figures in the history of the stage. His
nobility of character shone in everything he did,
both on the stage and off it, and I can assure
you that his loss is felt among us here at the
Comédie Française deeply and sincerely."

The testimony of Coquelin is full and so very
remarkable from its sincerity and obvious truth
that it should be given at length :—

" I hardly know how to find words in which
to express my sorrow," Coquelin said. " Irving
has been my friend for over thirty years. I have
never been to London without seeing him constantly, and scarcely a week has passed throughout
our friendship without some token of his affection
reaching me. Only last week two friends of his
came over who had seen him on his provincial
tour. They told me that he seemed better than
I had hoped, and in brighter spirits, and the news
of his death, coming as it did so quickly after
this good news, gave me a shock from which I
have not yet recovered. For we were like

brothers, Irving and I, and I am only, as you know, two years his junior. Yet there is little selfishness, I think and hope, in my sense of loss at this great man's death—*c'était une très belle mort*. He always said he hoped to die in harness. He was a great man, and not England only, but the whole world loses by his death. He was so much more than an actor. Irving's life work has raised the tone not only of the stage, but of all English art and of the art of the world.

"The man was kindliness incarnate, the manager was the greatest master of stagecraft and of scenery in dramatic history, and of such a man's productions it is almost impossible to speak in detail. I have seen him, I think, in every play he ever played.

"As a friend and as a comrade Irving was incomparable. I usually supped with him after the theatre when I was in London, and I remember more especially the last hours that I spent with him. We talked late into the morning of old times and old experiences, and when I left him I was permeated with the indefinable charm of the man— a charm which had for a basis an unconquerable and illimitable love for his fellow men, seasoned with a brilliancy of sparkling wit such as no other man I know, or have known, possessed.

"I have known brilliant talkers; I have known men who were leaders of men (M. Coquelin was a close friend of Gambetta), but I have never met anybody whose personal charm or whose personal nobility of character equalled Henry

Irving's. Everybody employed in his theatre, from the leading actors and actresses to the dressers and the call-boys, loved him, and one word from 'the Chief' was enough to smooth all difficulties.

"I could not if I would judge my old friend's art impartially. He was perhaps greater as a stage-manager than he was an actor, but he was truly great in either and every character, and greatest of all, perhaps, in private life. His grasp of detail was extraordinary, his power of work was wonderful. I am myself a worker, and I love my profession. Henry Irving was wrapped up in his. He lived for it.[1]

---

[1] I have already pointed out that the actor's temperament had something akin to that of Dickens. How strange and how little noted was the forecast of impending death, given in "Edwin Drood": "Cutting out the gravestones of the next two people destined to die at Cloisterham—curious to make a guess at the two, or say *at one of the two*." Within a few weeks he himself was gone.

SIR HENRY IRVING'S ROOM AT THE LYCEUM.

To face p. 284.

CHAPTER XX

ALL who knew Irving intimately must agree that he was one of the most charming, interesting men they ever met. He had a sort of simplicity and *naïveté* that was exceedingly attractive and engaging. That captivating smile of his worked as a sort of spell. He never said anything in a dictatorial way, or "laid down the law" as it is called. He usually put the matter in a doubtful, interrogatorial way, with a "Hey, hey—what d'ye think? Eh, now?" This was really Garrick's style. He was all the time a dreamy, half-poetical creature.

He was not a regularly educated man, but he had acquired a vast deal of knowledge in a wonderful way. Nothing was more characteristic than his notion that he knew *French*. He had really "picked up" a great deal about French and France generally, and he had a general instinct as to all that was French. He was so intelligent that he understood a little, and carried it off somehow—but still, he could not speak the language. He *acted* the knowing of French—made

his few words go far.   It really was highly dramatic
to see him carrying on a sort of conversation with
the French actors—all winning smiles and gestures,
and movement, but little language ; but so clever was
he that he always contrived to convey his meaning.

What a generous host he was ! how magnificent
in his treatment of his guest !   Everything was of
the very best.   How often did we hear his kindly,
most pressing invitation—" That's Pommery-Greno
of '93.   Try it.   Here !   Bring one of the—er—mag-
nums."   At one of his vast banquets, when there were
a couple of hundred folk, magnum after magnum
of this Pommery-Greno was emptied.   His great
caterer was Gunter, for the little snug supper or
the grand banquet.   When the *débacle* came there
was a huge sum owing to these caterers, but they
were honourably and faithfully paid off within a
short time.   His ideas were really magnificent in
every direction ; he would have nothing but of
the best—the very best.   Even if you went to
him for one of those midnight suppers in the
beefsteak-room in the Lyceum, you had an exquisite banquet.   There was a poor creature who
had to sit up till the guest departed between two
and three a.m., who had looked after the banquet
and then saw his master into the hansom.   But
this turning of night into day was a tremendous
strain, and it was wonderful how he bore it so long.

That sagacious man of business and shrewd
observer—his former manager also—Mr. Henry
Labouchere, used to try to advise him, and
begged of him to save : " Again and again I

urged him to put by a certain sum, so as to be independent under all circumstances. He would reply : 'This is all very well to advise, but a play at the Lyceum costs a great deal to produce ; it needs many full houses to get it back, and then it has to be spent in getting up the next play.' And I never could convince him that this was not business. Had it not been for his old friend Mr. Bram Stoker, he would have been eaten out of home and theatre very speedily."

" As a man," he goes on in his generous tribute, " I greatly admired him. He was ever the kindest and most generous of human beings. Money burnt holes in his pockets. No one who appealed to him for assistance—oh, and many did—ever appealed in vain.[1] He spent little on himself, but much in charity and on hospitality, and he wasted a good deal on superfluity of detail in his pieces."

The same friend gives one of the most accurate sketches of the actor's dreamy fashion of taking his pleasures. Once at Twickenham, about midnight, there entered Irving, who had been dining at Richmond, saying, " He thought he would look in on him." He had his hansom. He stayed an hour or so, went off to call on some one at Teddington, and promised to return. A friend staying with Labouchere was rather astonished. " Does he know how late it is ? " " Certainly," he replied,

---

[1] His kindly thought of his friends was once illustrated when he was in Scotland at Christmas time, when we, all of his intimates, received a jar of the choicest old whisky, despatched from one of the most famous distilleries of the North.

" but I have no doubt we shall have him back."
And so he did arrive about two, remaining till five,
then driving back to London. He was fond of
these late, or early, hours. Such was Irving all
over. Who of his friends cannot see him as he
would enter in those small hours with his engaging
smile and his " Eh! eh!"

This friend also discusses his professional merits
in his own impartial way. Irving's acting in Shakespeare was *always sensational*, " it depended on
something new or striking in the way of ' business '
or readings. Irving could impress an audience
with his own personality, but he never seemed to
me able to carry them away, and consequently
had to depend on other methods to capture
them. But he *never passed the line where art
ends and genius begins*." How true is this! He
was not capable of those natural outbursts of feeling which sweep the hearer off his feet. He had
no tempestuousness in his passion, when the words
tumble forth in confusion—on top of each other
as it were. On the contrary, he grew slow and
yet slower. Every one knows that when danger
is at hand, pressing us close—the voice trembles,
we hurry in speech—speak low for fear of being
heard. But with Irving—the greater the crisis, the
more his words became like " minute guns." [1]

---

[1] In the ' Lyons Mail,' when Dubosc was rifling the letter-bags,
this was shown conspicuously. At such a moment everything
would be excitement and hurry—not a moment to be lost—and
this would affect the spectator. But no ; Irving was as slow and
leisurely and making long speeches.

"WHAT A KNIGHT WE'RE HAVING!"

DAVID GARRICK: "Congratulate you, Sir Henry, in the Name of the Profession!
May you live long, and prosper!"

From the Cartoon by Linley Sambourne.   By permission of the Proprietors of "Punch."

[To face page 288

His unaffected modesty and total lack of "side," even at his greatest prosperity, were extraordinary, and recalled Dickens, who always seemed to me the most modest man of his time. He took no airs. I recollect him one night at supper, when he complained to me of a stage carpenter who would carelessly leave a pail in the wing, over which the actor would trip as he impetuously "came off." I hear him quietly stating his grievance. "I remonstrated with the man. He said he couldn't help it. 'But, my friend,' I said, 'you should try. Would it not be a serious thing for me if I broke my leg over your pail. I am sure you would be sorry, but that would be no good to me.' He went away grumbling." This was said in a gentle voice, as though the man had rights in the matter. Yet on a word from Irving he could have "got the sack." The legends of Irving's liberality are almost incredible. We hear of some tale of distress, with £100 or £50 sent off as a solatium. Any old friend fallen on evil time might rely on help. No doubt he had a satisfaction in this princely lavishness : it ministered to his state, though this was far from being the motive. And the variety of shapes his hospitality took seemed inexhaustible. Here was a delightful summer evening. He must gather all his friends on board a chartered Thames steamer, and go down to Greenwich. In those days whitebait dinners were still in vogue. What an agreeable, parti-coloured complexion had those feasts—actors, actresses, writers, lawyers, musicians—but all of the Irving "set," and therefore more or less homogeneous.

20

Those of his own theatrical household he never
forgot. Witness Alexander, then his ideal " young
first," with his charming, vivacious wife. Then
came the return at midnight, a delightful sail back,
on the river. I have mentioned how on one
summer Sunday morning a hansom cabman
arrived express with a letter from " the Chief,"
inviting to a day at Dorking with the French
Company of " La Comedie." What a delightful day that was! We had Delaunay, Mounet
Sully, Coquelin, I think, and another—with Sir F.
Pollock and his son, Campbell, the present Mr.
Burdett-Coutts, and some others. We had lunch
at one of the old inns, and I noted as we
walked about afterwards how careful was our
host to seize any opportunity to increase his
popularity. A young man staying at the hotel
spoke to him, and Irving answered him cordially
and presently offered one of his own choice
cigars. The Frenchmen were deeply affected by
his goodwill, and made ineffectual attempts to understand. Sumptuous as was the lunch, it did not
suffice, and we returned to dine at the Garrick
in superior style. So with the Meiningen Performers. There were great banquets for them, and
they were treated with the same lavish hospitality,
which was shared by us all.

Irving was extraordinarily fortunate in his figure
and general appearance. It was truly picturesque
and quite remarkable. It used to be said that there
were only three or four men whom people would
turn to look after in the street—Mr. Gladstone, Car-

dinal Manning, and Irving. He was fortunate in his spare figure, his dark wavy hair, and finely cut features. It is curious that this should not have been the original type, for in the days of his early youth we find him a rather conventional-looking young man with a full moustache. It is clear that he developed the later style by a sort of intellectual effort, by earnestly concentrating his thoughts on characters, feelings, passions, &c. He wore his features down and refined them : and so his face acquired a spiritual look. There was the fine forehead, well-cut nose, and beautifully expressive mouth. He added a slightly eccentric style of dress, a tall, broad-brimmed hat, a low collar, and a curiously cut coat, with " flowing " collar and skirt. In this he suggested Dickens. His voice—his natural voice—was low, sweet, and winning, but his walk in private, as on the stage, was straggling and ungraceful. Yet these oddities were interesting, and meant absence of affectation, and that he was careless about such matters. He was, indeed, a most attractive man, and had he been single would certainly have captivated some dame of high degree.

With such attractions it is a surprise that no fitting portrait has been left of the actor. Millais, Edwin Long, and Whistler have been the most conspicuous artists to whom he sat. Millais' effort is a side face of a sketchy sort, the colouring poor, and the likeness not very striking ; Long shows him as Hamlet, and is an interesting picture ; Whistler's is a shadowy thing in his own special style, and I well remember the ridicule with which it was greeted. It brought a high price at the sale. The sculptors have not been more successful. Onslow Ford's sitting figure of him as Hamlet is rather ungainly in attitude, and has little romance or feeling. There is an early bust by Joseph, I think— also prosaic enough—casts of which he used to give his friends. And there is a statuette of him as Mathias in 'The Bells.' The finest, most thoughtful and expressive reproduction of his face was assuredly the Cameron photograph of him as Becket, the frontispiece of this volume. His many admirers will be glad to have it.

Not many weeks after the actor's death, his numerous effects, curios, and general collections were " brought to the hammer " at Christie's. It was quite a gala time and caused some excitement. The fashionable dowagers with their daughters crowded into the rooms, certainly not with intention of purchase. *Que font ils dans ce galère ?* No one could answer that. It was the same at the time of Dickens' sale, when such extravagant prices were realised. Never was there such a heterogeneous collection as was now exhibited. It seemed like walking through the rooms of some old curiosity shop, for there were pictures, armour, china, bronzes, books, figures, ornaments. The effect, however, was not unpleasing. The actor seems to have followed his fancy and purchased whatever pleased him at the time. The attraction of the whole was the portrait of himself as Philip, by Whistler, and that gaudy presentment of Miss Terry, by Sargent, each fetching a large sum. Among the books the most interesting were the "Grangerised" copies of memoirs, notably that of Dickens's life, enriched with rare portraits, autographs, letters, &c.[1] The money received for the whole was close on £19,000.

Irving was much honoured in "Clubland." He was a member of four distinguished clubs—the Reform, the Garrick, the Athenæum, and the Marlborough. Rarely has an actor been so honoured. At the Garrick he was a power. There he received his friends to dinner and supper, and there he knew every one. To the Athenæum he was elected in its complimentary way, viz., under Rule 2, and by choice of the committee. It may be doubted, however, whether he would have been admitted within its august portals by the ordinary ballot. This we might forecast from the fate of another distinguished player, who was later excluded by a rather unhandsome combination. The Marlborough was truly "select," being at the time recognised as the Prince of Wales's own club, and who appeared to nominate its members.

Irving had ever a sort of romantic interest in the Roman Catholic Church and its ceremonial grandeur. I often think that he fancied he was somehow affiliated to it, from having so often

---

[1] The fluctuations of taste and fashion are shown by the loss of interest in this Grangerising process. For owing to the rise in the price of prints, portraits, and letters, it is found more profitable to "break up" these collections, made at such cost and trouble, and sell the component items separately.

figured as one of its ecclesiastics on the stage.
Cardinals, bishops, priests, religious processions,
rites, altars, sanctuaries—all these he was perfectly
familiar with, and he had "made up" by the most
careful inquiries all details that were necessary.
It was said that he obtained his Cardinal's robes
through a Catholic house of business, and certain of the faith were said to have advised him
in that department.   At all events, there was a
tenderness in his bearing towards the Church.
He knew the two Cardinals Manning and Vaughan,
and had many Catholic friends.   On the first
performance of ' Becket ' he, as usual, gave
his friends and acquaintances a handsome banquet
on the stage.   We remained on and on until
it came to nigh two in the morning.   I well
remember his coming down to the door in his
monastic robes and tonsure, which he had worn
through the supper.   He was dreamily placid,
delighted with every one and with himself—he
seemed to be half Irving, half the monk : for as I
passed into the street, wishing him good-night, he
wrung my hand slowly and warmly, uttering at the
same time a fervent benediction : " God bless you !
God bless you ! "   For a second he seemed to be in
real orders, or a sort of orders.   Cardinal Vaughan
invited him to give a reading at Archbishop's
House, for his schools.   And the actor agreed
cordially : he came and read ' Macbeth ' with great
spirit to a vast number of priests, who would
otherwise never have seen or heard him.   One of
the school girls came forward and prattled some

complimentary lines, and it was delightful to see the actor transformed into the good Vicar of Wakefield and smiling encouragingly on the child.

The question has been often discussed: Was Irving's stage system good? Was the Lyceum school conducive to the general effect? This really raises the question of actor-managership, which is a sort of amiable despotism. For it is admitted that any performer who attempts to take full scope and license would interfere with the ruler. Hence Irving's rigidity, compelling all to be subordinate: to indulge in no strong or distracting efforts. It was almost amusing to see how all this was unconsciously felt and quietly enforced.

And what has been the effect on the stage of this modern institution of actor-manager? In truth, Irving might be considered the first and most successful. Of course, there had been actors long before him who were also managers, such as Garrick, Macready, and Phelps. But these were not manager-actors in the modern sense. Garrick, Macready, and Phelps were all members of a company, and allowed members of the company to be as prominent as themselves. The play was dominant. Play succeeded play in the course of the week, so that every one's turn came round. Charles Kean and his wife, indeed, rather engrossed the whole attraction of a scene, and may be said to have been precursors of Irving and Miss Terry. This modern system is founded, strangely enough, on a *liking* for the person and character of a leading player. Audiences grow

to love their player ; they like to see him ; they
relish his ways, tones, defects even. *They go to see
him*, not his play or his " show." Hence he
naturally thinks that the more he can give of
himself to the exclusion of disturbing elements
the better. At another person's theatre, he must
take his place in the ranks ; for others have *their*
claims. He is thus gradually encouraged to seek
an exclusive domain of his own, where he can rule
and be the central figure. Irving set the example
for this system, which he carried on successfully for
twenty years. His example was duly followed by
every successful performer, and the motto, " One
man, one theatre," has become " your only wear."
Alexander, Tree, Maude, Seymour Hicks, Wyndham, Terry, Bourchier, and others all represent the
system in full force. It is obvious that it is hardly
a healthy one for the stage, as the result of
Irving's twenty years' experiment has shown. It
has indirectly destroyed the general taste for "the
play." It has all but extinguished the dramatist,
who ought to have a company to write for, not a
single actor or a "show." Curiously enough, Irving
was to exemplify this state of things, for when he
came to cast about for original plays he found none
that would suit him or his conditions. There is but
little dramatic interest in these " one-man " parts ;
and thus it came about that after this long series of
years the public showed signs of fatigue, if not
of indifference. Of course, as might be expected,
for their own credit audiences will cling to their
old favourite, but still the old idolatrous devotion

is a thing of the past. And now, as we look round, what do we find as the result of the system? The stage mainly in possession, not of the drama, but of showmen and shows!—for musical comedy, we are told, is " the natural expression of English taste." There are a few sketchy plays mainly furnished by a writer of foreign extraction, but these possess what attraction they have, not owing to the manager-actor, but to an equal distribution of interest among the characters. In short, then, two elements—the " one-man " play and the exhibition of shows—must destroy all interest in the purer intellectual delight of real drama. In fact, as Mr. Hare said recently with excusable exaggeration, " By and by there will be no ' play ' at all." No one could say that this was from selfishness or jealousy—it was the system. It must disturb the balance. There was one great central force and attraction, all the others were softened down and graduated. Thus there was a harmonious whole.[1]

But would we find further proof of the failure of this actor-manager principle we have only to consider the case of Irving himself. No one ever

---

[1] Once, and once only, I saw Irving actually " played down " almost to extinction by one of his own comrades, and in his own theatre. It was at a performance of ' Robert Macaire' for a charity, and Toole had good naturedly volunteered for Jacques Strop. Never was there such an exhibition. Poor Macaire could not get in a word. Toole completely overpowered him, " gagging" eternally, inventing " business," in fact dominating the whole to roars of laughter. Irving had virtually to look on. Yet this was all done with the best intentions.

received more money from the public ; in one year, and in perhaps more, he "took at the doors" close on £100,000. His yearly profit must have been always from £8,000 to £10,000. Yet at his death he left nothing. Nothing saved or put by. True, his curios and relics brought nigh £19,000 owing to the factitious enthusiasm of the moment. Here was the result of actor-management; it was so with Charles Kean, and will be so with many who are now actor-managing. The truth is, the actor and the manager are distinct professions, and cannot be combined. They are both most difficult professions, requiring skill, instinct, and training. The actor-manager really does not manage, for management means the controlling of a large *corps* of clever persons, with study of their special gifts with a view to setting them out profitably, and to the best advantage. The actor has none of this class to attend to, nothing but to set off his own personal advantages in the best way, and to make the most of his own popularity. When this popularity begins to wane his fortunes wane also.

Irving, I noticed, was never quite at home in other theatres than his own, as when he played in a grand combination version of 'The School for Scandal.' The best and choicest of the profession had volunteered even for the smallest parts. But Irving had Joseph. "How fine," said every one, "he will be. Suit him down to the ground! Fancy the screen scene!" Never was there a greater disappointment; it was really the worst Joseph one had ever seen. He was perpetually changing his legs, jumping up and down. Half he said was scarcely heard; it was at Old Drury, but it was clear to all that he had no conception of the part. He could only give it his own habitual resources; strange jerks, queer tones and general restlessness.

Still, it must be said, a vast deal has been done for Shakespeare at the Lyceum. What a long series, and how splendidly presented! What an education during twenty years! Nothing can be so true, and we are under infinite obligations to him. Even granting that the system of illustration is the best, if persisted in, it must lead to catastrophe. For it is too costly and over-whelming. Again, the list of performing Shake-spearian plays is not very long. Yet it would seem almost impossible to get the public to accept any beyond those they are well accustomed to. A strange phenomenon surely! The more favoured are 'Hamlet,' 'Macbeth,' 'As You Like It,' 'Henry VIII.,' 'Much Ado About Nothing,' 'Henry IV.' and 'Henry V.,' 'Midsummer's Night Dream,' 'Othello,' 'Richard III.' and one or two more. 'Richard II.,' 'Twelfth Night,' and 'Cymbeline' had been at-tempted by Irving, but with little success. One often wished that he had brought forward 'The Tempest,' which many conceived would have suited him and his theatre admirably; he would have declaimed Prospero in a noble, stately fashion, but he shrank from the duller and heavier moments. I have already insisted that the 'Twelfth Night' was one of his most beautiful and poetical efforts:

the scenery and his own acting were all but perfect.   But t'would not do, it was coldly if not hostilely received.

Irving will be recollected not so much for his acting as for these Shakespearian revivals.   Not that all can be considered to have been in the best and most complete taste ; indeed it may be that in a generation or two his revivals will be classed with those of Macready and the Charles Keans, which were just as much extolled.   Mr. Tree has long since entered the field as a competing revivalist, and has gone " one better," and is more " up to date." Irving's changes and illustration were often matters of critical taste.   But he ever showed a reverent respect for his art.   Mr. Tree's are guided by no principle but that of dealing with the bard as though be had lived in our day, and of making his humorous characters funny on modern lines.[1]

The absurdity of the modern system of decorating Shakespeare, or piling on him ornaments, can be shown by one specimen — the burial scene of Ophelia.   It will serve as a typical instance.   Every manager at once says, " Here we must have a procession—king, queen, priests, censers, lights, copes, &c., and solemn music from the organ in an

---

[1] Thus Bottom was fashioned into a sort of London clown. The part was amplified and extended for the benefit of the manager, who played it, so that it became the chief character of the play.   Yet, strange to say, this adapter gave us, beyond doubt, the finest representation of 'Julius Cæsar' that it was possible to imagine.   Antony's speech, and the whole scene of the crowds, &c., were really unsurpassable.   *O sic omnes !*

adjoining church." All wrong, for Ophelia was debarred from rites, and was buried as a suicide—a single priest officiating, with no procession. I myself doubt whether any great effect is produced by these processions, battles, armies, combats and such shows. They are never convincing. It is clear to the spectator that the "super" soldiers tumble down of their own motion, so as "to make believe" that they are killed. I was always rather astonished that Irving did not think out some new and original method of illustration, based on a profound study of the bard, and search out what is the minimum, not the maximum, of illustration. But he really favoured the old stagey and stale methods. Often did I all but implore him to discard the cumbrous and expensive "built-up" structures and revert to the "cloths," and he used to promise; or he would turn it aside with a pleasant smile. "Cloths" painted artistically, with vivid colour, have an exceeding dramatic effect. I am afraid his taste in many directions was a little corrupt.

It grew to be almost a custom that I had to collect for him for the particular play that was being got up, all the points, effects, readings of great actors, bits of emphasis, "business," &c., recorded in the scattered "Memoirs." He found this very useful. I thus found for him the criticisms on Le Maitre in 'Robert Macaire.' I even manufactured a sort of refrain of a song about "toiling and moiling," which he used to "hum" as he lounged about in his part.

As a training school for acting, and particularly for elocution, emotional emphasis and the rest, it must be said Irving's teaching and example were unsatisfactory. This was specially shown in his Shakespearian productions, and was the result of the manager's rigid, well-thought out system of effacing, as it were, his followers. They were to be figures—graceful, interesting figures—but without prominence. They seemed to be allowed to recite their beautiful lines in a sort of light, chattering style, as young men of our day would talk. The verses were turned into running prose, and the pace was so fast and the utterance so indistinct, that it was difficult to gather the meaning. All had the same methods and seemed indistinguishable one from the other. There was nothing illiberal in this; as I have said it was his system. The two principals were the real actors; on them was the whole attention to be concentrated, undivided and undistracted.

I think it is within the experience of many, that at dinner parties in those days, Irving usually came in for much good-natured attack. "I hate him, he is quite ridiculous," would the ladies say. The general voice, without exception, was for the enchanting and captivating Ellen, then in her prime, ever engaging and winsome. They "grew wanton in her praise." The truth was, Irving in those days preached much. When launched on a long verified soliloquy he fell into a lugubrious and most monotonous chant which, as in the case of Peter Magnus, "amused his friends very much."

The effect on persons who had never seen him before was often surprising, the extraordinary tones emitted by the actor at moments of agitation being truly unique and astonishing. When he would express passionate grief, it took the shape of strange croonings, yelpings, and animal noises. All his pronunciations such as " Gud" for God, " wammin" for " women" became intensified. Where, or why, or how he engendered this expression of emotion it is hard to say. It clung to him to the last, and his more fanatical adherents thought it all very beautiful. And the same emotion produced that queer, limping gait. He revelled in these long speeches, hence the secret of his fondness for Wills, who knew how to supply him.

Most of Irving's gifts were exterior. He had true glamour, a gracious presence, a romantic bearing, but little real passion, though he could simulate it in a sort of effective way. His curious tones in grief or anger were generally inappropriate and often opposed to the sense of the words ; strange as it may seem, he suggested a lack of training and education. And yet it was not always so. His early efforts were admirably finished, correct in style, his elocution good. I have mentioned the extraordinary deterioration of his playing in 'The Two Roses,' his making a complete and rough caricature of what was formerly the highest and sincerest bit of comedy. No doubt the absence of control, the want of some one to advise and tell him the truth, the abundant compliments and flatteries that pursued him only confirmed him in his ways, and could not encourage correction or improvement.

Again, it was extraordinary that one who gave certain characters so perfectly, should have done others so badly and poorly. What could have been more natural, easy and appealing, than his Vicar of Wakefield, so genuinely affecting and affectionate, so full of little engaging ways! It was, as I have always said, a perfect performance. He looked the part admirably. His Shylock, also, would pass anywhere, and in any theatre, as a really finished and finely interpreted character. Louis XI. also was remarkable, though the hypocrisy was a little too marked and panto-mimic.

It is sad that in almost the last words of this perhaps too partial account I should record that, though some months have elapsed since his death, the great actor's name is scarcely mentioned. He seems, indeed, forgotten. For many a "cheap" celebrity, there are committees and subscriptions and memorials and statues ; but nothing of the kind has been even suggested.

Looking back across the flood of criticism that since the actor's death has burst through the flood-gates, and weighing the absurd raptures— the unkind—the praises of the wrong thing, the appreciation that seems fairest and most just was the one in the *Times* the morning after his death. Nothing can be more temperate, more judicious.

Such was Henry Irving, the actor and the man.

An actor of high and unusual pretension, interesting and romantic, while he must be counted a reformer of the stage ; a man of a most attractive kind, of winning and engaging character.

INDEX

The Gresham Press,
UNWIN BROTHERS, LIMITED,
WOKING AND LONDON.